HITLER'S DEATH

HITLER'S DEATH

The Case Against Conspiracy

Luke Daly-Groves

OSPREY
PUBLISHING

OSPREY PUBLISHING
Bloomsbury Publishing Plc
PO Box 883, Oxford, OX1 9PL, UK
1385 Broadway, 5th Floor, New York, NY 10018, USA
E-mail: info@ospreypublishing.com
www.ospreypublishing.com

OSPREY is a trademark of Osprey Publishing Ltd

First published in Great Britain in 2019

A catalogue record for this book is available from the British Library.

ISBN: HB 978-1-4728-3454-6; ePDF 978-1-4728-3451-5;
ePub 978-1-4728-3453-9; XML 978-1-4728-3452-2

18 19 20 21 22   10 9 8 7 6 5 4 3 2 1

Typeset in Fournier MT Std by Deanta Global Publishing Services, Chennai, India
Printed and bound in Great Britain by CPI (Group) UK Ltd, Croydon CR0 4YY

Osprey Publishing supports the Woodland Trust, the UK's leading woodland
conservation charity. Between 2014 and 2018 our donations are being spent
on their Centenary Woods project in the UK.

To find out more about our authors and books visit www.ospreypublishing.com.
Here you will find extracts, author interviews, details of forthcoming events
and the option to sign up for our newsletter.

For Jessica

CONTENTS

ABBREVIATIONS

AIO	Area Intelligence Office [British]
BLO	British Liaison Officer
CAB	Cabinet Office [British]
CIA	Central Intelligence Agency [American]
CIB	Counter Intelligence Bureau [British]
CIC	Counter Intelligence Corps [American]
DDMI	Deputy Director of Military Intelligence
DMI	Director of Military Intelligence
ECIC	European Command Intelligence Center [American]
FBI	Federal Bureau of Investigation [American]
FO	Foreign Office [British]
G-2	US Army Intelligence
GCHQ	Government Communications Headquarters [British]
HJ	Hitler Jugend (Hitler Youth) [German]

HW	Government Communications Headquarters Records [British]
IB	Intelligence Bureau [British]
ID	Intelligence Division of the British Control Commission for Germany
ID EUCOM	Intelligence Division European Command [American]
IG	Intelligence Group of the British Control Commission for Germany
JCC	Joint Consultative Committee on Captured Enemy Documents [British]
JIC	Joint Intelligence Sub-Committee/Committee [British]
MGI	Major General Intelligence [British]
MI14	Military Intelligence Section 14 of the War Office [British]
MI5	Security Service [British]
MI6	Secret Intelligence Service [British]
NARA II	National Archives and Records Administration, College Park, Maryland
NKVD	Soviet Secret Service
OMGUS	Office of Military Government, United States
PW	Prisoner of War

QIC	Quadripartite Intelligence Committee [American, British, French and Soviet]
RIO	Regional Intelligence Office [British]
SHAEF	Supreme Headquarters Allied Expeditionary Force
SIGINT	Signals intelligence
SIS	Secret Intelligence Service (MI6) [British]
SMERSH	Soviet counter-intelligence agency; literally, 'Death to Spies'
SS	Schutzstaffel (Protection Squadron) [German]
TNA	The National Archives, Kew, Surrey
USLO	United States Liaison Officer
USFET	United States Forces European Theatre [American]
WO	War Office [British]

ILLUSTRATIONS

Figures

Plates

6   J. Edgar Hoover refutes rumours of Hitler's survival in Argentina.

7   Social media 'Hitler waves' increase popular interest in survival rumours.

8   During the Potsdam Conference Stalin claimed Hitler could have escaped to Spain or Argentina.

9   The Moscow Skull. In 2009, DNA tests proved that this skull, once thought to be Hitler's, is female.

10 Hugh Trevor-Roper in 1950 after leading the British investigations into Hitler's death.

11 A 'poor double' found by the Soviets.

12 Hitler's teeth are archived in Moscow.

13 According to Lev Bezymenski the mush photographed in these boxes is all that was left of Adolf Hitler and Eva Braun.

14 The sofa on which Adolf and Eva Hitler committed suicide photographed in July 1945 by Life correspondent Bill Vandivert. Note the blood stains on the armrest which match where Axmann saw Hitler's body slumped over.

15 Adolf and Eva sit beside each other in happier days for the Nazis.

16 British Prime Minister Winston Churchill enjoying his visit to the bunker.

17 Looters' paradise. The Reichschancellery in ruins.

18 Captain Eric Mundy of the British Intelligence Corps photographed the Führerbunker between 1945 and 1947. His incorrect captions reflect the confusion caused by the Soviets.

19 Vandivert captured several eerie photographs inside Hitler's bunker.

20 Unsecured crime scene: souvenir hunters even tore fabric from furniture in the bunker.

21 Long before the bunker, Hitler greets Hanna Reitsch, overlooked by Hermann Göring (centre) and Nicolaus von Below (left).

22 After the battle: the East–West Axis where Reitsch landed her Fiesler Storch before her last meeting with Hitler.

23 The 'normal' face of evil. Joseph and Magda Goebbels pose with their children.

24 Near the end: the Führer and Artur Axmann greet members of the Hitler Youth in the Reichschancellery Garden.

25 Hitler and his friend, Albert Speer.

26 The last government of the Third Reich. Albert Speer, Karl Dönitz and Alfred Jodl.

27 J. Edgar Hoover with President Harry Truman. In 1948, Truman gave Hoover's FBI permission to investigate rumours of Martin Bormann's survival in Argentina.

28 Martin Bormann's skull compared to a picture of him when alive.

Picture credits

1   GettyImages-613513772/Hulton Deutsch;
2   GettyImages-596285329/Peter Unger;
3   National Archives and Records Administration (US): NARA II, RG 242, P 26, Box 1, 12008425;
4   The National Archives: TNA, WO 208/3788;
5   The National Archives: TNA, FO 371/46749;
6   The FBI Vault: Adolf Hitler Part 02 of 04, p.174;
7   Author screenshot;
8   GettyImages-535794775/Photo 12;
9   GettyImages-145415076/Konstantin Zavrazhin;
10 GettyImages-57163095/John Chillingworth/Stringer;
11 GettyImages-104405173/Keystone-France;
12 GettyImages-907951596/Laski Diffusion;
13 Reproduced with permission of the Central Archive of the Federal Security Service of Russia (FSA);
14 GettyImages-50499148/William Vandivert;
15 GettyImages-871688128/Photo 12;
16 GettyImages-104408425 Keystone-France;
17 GettyImages-515619654/Bettmann.
18 Imperial War Museum: Eric Mundy Collection Photographs online refs: www.iwm.org.uk/collections/item/object/205313940 and www.iwm.org.uk/collections/item/object/205225002
19 GettyImages-50409450/William Vandivert;
20 GettyImages-159761535/William Vandivert;
21 GettyImages-545069913/Ullstein Bild Dtl;
22 GettyImages-548792397/Ullstein Bild;
23 GettyImages-537148347/Ullstein Bild Dtl;
24 GettyImages-566464355/Universal History Archive;
25 GettyImages-541077595/Ullstein Bild;
26 GettyImages-104419759/Keystone-France;
27 GettyImages-514946152/Bettmann;
28 GettyImages-79661965/Popperfoto.

PREFACE

I remember watching the news around the time when *Grey Wolf: The Escape of Adolf Hitler* was published.[1] Here was this man, on a television programme, telling the world that history and historians have been wrong all along. He has proof, concrete proof, that Hitler escaped to Argentina. Fascinated as I was and still am by contrarian thinkers, I received the book as a Christmas present and read it in a short space of time. I came away with more questions than answers. Could it really be that declassified FBI documents offer the proof their authors ascribe to them? Could British intelligence have really been so scheming or so foolish?

My interest in Hitler's last days deepened. Naturally, during my undergraduate studies, it reached its pinnacle during my visit to Hitler's bunker. My partner and I arrived in Berlin late in the evening on 31 March 2013, Easter Sunday. My hotel, unbeknownst to me until I stepped through the door, was opposite Friedrichstrasse railway station. This was, of course, the same station on the same street where a group of important officials from the Führerbunker gathered before unsuccessfully trying to break out through the Russian lines in 1945. More gruesomely, several fleeing soldiers were hanged from the station in April 1945 wearing signs reading 'I am hanging here because I did not carry out the Führer's orders'.[2] Unable to rest, we both left the hotel as soon as we could. The dark streets of Berlin were strangely empty of pedestrians in most areas. We headed to the Reichstag, which was likewise deserted and I enthusiastically recounted tales of the Battle for Berlin. Then we went to see what is left of the Führerbunker.

When we reached Hitler's bunker the hairs on my arms and the back of my neck stood up. The atmosphere was ghostly. I felt a strange sense of certainty that this must be the place where the murderer of millions took his own life. But feelings count for little in scientific enquiry. From that point on I was determined to investigate the stories of his escape and to analyse the investigations which determined that he had committed suicide and the circumstances in which he had done so. I approached the task with an open mind, being prepared to investigate wherever the evidence led me and report my findings according to what the evidence suggested.

As a result, when the time came to submit a proposal for my BA (Hons) dissertation, I chose to write about Hitler's death. This caused a minor stir in some quarters. In particular, I remember listening to a lecture in which we were warned (quite rightly) that undergraduate dissertations should not try to rewrite world history or discuss such well-covered topics as Hitler's rise to power. Thinking I was in trouble, immediately after the lecture I made my way to that lecturer's office and tried to defend my case. It was a risk, he said, a gamble. I thought it over. After conversations with more of my tutors (including a memorable discussion with Dr Billy Frank), it was, in the end, as often is the case in history, the words and support of my partner that finally gave me the courage to take up the challenge. I was going to reinvestigate what better historians than I had investigated before. My superiors kindly conceded. Don't mess it up, I was told, though in stronger words. I was determined not to. I am forever thankful for being given the opportunity to research, and now publish, what I consider to be a strong case against theories of Hitler's escape.

I spent the entire summer of 2014 reading all the books about Hitler's death that I could find, from cover to cover. Every day, all day, I read the memoirs of intelligence officers, eyewitness accounts from the bunker, general histories of the last days, Soviet files published verbatim, detailed histories of Hitler's death and conspiracy theories. I stuck notes to almost every page in some books, highlighting each detail of interest. By the time I submitted my thesis in 2015 I had read all the main British intelligence files concerning Hitler's death that were available to the public at the National Archives in Kew. Surprisingly, I had managed to dig up new evidence concerning Hitler's death and the British investigations that has never been published. The thesis was well received and forms the basis of this book. In the years since then I have had the opportunity during my master's and doctoral studies to further my knowledge of Anglo-American intelligence in post-war Germany. This has enabled me to correct several errors in my undergraduate thesis concerning intelligence organisations. Any remaining errors are of course my own. I have now also studied in detail the files preserved by numerous American intelligence agencies concerning rumours of Hitler's survival and these have bolstered my original conclusions. Moreover, I have been fortunate enough to talk to veterans of Anglo-American intelligence and to visit the site of the British Intelligence Division Headquarters in Herford, North Rhine-Westphalia, from where several secret investigations discussed in this book were directed.

Although this book is critical of conspiracy theorists who argue that Hitler lived beyond 1945, they cannot be faulted for asking difficult questions, reinvigorating debate and inspiring public interest in historical topics that many historians avoid. However, they should be faulted for their poor research methods, their distortion of historical facts and the negative (albeit possibly unintended) consequences of their publications. Consequently, this book sets out the case against conspiracy theories of Hitler's escape. Rather than recounting the familiar story of Hitler's last days in detail, it investigates the Anglo-American intelligence investigations into Hitler's death and rumours of his survival in order to provide ample proof of the Führer's suicide on 30 April 1945.

Luke Daly-Groves
Maghull, 2018

*It was a scene not only of hideous ruin but of the
total dissolution of his empire, his system and his
supporters.*

—Intelligence Bureau,
Control Commission for Germany
(British Element), 1946[1]

Introduction

Is History Wrong?

Many books about Adolf Hitler end the same way. A defeated but still furious dictator shuffles around his Führerbunker deep below the streets of Berlin. Sick, old, increasingly frail, he frequently loses touch with reality, oscillating between overconfidence and anxiety, despair and hope.[2] He directs ghost armies from his map room, roars at generals to carry out impossible orders and hopes for a miracle.[3] Maybe the British and Americans will fall out with the Soviets, he thinks; capitalism is, after all, the enemy of communism.[4] Is President Roosevelt's death on 12 April 1945 a sign from providence that Nazi Germany can at the last minute, like Frederick the Great, prove victorious against the Russians?[5]

In the last week of April, the unrelenting shellfire ripping holes in his previously tranquil Reichschancellery garden suggested otherwise. Many of his close comrades knew this was the end. The Second World War was drawing to a close. The so-called thousand-year empire was to last barely 12 miserable years. All that was left defending the capital of Hitler's Reich was a hotchpotch of Hitler Youth (young boys), Volkssturm (old men), foreign SS units with everything to lose, and whatever could be scraped together from the Luftwaffe, the Wehrmacht and the Kriegsmarine against millions of Soviet soldiers.[6] Outnumbered and outgunned, many high-ranking Nazis asked Hitler to escape to Berchtesgaden on several occasions, believing that arrangements could have been made for a last stand in the mountains with more troops, more equipment and under more favourable conditions.[7] But Hitler did not want to abandon the capital of the Third Reich. Death in a countryside holiday home was unbefitting for the commander, and murderer, of millions.[8] If his Reich was going to go down, he wanted it to descend in a glorious hail of bullets, a final act of defiance, a signal to future generations of Jew-hating admirers that even in defeat the Nazis placed loyalty, fanaticism and honour above all else. At least that was how Joseph Goebbels, the Reichsminister of Propaganda, tried to spin things.[9] The reality was much more sordid.

On Hitler's 56th birthday, just ten days before his suicide, in the company of Artur Axmann, head of the Hitler Youth (HJ), he emerged from the bunker to inspect several young boys who were fighting this last bloody battle for him — in the same garden where his blood-stained corpse would later burn.[10] The day before this birthday 'celebration', Eva Braun, Hitler's lover, known at this time only to a select few, dyed her hair in Hitler's favourite shade of blonde for the last time.[11] According to her hairdresser, Heinz Bernhard, Braun recited 'melancholic verses from one of Goethe's famous poems' before bidding him farewell.[12] At this point, Eva suspected that she might die in Berlin, but, like her lover, she was experiencing fluctuating emotions, including hopes of victory.[13]

Hitler's refusal to leave the bunker has since become infamous thanks to a particularly memorable and mostly accurate scene in the 2004 film *Downfall*.[14] On 22 April

1945, the Führer threw his coloured pencil across his map table and admitted for the first time in a rage, 'The war is lost! But if you gentlemen think that I am going to leave Berlin you are making a very big mistake! I'd rather blow my brains out!'[15] This did not stop others such as Hermann Göring, head of the once mighty Luftwaffe, from fleeing to Berchtesgaden. From here, Göring offered to take control of Nazi Germany. Hitler considered this a betrayal. Martin Bormann (Hitler's powerful private secretary and an old rival of Göring) stoked Hitler's anger and ensured Göring's arrest.[16] Contrastingly, just hours before news of Göring's 'betrayal' filled the bunker, Albert Speer, Hitler's architect, Reichsminister of Armaments and War Production, and long-time friend, took a risky journey from Hamburg to Berlin to say his final goodbyes.[17] This meeting reminds historians that Hitler was not a monster who was incapable of friendship but a human being with terrible ideas. Hitler's crimes are much more frightening when viewed in this light. The man who fussed his beloved German Shepherd Blondi and her puppies in the bunker and enjoyed walks followed by tea parties with cake in the mountains of Obersalzberg was also capable of murdering millions of innocent people.[18]

On 26 April, Hitler received another surprising visitor. The wounded Robert Ritter von Greim had arrived to take control of the Luftwaffe.[19] He was accompanied by the test pilot Hanna Reitsch, who had just undertaken one of the most remarkable acts of courage during the Battle of Berlin. She had flown a Fieseler Storch through the heavy Russian fire over Berlin, taking a severe direct hit but still managing to land on the East–West Axis (the road between Brandenburg Gate and the Victory Column), which was then a temporary runway.[20] On 28 April, news that Heinrich Himmler, head of the SS and orchestrator of Hitler's worst crimes against humanity, had been secretly attempting to negotiate peace with the Western Allies aroused further fury in Hitler.[21] This was the worst betrayal of all for him.[22] Hermann Fegelein, husband of Eva Braun's pregnant sister Gretl, and Himmler's liaison officer to Hitler, paid the price with his life.[23] Ritter von Greim and Reitsch got to keep theirs – Hitler ordered them to fly out of Berlin to ensure Himmler could not take control of the Reich.[24] Those who now remained in or near the bunker would become the key witnesses to Hitler's last forty-eight hours alive.

On 29 April, Eva Braun boasted that she could now be referred to as Frau Hitler.[25] Her lover had finally officially acknowledged their relationship in marriage. As British intelligence interestingly speculated, 'The suggestion probably came from her. She had always wished for the glory of dying with Hitler, and on all recorded occasions had used her influence to persuade him to stay and die in Berlin.'[26] Shortly after this bizarre wedding ceremony had concluded, Hitler dictated his last private will and his political testament to his secretary, Traudl Junge.[27] In his personal will, Hitler explained his decision to marry Eva:

Although during the years of struggle I believed that I could not undertake the responsibility of marriage, now, before the end of my life, I have decided to take as my wife the woman who, after many years of true friendship, came to this town, already almost besieged, of her own free will, in order to share my fate. She will go to her death with me at her own wish, as my wife.[28]

For Hitler, marriage clearly indicated that his work as Führer was over. He no longer had to devote himself entirely to Germany; suicide and matrimony went hand in hand, one partially explaining the other. He later stated more bluntly:

> My wife and I choose to die in order to escape the shame of overthrow or capitulation. It is our wish that our bodies be burnt immediately in the place where I have performed the greater part of my daily work...[29]

The following day, the most powerful and closest members of Hitler's staff assembled near his private quarters.[30] Hitler shook hands with each of them.[31] The day before he had done the same with several female members of staff, but this was now the final goodbye.[32] Otto Günsche, Hitler's personal adjutant and bodyguard, having received orders from both Hitler and Bormann, set about making preparations for the disposal of Hitler's body.[33] Heinz Linge, Hitler's valet, remembers the last words the dictator spoke to him. Linge asked his boss what there was left to 'fight for now', to which Hitler replied, 'For the Coming Man.'[34] Magda Goebbels, wife of the skeletal Propaganda Minister, ensured that Hitler's final farewell was not to be all orderly and stoic. She frantically begged Hitler on her knees to reconsider his decision to commit suicide.[35] Hitler lifted her up, politely refused and returned to his room.[36]

A few moments later, the lifeless bodies of the newly-wed couple were carried outside the bunker into the Reichschancellery garden. They were doused in petrol, but the ritual was interrupted by relentless artillery fire from the Red Army. Shells were landing so close to the funeral party that they were forced to retreat to the precarious shelter provided by the garden exit of the bunker.[37] This block-shaped structure would later become the feature of many post-war photographs. It has come to symbolise the end of Hitler's Reich. From this doorway, a rag doused in petrol was lit and thrown on to the bodies, causing them to burst into flames.[38] The group raised their arms in a final, no doubt eerie, Hitler salute, before retreating to the bunker.[39]

Frau Goebbels now prepared to commit one of the most appalling crimes of the Nazi regime. With the help of Dr Ludwig Stumpfegger, she killed all six of her little children with cyanide as they lay in their beds.[40] This act of filicide further demonstrates how fanatical belief in Nazi ideology resulted in genocide. Photographs of their lifeless corpses, along with chilling images of their semi-cremated parents, can be found in several publications analysing Soviet documents. After Joseph and Magda committed suicide, there was very little petrol left to burn their bodies, most of it having been used earlier on Hitler and Eva.[41]

Many of the remaining Nazis now turned their attention to escape. General Wilhelm Mohnke organised ten battle groups, which attempted to break through the Red Army encirclement of Berlin.[42] These groups, which contained many important personalities, including Bormann, met with varying success, as will be seen. Other Nazis, such as General Hans Krebs, chose to add to the bunker's suicide rate.[43] Shortly before the breakout, he was sent by Goebbels to negotiate a more agreeable surrender with the Soviets. This farcical white-flag affair was a last desperate attempt to salvage something like an honourable defeat. Unsurprisingly, the Soviets refused.[44] In 1943, Goebbels had called for total war. In 1945, his defeat was total, the surrender unconditional.

There was to be no glorious emergence from the bunker for Hitler. The soldiers in the mountains surrendered. Germany was divided into British, French, American and Soviet zones of occupation. Nazism as a mass popular movement died a quick death. The location of Hitler's suicide was paved over with a bland car park, his Reichschancellery destroyed. Today, only a sign reading 'Führerbunker' marks the eerie concrete grave under which Hitler's final headquarters and the hub of multiple murder-suicides lies.

For the past few years, the general public would be forgiven for thinking that history as we had known it has been proved wrong. Countless documentaries, newspaper articles and internet pages written by conspiracy theorists have led the ongoing debate concerning Hitler's suicide. The most popular of these claim that the Führer did not end his life in his dark and gloomy underground shelter in war-torn Berlin but in fact escaped the Russian onslaught and lived to an old age with other Nazi fugitives in Argentina.

The historians, it seems, have been silenced, swamped by contrary opinion, or maybe even (some would argue) disproved. Until now. This book returns to the evidence of Hitler's suicide in order to scrutinise the arguments of conspiracy theorists using scientific methods. It's not that historians haven't dealt with this subject before – they have – but since the discovery in 2009 that a skull fragment once thought to belong to Hitler actually came from a female, no thorough attempt has been made to examine the vast array of conspiracy theories surrounding this subject through analysis of the files created by the intelligence agents who investigated Hitler's end. This is perhaps unsurprising, because 'conventional wisdom' arguably considers such theories to be 'too silly to deserve the effort of a serious refutation'.[45] Moreover, academic accounts tend to be buried in scientific journals or within lengthy studies of Hitler's life, hidden away from the general public, who are unlikely to delve into such works. Most people do, however, watch television. Many readers have likely seen or heard of documentaries describing elaborate hunts for Hitler's reported final resting place in South America. Central Intelligence Agency (CIA) veteran Bob Baer's claim on the first episode of the History Channel's *Hunting Hitler* is typical of these programmes: 'All the stories we've been told about Hitler's bunker, there is nothing to back it up.'[46]

The last detailed academic publications concerning Hitler's death appeared before this recent surge in popular conspiracy theories, and a reconsideration of the evidence using academic methods is long overdue. How did the debate reach this stage? When did conspiracy theorists take over? What inspired them? What have historians previously argued? It is essential to trace how the story of Hitler's death, together with the many conspiracies surrounding it, has evolved before reconsidering the evidence which convinced intelligence officers that he did in fact commit suicide on 30 April 1945.

I am disinclined to believe anything that is stated by that flatulent ass Musmanno.

—Hugh Trevor-Roper, 1966.[1]

The Evolution of Facts and Conspiracies

I: Hitler Waves

A historical consensus is yet to be reached regarding how Adolf Hitler died. Many publications have sought to solve the mystery. Contradictory theories arguing variously that Hitler committed suicide by shooting and/or poisoning, that he was murdered or that he escaped have produced a somewhat confusing array of explanations. Historians such as Hugh Trevor-Roper have attributed the reason for such confusion to Soviet conduct.[2] Having captured Hitler's bunker in May 1945, the Soviets were in the best position to produce evidence of Hitler's death.[3] Instead, they embarked on a campaign of misinformation, claiming in May 1945 to have identified Hitler's body with near certainty, but then later asserting that he had escaped to Argentina, or that he was hiding under British protection in Germany.[4] Theories of Hitler's escape have gained increasing popularity since 2009, when DNA tests revealed that a piece of skull in a Moscow archive that had been thought to be Hitler's in fact belonged to a woman.[5] In this climate of historical uncertainty, the existing historiography concerning Hitler's death must be analysed to show how such theories have developed and to expose the gaps in historical knowledge, many of which will be filled by this book's return to primary sources. As I will demonstrate, few historians have analysed British documents relating to Hitler's death, and so have overlooked evidence that could have brought further clarity to this important historical issue.

In 1947, Hugh Trevor-Roper published *The Last Days of Hitler*. Using evidence collected during the time he was leading the British investigations into Hitler's death, he concluded that Hitler and Eva Braun committed suicide in the Führerbunker on 30 April 1945, Hitler by shooting and Eva by poisoning, that their bodies were burned in the Reichschancellery garden and that the final location of their corpses was unknown.[6] The evidence analysed by Trevor-Roper is mainly eyewitness testimony (the limitations of which he acknowledges) combined with documentary evidence such as Hitler's last will and testament.[7] In later editions, Trevor-Roper describes his frustration with the Soviets for denying him access to prisoners of war and their accounts, as well as other evidence.[8] Following the release of important eyewitnesses from Soviet captivity in the 1950s, Trevor-Roper updated his book to include new testimonies, which, he argues, agreed with his initial conclusions.[9] Also in 1947, Lieutenant-Colonel Byford-Jones published his perspective on the Hitler investigations.[10] Byford-Jones had limited involvement in the British investigations and withheld information due to intelligence restrictions that were in place at that time.[11] Nevertheless, his book is useful in demonstrating the differing opinions that existed regarding the evidence obtained by British intelligence (Byford-Jones, contradicting Trevor-Roper, questions the authenticity of Hitler's marriage certificate) and the early

Cold War tensions in Berlin, which coincided with the British investigations.[12]

Trevor-Roper's book was immediately criticised by the former 'chief' American intelligence officer in Berlin, W. F. Heimlich, who concluded, using eyewitness testimony, that Hitler was murdered by his doctors on the orders of Himmler.[13] He argues that Trevor-Roper ignored crucial evidence, rushed the investigation, led a one-man show, and that his conclusions were preconceived.[14] Heimlich's arguments have been dismissed by historians as the result of wounded pride (as his references to Trevor-Roper's lack of consultation with American colleagues suggest).[15] Nevertheless, due to Heimlich's status as an intelligence officer, his criticisms deserve deeper analysis than has so far been conducted in existing publications. Recently declassified American military intelligence files available at the National Archives and Records Administration (NARA II) make this possible.

Heimlich was not kept fully informed about the investigations into Hitler's death because higher-ranking American intelligence officers were aware that he was attempting to capitalise on sensational rumours.[16] In November 1947, when initiating investigations into the alleged identification of Hitler's jawbone, one officer noted that the Americans, like the British, desired to 'end once and for all rumors recently persistent that Hitler was not burned or that he is still alive. In addition it is known that many persons are at present capitalizing in various ways, particularly in the literary field, on the above mentioned rumors. One such person ... who is believed capable of participating in such activities is Mr. Heimlich.'[17] Therefore, the officer went on, '[i]t is particularly desired that Mr. Heimlich NOT be consulted and that he NOT be given any hint that the above requested investigation is taking place'.[18] These suspicions about Heimlich turned out to be correct, as revealed by his comments in the book *Who Killed Hitler?*, published later that year. This evidence demonstrates that Heimlich's criticisms cannot be considered fully informed. Moreover, his suspected motives for publishing this book were the same as those of many others disseminating rumours of Hitler's end. Clearly, the Counter Intelligence Corps (CIC) failed in its objective of 'permanently spiking' rumours of Hitler's survival, as will be seen.[19]

Despite the general unreliability of Heimlich's work, his impression that Trevor-Roper was running a one-man show is somewhat valid, as other aspects of the British investigations not involving Trevor-Roper have been overlooked by most historians. The theory that Trevor-Roper arrived at preconceived conclusions is furthered by authors such as Peter Levenda. Levenda claims that Trevor-Roper was appointed to lead the Hitler investigations by Dick White, an influential MI5 (British Security Service) officer who would later lead MI6 (the British Secret Intelligence Service), because as a historian he would be able to manipulate evidence in such a way as to counteract Soviet claims of Hitler's survival, whilst overlooking evidence indicating Hitler's escape.[20] However, historians have not yet analysed recently declassified MI5 files containing correspondence between White and Trevor-Roper concerning the purpose of the latter's book. This evidence will be analysed later in this book to shed more light on whether political considerations overshadowed the need to establish the truth about Hitler's death.

Heimlich was not the only American who attempted to rival Trevor-Roper's work. In 1950, Judge Michael A. Musmanno published *Ten Days to Die*.[21] This book was based on several years of interrogations undertaken by Musmanno during his time working for the American Navy.[22] Musmanno's account, unsurprisingly, accepted the fact of Hitler's suicide but seemingly added little to Trevor-Roper's earlier work other than a more sensational writing style.[23] During later discussions of Musmanno's book, Trevor-Roper, with typical harshness, claimed, 'I am disinclined to believe anything that is stated by that flatulent ass Musmanno; but I suppose I ought not to be prejudiced!'[24] Trevor-Roper's criticism was not entirely unwarranted because there were several inaccuracies in Musmanno's book, particularly concerning the writing of Hitler's last will and testament.[25] Nevertheless, Musmanno should be praised for his continued refutation of rumours about Hitler's survival.[26] Moreover, some mistakes in such earlier publications can be forgiven because the evidence available for analysis in 1950 was incomplete.

Indeed, certain questions raised by early accounts of Hitler's death could not be answered at the time because Moscow maintained an official silence on the issue.[27] The Soviets released evidence only gradually. In 1955, Heinz Linge (Hitler's valet), having been tortured and interrogated by the NKVD (the Soviet Secret Service) concerning his knowledge of Hitler's last days, was released from Soviet captivity into West Germany along with other witnesses.[28] He related his account of Hitler's suicide to the press that year.[29] In May 1956, Linge's fellow ex-prisoner, Otto Günsche (Hitler's adjutant/bodyguard), did the same.[30] Almost a decade later, a member of

SMERSH (a Soviet counter-intelligence agency) cast doubt on Trevor-Roper's conclusions by claiming that a Soviet autopsy on Hitler's body showed that Hitler died from cyanide poisoning.[31] In 1968, Lev Bezymenski published documents from the Soviet investigations that included an official autopsy report on what was claimed to be the corpses of Hitler and Eva.[32] The autopsy concluded that Hitler died from cyanide poisoning.[33] This enabled forensic scientist Reidar Sognnaes to compare the autopsy with evidence from American archives, such as reports from Hitler's doctors and dentists, which, Sognnaes claims, proves that the body analysed in the autopsy was that of Hitler.[34]

Some western authors such as James O'Donnell acknowledged the findings of the autopsy and combined it with eyewitness testimony to conclude that Hitler simultaneously took cyanide and shot himself.[35] This theory has been challenged by Anton Joachimsthaler, who argues that this would have been virtually impossible due to the instantaneous nature of death from cyanide poisoning.[36] The autopsy has been criticised by scientists and historians for various scientific oddities and inconsistencies.[37] Consequently, historians such as Joachimsthaler and Joachim Fest argue that Hitler's body was never found and the autopsy was fabricated Soviet propaganda.[38] Donald McKale argues that the method of Hitler's suicide became a political issue as Soviet officials were concerned that stating Hitler shot himself (that is, that he died a soldier's death) would encourage neo-Nazism and thus insisted that Hitler poisoned himself, ignoring evidence that indicated the possibility of shooting.[39] On the other hand, McKale accuses western historians of arrogantly dismissing the autopsy results and, by insisting that Hitler shot himself, of defending him in death as an anti-communist crusader.[40] McKale concluded that such ideological squabbles would continue to cloud the issue.[41] However, as the Cold War ended, new forensic evidence came to light.

In the 1990s, the policy of glasnost enabled Ada Petrova and Peter Watson to analyse Moscow's files on Hitler's death.[42] The files included what was claimed to be a piece of Hitler's skull damaged by a bullet hole.[43] Many Soviet documents were published verbatim in *Hitler's Death*, which claimed, like Petrova and Watson, that the skull provided the definitive conclusion to the mystery.[44] The documents state that Hitler and Eva's bodies were captured by the Soviets, that two investigations into Hitler's death were completed in which Hitler's teeth were positively identified by his dentists, that his cause of death was determined by autopsy, that the results were given to Joseph Stalin, that the bodies were destroyed in 1970 and that a piece of Hitler's skull and his jaws were archived in Moscow.[45] Authors such as Hugh Thomas remained sceptical. Thomas claimed through detailed analysis of the Soviet evidence that forensic fraud had been committed to disguise the fact that Hitler was murdered and Eva escaped.[46] Aside from its extremely dubious conclusions, which lack supporting evidence, Thomas's book, like most published since Soviet evidence became available, fails to refer to any British primary source documents.[47] Thomas himself admits that 'the part played by British Intelligence ... has never properly been acknowledged'.[48]

The new evidence from Russia provided the impetus for a large variety of publications concerning Hitler's death. These included various memoirs of eyewitnesses from the bunker, each providing different perspectives on Hitler's last days.[49] The numerous discrepancies amongst eyewitnesses have been analysed in detail by many historians.[50] For example, Trevor-Roper's reliance on the testimony of Hitler's chauffeur Erich Kempka, who admitted to O'Donnell in 1974 that he told his interrogators whatever they wanted to hear in 1945 to save his own skin, has been heavily criticised.[51] Fest concluded that the method of Hitler's suicide will never be discovered due to the many eyewitness discrepancies.[52] O'Donnell criticises Allied interrogators for lacking objectivity and for asking the wrong questions. [53] However, little research has been conducted into how British intelligence selected eyewitness testimonies and determined the reliable from the fictitious.

Fest's book inspired the 2004 film *Downfall*, which has received widespread acclaim from historians for its attention to detail.[54] However, the film has been criticised for failing to show how Hitler committed suicide.[55] This omission perhaps reflects Fest's argument that Hitler's method of suicide remains unknown. The revived interest in Hitler's last days also saw the publication of more wide-ranging studies. Historians such as Luke Bennett noted how the narrative of Hitler's death has become ingrained in popular culture symbolically and metaphorically, with phrases such as 'bunker mentality' being frequently used in recent political discourse.[56] Other historians, such as David Beisel, focused on the mass wave of German suicides that plagued Germany in 1945 and demonstrated that Hitler's suicide was neither unique nor inconsistent with his character, as some authors and eyewitnesses claimed.[57] Such accounts supported Trevor-Roper's theories on the inherent nihilism in Nazi ideology, which arguably stemmed directly from Hitler's suicidal tendencies.[58] When combined with analyses of Hitler's medical condition in April 1945, they undermined theories of Hitler's escape by supporting Trevor-Roper's argument that Hitler was physically and psychologically unable to escape from the bunker.[59] However, as numerous scientists argued in 2005, only DNA analysis of the remains thought to be Hitler's could completely solve the issue.[60]

Due to the extensive amount of literature that has been produced about Hitler's death, numerous historical inaccuracies have been perpetuated by historians reproducing the mistakes in other publications.[61] Joachimsthaler sought to rectify this situation. Through analysis of international documents and eyewitness testimonies he concluded that Hitler shot himself in the right temple.[62] However, he did not scrutinise any British primary source documents, his analysis of a British perspective extending only to Trevor-Roper's investigations.[63] Consequently, he presented an incomplete account. Nevertheless, Joachimsthaler's methodology demonstrated that when a historical issue is clouded by a mass of literature disseminating inaccuracies, it is essential to return to primary sources in order to regain perspective on official conclusions. This methodology is useful when new evidence emerges that confuses the issue further, such as the 2009 DNA results that inspired a series of publications claiming that Hitler escaped from the bunker.

In *Hitler: The Survival Myth*, Donald McKale shows how many survival rumours that are popular today – such as Hitler escaping to Argentina, leaving a double to be burned in Berlin – have been repeatedly published in newspapers since 1945.[64] McKale does not blame such rumours solely on Soviet conduct but argues that western journalists, through their widespread publication of survival rumours and statements by such officials as Dwight Eisenhower that Hitler could be alive, aided their dissemination.[65] However, through detailed analysis of Soviet Cold War foreign policy, McKale, like many historians, argues that Stalin's political aims (discussed further in Chapter Four) provided the main impetus for the spread of such rumours.[66] Methodologically, McKale focuses primarily on newspaper analysis. Whilst this has certain advantages, such as demonstrating how various 'Hitler waves', consisting of widespread media coverage about Hitler, occur when new evidence emerges, newspaper analysis can only provide a limited perspective.[67] For example, although McKale refers to public opinion by assessing opinion polls, his analysis of the views of government officials is minimal and derives mainly from memoirs and other published works.[68] This leaves a crucial gap in perspective, as only by analysing the opinions of officials in classified documents can the true effect and substance of survival rumours be assessed. Analysing such documents is arguably necessary to disprove the new 'Hitler wave' of conspiratorial publications produced as a result of the 2009 DNA results.

There is much academic discussion in the pages of scholarly journals concerning the most useful definition of a conspiracy theory and/or theorist.[69] Some (as is typical in such debates) have even suggested that the quest for a definition be abandoned altogether.[70] When applied to Hitler's death, the conspiracy theorists are considered in this book to be those who argue that Hitler did not commit suicide in 1945 but escaped or was murdered. They therefore go against the 'official story', or at least that accepted by experts (in this case, historians,

scientists and intelligence agencies).[71] Both the escape
and the murder scenario involve plotting in secret by an
individual or individuals to bring about a historical event.
However, for some scholars, for it to warrant the label of
conspiracy, the secret plotting must be undertaken by a
group of individuals.[72] Perhaps, then, if one wants to be
more specific, that term should only be applied to those
who argue that Hitler escaped with the knowledge and/
or help of Anglo-American intelligence agencies, since
this would have involved plotting by several government
agencies. This is one of the popular theories (if not
the most popular) put forth so far, and it is also, as will be
argued, the theory that has the potential to produce the
most undesirable consequences. By various definitions, all
theories and theorists claiming that Hitler did not commit
suicide in April 1945 can be considered conspiratorial, as
they are in this book.

Since 2009, the historical debate regarding Hitler's
death has been dominated by conspiracy theories. The
most popular of these is provided in *Grey Wolf*, which
received considerable media coverage.[73] Like similar
theories, the book emphasises the 2009 DNA results,
statements made by Soviet and American officials that
Hitler had escaped and criticises historians for using
unreliable eyewitness testimonies.[74] It argues that Hitler
fled to Argentina in 1945 along with Martin Bormann
and other Nazi cronies.[75] Although the authors analyse
many Federal Bureau of Investigation (FBI) documents
concerning the possibility of Hitler's escape, they fail
to analyse any British War Office documents relating to
Hitler's death and consequently overlook documents
that arguably disprove their theory.[76] Gerrard Williams,

co-author of *Grey Wolf*, recently gained further publicity for his ideas when he appeared on several episodes of the three-season History Channel series *Hunting Hitler*.[77] Academic historians such as Richard J. Evans have dismissed such theories but have not acknowledged or reassessed the evidence surrounding Hitler's death in light of the recent DNA results.[78] As Charles Pigden argues, it is 'the conventional wisdom' that 'conspiracy theories should be neither believed nor investigated'.[79] The desire of historians to dismiss such theories is understandable, especially when one considers the flawed reasoning and fantastic conclusions expounded by some conspiracy theorists discussed in this book.[80] But such theorists should not simply be dismissed out of hand if they claim to have new or extraordinary documentary evidence to back up their statements, as many Hitler theorists do. To dismiss them simply for being conspiratorial is to contribute to a form of belief without proper scrutiny of evidence.[81] To avoid this, these theories should be properly challenged with evidence before any conclusions are drawn. As this book will show, this was the method that intelligence officers themselves utilised in the 1940s.

The failure of academic historians to engage sufficiently in such debates has arguably fuelled the increase in conspiracy theories. Indeed, similar theories have recently been put forward, in publications such as *Hitler in Argentina*, which claims to provide 'solid proof' of Hitler's escape.[82] As recently as 2018, popular social media pages have given much publicity to such rumours in a variety of articles repeating sensational stories of Hitler's post-war survival.[83] As Anne-Marie Bojan, who writes for *UNILAD*, the 'university student lad's magazine', exclaims, 'Anyone who loves a good conspiracy theory will have heard a shed load about Hitler.'[84] At best, these articles give equal weight to the arguments of historians and conspiracy theorists, but their headlines, tone and focus usually favour the latter. Such publications raise questions regarding the role of public history and highlight the issues that arise when academic historians fail to fully engage in public history debates. Christopher Gilbert analysed public interpretations of Hitler's death in the form of *Downfall* parodies and concluded that such interpretations are harmless when presented as fiction.[85] However, as McKale argues, when presented as historical fact, the idea that Hitler escaped, thereby fooling the Allies, can be dangerous because it romanticises Hitler and ignores the inherent nihilism in Nazi ideology that resulted in his demise. Further, suggestions made by books such as *Grey Wolf* that the Western Allies allowed him to escape may encourage neo-Nazism and foster distrust in democracy.[86] The latter consequence was a concern of British intelligence officers investigating similar theories in occupied Germany, as will be shown in Chapter Four. Indeed, such theories and the incorrect knowledge they spread about intelligence could undermine public confidence in Anglo-American intelligence services, which would hinder the important work they do in safeguarding democracy and those who live under it.[87] As John Bruce Lockhart, the former head of MI6 in Germany (1948–1951), argues, intelligence is largely based on public trust.[88] Conspiracy theories about Allied participation in Hitler's escape should therefore be properly challenged.

Much of the literature about Hitler's death is written by 'amateur historians', authors who, unlike academic historians, are not trained to practise history but are often skilled in other areas, such as journalism.[89] Professor William Rubinstein analysed a variety of similar historical subjects that have attracted a large amount of attention from amateur historians, with the ensuing conspiratorial publications, but which academic historians have generally ignored.[90] Rubinstein argues that this is because subjects such as 'Who was Jack the Ripper?' tend to lack the wider context that academic historians consider important in order to engage in a detailed study.[91] Some historians may therefore question why the seemingly narrow topic of Hitler's death requires a detailed analysis. However, as Petrova and Watson point out, the search for Hitler's method of death became a search for his character.[92] The way in which his regime ended was intended to be a Wagnerian twilight of the gods, an example for posterity. Aided by the recent surge in survival rumours and media coverage, the question of Hitler's death has acquired further cultural significance. By researching Hitler's death, one is researching not merely the death of one man, but rather the death of the Nazi regime, a vision of Europe, the legacy and character of the ideas behind that vision and the beginning of the Cold War.

This assertion of historical importance that featured in my thesis concerning Hitler's death was intended to serve as a call for fellow historians to reclaim dominance in a debate hitherto directed by conspiracy theorists. Thankfully, since its completion in 2015, the balance has gradually been redressed. For example, Dr Caroline Sharples recently drew attention to the lack of works explaining 'the origins and persistence of survival myths'.[93] She places Hitler's death in the context of Nazi ideology, making the excellent point that ideas surrounding the immortality of fallen Nazis during the Third Reich likely contributed to the initial refusal of some Germans to believe that their Führer was dead after its fall.[94] Sharples also believes that 'we do not have the sufficient data to fully understand the motivations' of those disseminating survival rumours owing to the Allied focus on 'leads to Hitler, rather than [on] the characters of those making the sightings or spreading the rumours'.[95] However, as this book will demonstrate, Anglo-American intelligence agencies were often more concerned with those spreading rumours than with the rumours themselves. This fact is crucial for effectively challenging the claims made by numerous conspiracy theorists.

In May 2018, the forensic intricacies surrounding Hitler's suicide once again made newspaper headlines.[96] An article in the *European Journal of Internal Medicine* written by a team of scientists and journalists claimed to have proved definitively through forensic analysis that the teeth held in Moscow belonged to Hitler.[97] This analysis is valuable and supports my original conclusions, as will be seen in Chapter Six. However, journalists Jean-Christophe Brisard, Lana Parshina and their colleagues have questioned the reliability of the 2009 DNA results, suggesting that the skull in Moscow could in fact still be Hitler's.[98] But despite their claims to the contrary, theirs cannot be 'the final word' on the subject.[99] Such absolute statements render these authors vulnerable to falling into the same trap that researchers fell into following the rediscovery of the skull fragment, leaving them open to future attack from conspiracy theorists. Indeed, despite their claims to finality, their own scientific article is (rightly) full of uncertain statements. For example, 'tiny blue deposits' identified on Hitler's teeth can only produce 'various hypothesis … without any certitude due to the absence of any elemental analysis'.[100] Moreover, the authors admit that further DNA tests are still needed before definitive conclusions on the skull may be drawn.[101] With so many documents left unread and so much further scientific analysis to be undertaken, no author can seriously claim to have provided the final word on this subject. But this does not mean that recent conspiracy theorists should remain unchallenged by historians, who, in the recent literature on Hitler's death, have largely neglected to analyse the documentary evidence produced by Anglo-American intelligence agencies, which conspiracy theorists claim provides proof of Hitler's escape. Analysis of these documents can bring clarity whilst the forensic evidence remains in a state of (hopefully temporary) uncertainty. Although historical context is being increasingly explored by scholars such as Sharples and forensic evidence is being usefully deployed by Brisard and his colleagues, the important context of secret intelligence remains largely neglected by historians. Consequently, although conspiracy theories are coming under increasing attack, several of their arguments have not yet been properly challenged in print. This book provides such a challenge.

II: A New Approach

Although a vast amount of literature has been published about Hitler's death, insufficient attention has been given to the British investigations. Such investigations, which extended beyond Trevor-Roper's account consisted of international and interdepartmental co-operation conducted before and after Trevor-Roper's investigations. Although a large amount of research has focused on Soviet documents, there has never been a full analysis of the British investigations into Hitler's death. This book will provide such an analysis. A wide variety of documents held at the National Archives in Kew and the private papers of several British intelligence officers held in multiple archives will be analysed to provide as full a perspective on the British investigations into Hitler's death as can be obtained with the documents currently available to historians. Analysis of Foreign Office documents will distance this book from the narrative of Trevor-Roper's 'one-man show' that is prevalent in the existing historiography. Trevor-Roper's investigations will be analysed, but from fresh thematic angles using new evidence from recently declassified MI5 and Cabinet Office documents not present in the existing historiography. By returning to such underused and overlooked documents, this book will shed further light on the mystery surrounding Hitler's death. However, as conspiracy theorists have recently focused mainly on files produced by the FBI, contextual analysis of these files, and of those declassified by the CIA, will also be conducted in order to provide readers with an alternative way of interpreting these documents, which are likely to continue inspiring 'Hitler waves' in newspapers for the foreseeable future. This book will therefore challenge conspiracy theorists by analysing the evidence they have produced to support their theories, whilst also contributing new evidence to the historiography.

Historians have also paid too little attention to the motives of those disseminating conspiracy theories. Much evidence concerning these motives is contained within documents produced by numerous American intelligence agencies preserved at the National Archives and Records Administration (NARA II) at College Park in Maryland. Some, such as large volumes of FBI files concerning Adolf Hitler, are available online. Further insight into the motives of those spreading rumours will be derived from analysis of the vast array of weekly, fortnightly and monthly intelligence summaries and reviews produced by several British intelligence organisations on the ground in Germany. This, together with analyses of the motives of the investigating intelligence officers, will enable this book to assess the credibility of numerous popular conspiracy theories in a level of detail that was previously impossible.

There are some limitations to relying solely on official documents. It is particularly difficult for historians to research the workings of intelligence agencies, which are by their very nature intent on remaining as secretive as possible.[102] All records of MI6 are withheld from public use on grounds of secrecy.[103] However, recent legislation has enabled various MI5 documents to be released, and these, as will be seen, sometimes contain MI6 papers that provide an insight into that agency's activities.[104] However, even declassified documents provide challenges to historians. For example, important decisions made by officials are sometimes not documented, and they can even be made over the telephone.[105] Moreover, declassified intelligence files go through a selection process and only a minority of them enter the public domain; the majority are destroyed.[106] This limits the scope of the perspective that historians can provide. Nevertheless, as Keith Jeffery argues, assembling fragments from a wide variety of documents can provide a bigger picture.[107] Furthermore, the majority of intelligence files available to the public concern Second World War topics, which has enabled this book to provide more detail than studies about later periods of intelligence history. Indeed, the War Office files on Hitler's death are so extensive that this book is able to provide a detailed analysis of official conclusions and methodologies, and to acknowledge the previously unpublished contributions of intelligence officers.

Drawing extensively on files preserved at the British and American National Archives, this book is the first to combine all elements of the British investigations, including new evidence from recently declassified files, along with an analysis of FBI, CIA and American military intelligence files, in a single publication, thus filling the gap that exists in the literature between case studies of Soviet documents and works that do not analyse British documents in sufficient detail, if at all. New ground is also covered by looking in detail at why Anglo-American intelligence agencies investigated rumours of Hitler's survival and why people all over the world chose to spread them. Most importantly, this book challenges recent conspiracy theories using Anglo-American intelligence files and is the first to assess the significance of the 2009 DNA results without asserting their inaccuracy or resorting to conspiratorial conclusions of Hitler's escape.

*Forgotten were the elementary rules of logic,
that extraordinary claims require extraordinary
evidence and that what can be asserted without
evidence can also be dismissed without evidence.*
—Christopher Hitchens, 2003[1]

British Intelligence and Rumours of Survival

I: 'Sheer Poppycock': The Foreign Office Investigates

Most publications about Hitler's death only discuss Hugh Trevor-Roper's investigations.[2] In doing so, they give the impression that Britain was inactive throughout the summer of 1945 and only began investigations when the Soviets claimed Hitler was hiding in the British Zone. However, the Foreign Office was in fact investigating the 'Facts about Hitler's Death' as early as 2 May 1945.[3] Indeed, British officials were receiving and commenting on information about Hitler's last days from international sources, and providing details to Winston Churchill to enable him to respond to parliamentary questions on the subject, prior to Trevor-Roper's involvement.[4] Much of the information analysed by Foreign Office officials concerned survival rumours, many of which derived from newspaper articles. A more detailed assessment of the basis and credibility of recent conspiracy theories can be provided by analysing the opinions of British officials, and existing historical knowledge can be enhanced by providing an official perspective on the survival rumours analysed by the Foreign Office.

'Hitler Still Alive Says Moscow' is a headline typical of many British newspaper cuttings collected by the Foreign Office in July 1945.[5] British reporters had been told by a Russian officer who discovered a charred body believed to be Hitler's that it was a 'very poor double'. From 11 September 1945, a plethora of survival rumours sent from the British Embassy in Moscow accumulated in the Foreign Office, beginning with the claim that Hitler was seen in Hamburg, living under an assumed name.[6] In a telegram dated 12 September 1945, Frank Roberts informed the Foreign Office of an article in the Russian newspaper *Pravda* which claimed that the deputy Bürgermeister of Berlin was 'convinced Hitler was alive' and that all Russian newspapers dated 11 September stated that British intelligence officers were searching for Hitler (who had recently changed his appearance by 'plastic operation') in Hamburg.[7] One puzzled Foreign Office official wrote, 'This peculiarity that Hitler is still alive in the British zone or in the Argentine keeps cropping up' and requested clarification.[8] In a reply that arguably summarised the views of British intelligence on all survival rumours, one official responded, 'I believe this to be sheer poppycock. The "plastic operation" which "changed Hitler's appearance" was probably carried out with a service revolver in the Führerbunker.'[9]

The Foreign Office was confident in its dismissal of survival rumours due to the evidence that had been accumulated suggesting that Hitler was dead (this is discussed further in Chapter Six). It is sufficient here to comment that the Foreign Office was impressed by an intelligence report produced by the Supreme Headquarters Allied Expeditionary Force (SHAEF) on 30 July 1945 that concluded: 'Despite Russian scepticism, it seems probable from all we know of Hitler's last days, he chose to die in Berlin.'[10]

Not all of the survival rumours investigated by the Foreign Office came from Moscow, although it appears that most rumours were initially inspired by the Soviet accusations. In October 1945, Eisenhower was temporarily convinced by his 'Russian friends' that Hitler was alive, but later retracted his statement after a discussion with Trevor-Roper on the evidence available to the contrary.[11] Despite the initial confusion caused by Eisenhower's remarks, officials at the Foreign Office believed that 'there are no reasonable grounds for supporting that Hitler is anything but dead'.[12] Having confidence in that conviction must have made it tedious for them to receive reports from the Dominions Office stating that 'in view of the suggestion that Adolf Hitler ... may be in Argentine, it might be of interest to the authorities concerned to know' that 'an ardent Nazi' named 'Major R.L. Berghammer' had once lived in Buenos Aires and should be located 'if there is any substance whatever in the rumour'.[13] One official replied, 'It is very doubtful if this will be of useful help to anyone.'[14] 'Very doubtful indeed', confirmed his colleague.

At other times, the Foreign Office viewed such reports with a sense of humour. A report received in November 1945 from the British Legation in Copenhagen claimed that a Danish lady informed them that her friend, who had previously predicted an RAF raid before it happened, had dreamed that Hitler was disguised as a monk, having shaved off his moustache.[15] Commenting on this, one official stated, 'I hope the lady's dream is true' as 'we could then await with suspense' the amusing scenario of Hitler's return as a monk.[16] As Major-General Kenneth Strong, head of intelligence at SHAEF, commented on the quality of some intelligence reports during World War II, 'All paratroops *always* seem to disguise themselves as nuns and priests.'[17] So, apparently, do deceased war criminals! The statement of one Foreign Office official that 'there will be no end to stories of this kind' has proved to be prophetic.[18] Indeed, some authors have attempted to publish such rumours as fact as recently as 2011, and British intelligence continued to investigate similar stories for years. The reasons why they were continually investigated, however, was not because of any doubt that Hitler was dead, as will be made clear in the following analysis of the War Office files which describe detailed investigations into rumours of Hitler's survival.

II: 'Baumgart is Telling Lies': The War Office Files

It has become something of a tradition in publications about Hitler's death for historians to describe the fantastic locations all over the world in which he has been reported to have been seen alive after April 1945. The survival rumours received by the War Office and preserved in its files are no exception to this. In a 'Dossier on Adolf Hitler' produced by MI14 (an intelligence agency of the War Office established in 1940 to provide information on Nazi Germany) prior to Trevor-Roper's investigations, Hitler was reported to have been seen in Ireland disguised as a woman and in Egypt, having converted to Islam.[19] Such rumours were described as 'wild' and usually received little or no comment. However, other rumours were taken more seriously and were investigated thoroughly during and after Trevor-Roper's investigations. For instance, in September 1946, the British Intelligence Division (ID) launched an investigation named 'Operation Conan Doyle' following 'spiritualist revelations' that a woman named Eva Hücker was in fact Eva Braun.[20] This investigation was inspired by a Mr and Mrs Hall, who informed the War Office that they had received messages from Mr Hall's dead father, who was a spiritualist, regarding a man named Stanley Knight who committed suicide after contracting venereal disease from Hücker. It was claimed that Hücker lived in Hanover with Hitler, who had undergone a 'facial operation' and was disguised under the name Heinrich, wearing a blond wig.[21] Although the War Office considered the story unlikely to be true, they requested that it be investigated as many people still believed Hitler was alive, and disproving such rumours would help prove his death. Accordingly, British intelligence officers managed to trace Hücker and discovered that she was a prostitute who bore no resemblance to Braun.[22]

One survival rumour was taken more seriously by British intelligence in September 1947 and was investigated for six months. This was the report of Frau Grape-Anderson, given to a Royal Air Force intelligence officer in Germany. She was concerned that not many people in Berlin believed that Hitler was dead, and she reported that it was widely believed in Hohenlychen that 'Hitler was definitely seen to take a lake-side walk on 24th April 1945'.[23] She also claimed that it was believed that a Fieseler Storch (a German light aircraft) carrying Hitler used to land frequently on a grass slope in the area so that he could visit Dr Karl Gebhardt in the SS sanatorium there.[24] Although it appeared to be a 'wild goose chase', the ID initiated investigations.[25] The story was reported to the ID's American counterparts at HQ EUCOM (European Command) with a note stating that Grape-Anderson's story coincidently echoed a similar story reported by Carmen Mory in July 1945 that Otto Skorzeny's paratroopers (famous for rescuing Mussolini) had rescued Hitler and other top Nazis from Berlin, taken them to a secret airfield in Hohenlychen and helped them escape.[26] It was stressed, however, that Mory was most unreliable as she had made a series of inaccurate statements before her suicide after being sentenced to death as a war criminal for her activities in Ravensbrück concentration camp.[27] This particular survival rumour was disproved on 11 March 1948 when the ID received interrogation results from both Gebhardt and Skorzeny.[28] Gebhardt was certain that Hitler had not visited him and that no plane had landed near the sanatorium in the last days.[29] Skorzeny stated that no high-ranking Nazis were evacuated by his unit and that if Hitler had been evacuated by his men, he would have known.[30] It was emphasised in correspondence with EUCOM that 'no undue importance' was attached to the 'implication of Hitler's survival' and that the reason for investigating was in case 'other leading Nazis had visited the Sanatorium'.[31] Clearly, British intelligence did not doubt that Hitler was dead, but it was felt to be important to 'properly evaluate' such rumours in light of any information they may provide with regard to other top Nazis. As will be demonstrated, this was the policy in all future investigations of survival rumours.

The longest and arguably most important ID investigation into any survival rumour began in December 1947 and continued until June 1948. This rumour originated with the testimony of Luftwaffe Captain Baumgart at his trial in Poland in December 1947 for war crimes. In a statement reported in the Polish newspaper *Express Wieczorny*, Baumgart claimed to have flown Hitler and Eva Braun to Denmark in April 1945.[32] Due to Allied bombing, he said that on 28 April he landed and stayed overnight in Magdeburg before continuing to Denmark the following day. Upon landing, Baumgart asserted, Hitler shook his hand and gave him a cheque for 20,000 RM (Reichsmark). This statement was reported in newspapers throughout the world. Further weight was added to this story when the ID received information from an informant (presumably ex-Nazi) working for a British Area Intelligence Office (AIO) stating that a plane had landed unexpectedly at Hadersleben airfield in Denmark between 26 and 28 April 1945. The informant claimed that '[o]nly the higher ranking officers were allowed to approach the plane and the purpose of the flight did not become generally known'.[33] Rumours spread that the plane had been carrying important personnel from Berlin. The ID had also collected cuttings from a German newspaper suggesting that Hitler could have escaped to Argentina in a U-boat, a rumour that was also stated in a German civilian communications intercept.[34]

Accordingly, the ID began tracking down Luftwaffe pilots to verify Baumgart's claims. However, Captain Hodges of the ID emphasised in several letters to intelligence officers that 'from the evidence available at this HQ', it is considered 'practically certain' that Hitler and Braun committed suicide on 30 April 1945, but, he added, it is 'still the policy to investigate leads which hold any promise of yielding useful historical information' and also to investigate in instances where it is 'thought possible that other high ranking personalities might have escaped from Germany by the method indicated'.[35] Conspiracy theorists such as Harry Cooper pose the following question to their readers: 'If Adolf Hitler killed himself in Berlin ... why were the world's spy services still looking for him into the middle of the 1950s?'[36] However, far from doubting the evidence of Hitler's death, British intelligence officers went on investigating survival rumours simply to gain information on other Nazis who may have escaped and to provide evidence for future historians to disprove rumours of Hitler's escape. After interviewing various Luftwaffe pilots who were stationed in Berlin and Magdeburg at the end of April and who all refuted Baumgart's story, and after confirming that Magdeburg was overrun by US forces on 18 April 1945, the ID concluded that 'Baumgart is telling lies'.[37] These conclusions undermine the argument in the most popular conspiracy theory book to date, *Grey Wolf.*

III: Double Trouble: Debunking the Escape Theories

In *Grey Wolf,* pages of documents concerning 'Hitler's Escape' are published verbatim.[38] Such documents bear the official stamps of American intelligence agencies and are often reproduced with statements of prominent officials such as Eisenhower and Stalin alleging that Hitler had escaped. Such documents and statements, when selectively removed and analysed in isolation from their context, may give the impression that Hitler did escape. Indeed, if the numerous British documents analysed in this chapter concerning 'Hitler survival rumours' were published without the opinions and conclusions of officials being included, the same impression could be created. However, the views of British intelligence officers make it clear that all such stories amounted to nothing. This selective methodology has been employed in various publications, including *Hitler in Argentina*, which claims that similar documents published verbatim constitute 'documented proof of Hitler's escape'.[39]

It is clear that when the documents employed by conspiracy theorists are analysed in such a way as to include the entire context, no conspiracy theory stands up to close scrutiny. Williams claimed in a television interview that 'we have the testimony from a Warsaw court of the pilot who flew them out'.[40] That pilot is Baumgart, the same Baumgart whom British intelligence established in 1948 was telling lies. *Grey Wolf* repeats his disproved story about landing at Magdeburg.[41] Williams concludes that Hitler escaped to Argentina, a rumour that was dismissed as 'sheer poppycock' by the Foreign Office as early as 1945. Williams even claimed that Trevor-Roper was unsuitable to lead the Hitler investigations.[42] However, Trevor-Roper had much experience as a member of MI6 during the Second World War deciphering German signals and interrogating Nazis.[43] Yet, despite these caveats, *Grey Wolf* still received considerable media coverage, and similar rumours of Hitler's survival are still published in newspapers today.[44] McKale's argument that the press takes advantage of the general reader, who would not have read the factual evidence concerning Hitler's death, in order to make money selling survival rumours is arguably confirmed by the extensive coverage received by conspiracy theories today.[45]

Another crucial argument put forward by Williams and similar conspiracy theorists is that a double was killed and burned in Hitler's place, allowing Hitler to escape.[46] The 2009 DNA results seemingly added further weight to this argument, and have been exploited in *Grey Wolf* to this end. However, as will be demonstrated in Chapter Six, those DNA results are in no way suitable evidence to support such conclusions. McKale's contention that the western press is partly to blame for the widespread perpetuation of survival rumours is bolstered by Trevor-Roper's interrogation of Baroness von Varo, filed in MI5 documents that have recently been declassified. She was among the women summoned by Hitler to say his final goodbyes, and she claimed that a newspaper reporter tried to force the opinion on her that the man who said goodbye to her was a drugged double, an idea she described as 'absurd', going on to reiterate that 'it was Hitler'.[47] The same reporter, Leslie Randall, was later denied access to the British files on Hitler's death in 1948 as intelligence officers were suspicious about him trying to 'rehash this very old history'.[48] The idea of Hitler being replaced by a drugged double who said the final goodbye to his staff with bleary eyes whilst the real Hitler escaped is repeated in various conspiracy theories. But Hitler's bleary eyes are in no way an indication of a drugged double. An analysis of Hitler's medical records reveals that 'the Führer complained' of seeing everything as through a 'thin veil over his right eye' in March 1944, a problem that could have returned in 1945 under the stressful circumstances of the bunker.[49] British intelligence gave a powerful argument against a similar rumour reported by Randall in 1945. Indeed, the rumour was described as 'ludicrously garbled', 'pure speculation' based on 'theory', not fact. Further:

'Hitler was not in a state of Coma when he said goodbye to the women; he was not supported by anyone', and 'it is important that such uncritical versions of the Hitler Story should not receive circulation as fact. We are satisfied that the first hand evidence at our disposal is now so full and consistent that, apart from direct eye-witness accounts of events in the bunker after midday on April 30th, no further material is likely to add anything significant to the story; and mere theories, unsupported by any eye-witness testimony, are worthless.'[50]

Indeed, the ID remained confident that the evidence British intelligence had collected 'does more than offset the numerous and vague reports of Hitler's survival which have circulated'.[51] The double theory, as numerous historians have argued, also fails to stand up to logical argument. Would Magda Goebbels have poisoned her children in the bunker because she did not want them to live in a world without National Socialism had she known her Führer would live on?[52] Her last hysterical plea for Hitler's life at his feet, most excellently depicted in the movie *Downfall*, was also a plea to spare her children, for in her warped mind, if Hitler died, her children must also die. The photographs taken by Russian soldiers depicting the lifeless bodies of these poor children are evidence enough that Mr and Mrs Goebbels were so convinced that Hitler had committed suicide that they took the lives of their children along with their own in 1945.

The evidence analysed in this chapter demonstrates that every British intelligence service involved in investigating Hitler's death considered rumours of Hitler's survival to be 'sheer poppycock'. This does not mean that all survival rumours were dismissed out of hand; on the contrary, those rumours which appeared to be more plausible were investigated in quite a lot of detail. Since many of the survival rumours investigated have been recycled and used again in more recent conspiracy theories, the British investigations provide a powerful argument against them. Those investigations also support McKale's argument that the western press bears some responsibility for the seemingly never-ending perpetuation of survival rumours, although, as will be seen in the following chapters, the brunt of this responsibility lies with the Soviets. But the recent surge in popular conspiracy theories has been largely inspired by the declassification of numerous FBI files which contain evidence of American investigations into rumours of Hitler's survival. The following chapter will therefore analyse these investigations in an effort to further determine the credibility of Hitler survival rumours and, for the first time, provide a detailed contextual analysis of the FBI files that have aroused so much interest over the past few years.

*Hitler was reported to have been aboard the
second submarine and with two women, a doctor,
and several other men ... pack horses were
waiting for the group ... at dusk the party arrived
at the ranch where Hitler and his party are now in
hiding.*

—FBI report, 1945[1]

American Intelligence and Rumours of Survival

I: 'A Dollar to a Doughnut': Hitler in America?

Late one night in February 1948, the FBI received an alarming telephone call. On a 'Central Railroad' train from 'New Orleans' an informant had 'observed a man in Seat 40, Car 10, whom he believed was Adolf Hitler. This individual was accompanied by a woman'.[2] No doubt out of a sense of duty, and perhaps curiosity, 'two Special Agents ... got on the train and had closely observed the person in question and his woman companion. It was so obvious to the Agents that this person was not Adolf Hitler that they did not make a positive determination of his identity, feeling that it would possibly create a situation causing absurd publicity.'[3]

Absurd as this incident was, reports of Hitler sightings in America were not unusual. Indeed, it may come as a surprise to some readers to learn that Adolf Hitler was often reported to be sighted in post-war America. Importantly, such reports were filed alongside the same documents that conspiracy theorists cite as evidence to claim the Führer escaped to Argentina.

Beginning in late 1945, regional FBI offices throughout America received odd stories from concerned residents claiming that Hitler could be living in their midst. In

October that year, one handwritten letter read: 'Dear Sir, I'll bet a dollar to a doughnut that Hitler is located right in New York City! There's no other city in the world where he could so easily be absorbed, no doubt you have considered this possibility...'[4] One year later, a lady from Virginia reported 'that she recently saw a man who looked like Hitler in Charlottesville'.[5] According to some Americans, on his tour around the United States, Hitler had even developed a liking for American food! As one report from October 1946 recalled, a lady sat down for lunch in Washington, DC at a crowded restaurant and asked to share a table with a man who sported a 'black mustache'. The man agreed, but during her meal his 'nervous' behaviour and appearance led her to worry that he could be Hitler himself. The lady, who seemingly worked for the Department of State, consequently called the FBI to tell them that she thought Hitler was 'right here in Washington D.C.'[6]

Conspiracy theorists unsurprisingly ignore such tales of Hitler in America, which swept FBI offices throughout the 1940s and 50s. This is likely because the outcome of these investigations, and the motivations of those who spread such rumours, cast further doubt on similar stories of Hitler living in Argentina that are filed alongside them. For example, in the early hours of the morning in October 1948, the FBI office in Washington, DC received a concerned telephone call from a lady who 'operates a rooming house' reporting 'that she believes a guest who has been at her home for the past few weeks is Adolf Hitler, this belief being based solely on the fact that he looks somewhat like him'.[7] Tragically, this story could have been a cry for help as the lady was 'incoherent and repeatedly stated that she is being persecuted by her neighbors'.[8] The FBI concluded that she was 'obviously demented' and likely referred her to the police, as they had done so in the past.[9]

Other reports of Hitler sightings in America were motivated by spite. For example, in 1949 the FBI interviewed a man who claimed 'Hitler was in St. Louis'. However, it was found that the interviewee had no reason for thinking that the accused gentleman was Adolf Hitler except that he 'speaks with a definite German accent and refused to sell [the name has been censored here] his life's history'. As a result, the case was closed, with the conclusion that the story was reported due to the man's 'intense dislike' of the accused, and 'not because of any real evidence indicating that' the man was Adolf Hitler.[10] By 1960, the FBI appears to have grown tired of such stories, as it was recommended that a lady who reported seeing 'Hitler in a cafeteria in Los Angeles on Easter Sunday, 1960 ... accompanied by a woman closely resembling Eva' be ignored because a response 'may encourage her'.[11]

As these reports of Hitler in America demonstrate, Hitler survival rumours could be inspired by mental illness and/or spite. The lady who reported spotting Hitler in 1960 claimed that she would 'like to be of assistance in helping to find Hitler'.[12] Therefore, her motive in reporting this story was possibly to gain employment and/or financial reward, something that was also undoubtedly true of many of the reports claiming that Hitler was in Argentina, as the following analysis will make clear.

II: Hitler in Argentina?

Like their allies in the British Foreign Office, from May 1945, FBI agents in America collected many newspaper cuttings concerning contradictory stories of how Hitler died.[13] Also like the British, the FBI was aware that much of this initial confusion stemmed from the Soviets. On 9 June 1945, the *Washington Times-Herald* ran a story with the headline 'Hitler's Corpse Found By Reds'.[14] The next day, the same newspaper stated that the 'Russian garrison commandant of Berlin' believed that 'Hitler has gone into hiding somewhere in Europe, possibly with (Generalissimo Francisco) Franco'.[15] In July, a 'Red Staff Officer' reportedly revealed that the body initially thought to be Hitler's 'was a double, and a rather poor one at that'.[16] Perhaps unsurprisingly, given the apparent confusion on the ground in Berlin, it was around this time that information concerning rumours of Hitler's escape to Argentina began to accumulate on the desks of FBI agents.

On 14 July, the FBI received a report from a 'source of unknown reliability' in Buenos Aires claiming that Hitler may have 'landed in Argentina approximately June 20' via submarine, possibly the 'U530' that surrendered to Argentina in July.[17] Fortunately for historians, the FBI contacts in Argentina reassuringly confirmed that all such rumours were 'being investigated'.[18] On 21 July 1945 the FBI collected a newspaper clipping in which a 'Nazi Sub Chief' who had captained the 'U-530' described reports that he had taken Hitler and Eva to Argentina as 'wild rumors'.[19] Like Otto Skorzeny, who was questioned by Anglo-American intelligence about a similar rumour, Admiral Eberhard Godt informed the press that he 'certainly would have known if the U-530 had been ear-marked for any special mission'.[20]

Another German fleet commander, 'Heye', supported Godt's statement, claiming that if Hitler had 'intended to escape it would have been by air, not by sea. He didn't like ships – he even got sick riding on his yacht on the Rhine.'[21] Perceptively, the naval officer added, 'The Fuehrer could not live anywhere as Mr. X.' Herr Heye clearly considered the idea of the bellowing, over-confident Hitler – who saw himself as the saviour of Germany – living life as an 'unknown man' to be ridiculous. As for the reason behind such rumours, he claimed that 'there is an organized effort to keep the Hitler myth alive', and that if Hitler was to 'return someday', then the Hitler Youth wanted to make sure they were 'worthy of receiving him'. This meant keeping Nazism alive in occupied Germany, in anticipation of Hitler's return. As will be shown in the following chapter, this was a key concern which inspired Hugh Trevor-Roper's detailed investigations into Hitler's death.

On 31 July 1945, the FBI finally received conclusions from its overseas contacts concerning the submarine-escape rumour. Despite its efforts to learn from him 'the source of his information concerning Hitler's presence in Argentina', the informant (whose name, like so many in FBI files, is censored) 'consistently refused to furnish any information in this regard'.[22] It was therefore 'concluded that newspapers and political circles in Uruguay are inclined to discredit the report that Hitler and Braun are in Argentina'.[23] Nevertheless, unreliable sources or not, the reports of Hitler in Argentina kept coming.

On 11 August 1945 the Washington, DC FBI division filed a rather lengthy report from an informant who claimed that his 'friend whose name he refuses to disclose' flew to a 'ranch' in Argentina that was supposed to be in 'the vicinity of the hideout of Adolf Hitler', who was living there with a 'group of his former henchmen'.[24]

Despite interrogation, the informant 'refused under any circumstances to reveal the source of his information'.[25] Three days later, a similar report was filed by the FBI field office in Los Angeles detailing the story of a censored informant who met a 'Spanish-Argentinian' man at 'a club in Hollywood' who claimed he was 'one of four men who met Hitler and his party when they landed from submarines in Argentina two and a half weeks after the fall of Berlin'.[26] According to this report, Hitler arrived at his Argentinian ranch on horseback! However, a few days later, the FBI received a radiogram from Buenos Aires informing them that 'possible clandestine landings from U 530 and similar craft' had been investigated 'with negative result to date'.[27] Moreover, it went on, 'It is consensus of USA Military, Naval Attaches, British and Argentine authorities that reports that Hitler and Eva Braun in Argentina are unfounded.'[28]

As newspaper reports of Hitler sightings in Argentina continued to inspire unfounded reports to intelligence agencies, on 25 August 1945 the American 'War Crimes Commission' asked the FBI whether they had 'any "probable cause" for believing that Hitler or any of his associates were hiding in the Argentine'.[29] Accordingly, the bureau replied that it had 'no tangible evidence of any such hiding'.[30] However, the FBI did not have to wait long for tangible evidence to disprove the rumours that Hitler was living in an Argentinian ranch.

On 6 September, the Director of the FBI, J. Edgar Hoover, informed the American Military Intelligence Service that 'it has now been learned that the source' of the original Hitler ranch rumour was 'a 97 year old spiritualist, leader of a spiritualist cult and a spiritualist prophet'. Most damningly for conspiracy theorists, Hoover concluded: 'To date no serious indication has been received that Adolf Hitler is in Argentina.'[31]

Despite the announcement to the press of Hugh Trevor-Roper's findings on 1 November 1945, the FBI continued to receive and investigate rumours of Hitler's survival in Argentina. Its possible reasons for doing so are discussed later in this chapter. For now, it is important to note that the great majority of these stories turned out to be nonsense reported by individuals with questionable motives. For example, on 28 November 1945, an FBI contact in Uruguay informed Hoover that the source of numerous publications claiming that Hitler was in Argentina was a 'journalist of the most sensational and unreliable nature'.[32] One year later, the FBI, like British intelligence, was still investigating rumours of Hitler's survival. In Philadelphia, special agents investigated the discovery of several suspicious documents containing notable passages such as: 'I saw Adolf Hitler the other day while in Argentina. He is considerably nervous, but has stopped taking drugs. He is hiding very safely while we take the chances...'[33] The investigating agents believed this material 'was possibly prepared as a childish prank, or by a person of unsound mind'.[34]

This was not the only incident of its kind that was investigated by the FBI. For example, in September 1947 San Francisco agents confiscated a hoax letter from an individual who proposed reading it out loud on the radio to cause a 'startling sensation'.[35] The letter read:

No doubt it is well known that little has happened in my life that could be called laughable, but when at the time of the Russian attack on Berlin I found refuge in the basement of the Imperial Chancellory building I was informed that my body and that of my wife (nee Eva Braun) had been covered with naptha and burned in the Chancellory garden. I could not help smiling for at this time we were many kilometres south west of Berlin on our air journey to Argentina.[36]

It was signed 'Adolf Hitler, Reichskansler, Berlin'. The FBI concluded that its real author, who was '77 years old and seemed to be a psychopathic case', was motivated purely by the desire to create sensation.[37]

Although the desire to cause a sensation may have been sufficient on its own to motivate American pranksters to spread rumours of Hitler's survival, for others, the motive was financial gain. As a letter from Mexico in May 1948 claimed, 'Hitler is neither in Spain nor in Argentina'.[38] To find out where he was, however, would cost 'about twenty million dollars'.[39]

III: Recurrent Legends: The CIA Investigations

The FBI was not the only American intelligence agency to investigate rumours of Hitler's survival. The CIA has also declassified some files which show that it too received reports of Hitler's supposed wanderings.

Unfortunately, the fragmented and censored nature of such files, like the FBI files, makes it impossible for historians to trace the conclusions of every survival rumour that was investigated. Nevertheless, it is clear from all the rumours for which the outcome of the investigations is preserved that there is no evidence whatsoever to prove that Hitler survived World War II. In reports for which conclusions are not provided or obvious, hints at the attitude of intelligence officers can still be retrieved, and general statements on the subject are revealing.

Of the many documents preserved by the CIA concerning Hitler, one stands out as useful for conspiracy theorists. This is a grainy photograph of a man, alleged to be Adolf Hitler, passed to a CIA agent in September 1955 by a former 'SS trooper', Phillip Citroen.[40] According to the latter, 'the Germans residing in Tunja follow this alleged Adolf Hitler with an "idolatry of the Nazi past, addressing him as 'der Fuhrer' and affording him the Nazi salute and storm-trooper adulation"'.[41] Conspiracy theorist Harry Cooper somehow uses the CIA documents concerning this rumour to bolster his theory that Hitler escaped to Argentina, despite the fact that Tunja is in Colombia.[42] This photograph was also viewed by thousands when it was posted on some popular social media pages in October 2017 (although the comments reflect a healthy scepticism).[43] Hitler, it seems, according to some conspiracy theorists, liked to travel a lot after the war!

The CIA clearly didn't think much of this photograph or of the informant who provided it. As the reporting agent noted, due to the 'apparent fantasy of the report, the information was not submitted at the time it was received'.[44] Moreover, Citroen and his brother were co-owners of a local newspaper, the *Maracaibo Times*. Perhaps the CIA suspected Citroen of trying to stir up sensation, like so many other journalists had done with previous Hitler survival stories. The investigating agents certainly considered it to be a 'fantastic story'.[45] Perhaps unsurprisingly then, CIA 'Headquarters ... felt that enormous efforts could be expended on this matter with remote possibilities of establishing anything concrete. Therefore, we suggest that this matter be dropped.'[46]

The CIA, having in its possession convincing evidence of Hitler's death from British and American intelligence sources (discussed further in later chapters), and most likely also having knowledge of the unfruitful efforts of Anglo-American intelligence to establish any substance in reported rumours of Hitler's survival, clearly felt that investigating the Citroen rumour was a waste of time. Considering the FBI's previous experience with journalists claiming to bear 'evidence' of Hitler's survival, this was probably the correct decision. Even the authors of *Grey Wolf* found the Citroen story and photograph to be 'ultimately unconvincing', again showing how conspiracy theorists can't even agree among themselves about which sources are reliable, which sources are not and where 'Hitler' was at certain times after the war.[47] The criteria for selection seem to be dictated by the personal theories of certain authors rather than by the quality of the evidence itself.

Other comments preserved in the CIA files concerning Hitler are particularly revealing of the opinion that many American intelligence officers held concerning these survival rumours. In a passage about the interrogation of Erna Flegel (a nurse who worked in the Führerbunker during Hitler's last days), an agent wrote, 'The Soviets controlled the evidence of Hitler's death and many of the Fuehrerbunker staff were imprisoned in the Soviet Union for years thereafter. More than two decades passed before Moscow decided to publish forensic proof of Hitler's death, thus spiking recurrent legends about his appearance in

Argentina.'[48] A synonym of the word 'legends', of course, is 'fairy tales'.

IV: 'Is Hitler Dead?' American Military Intelligence Investigates

Although most conspiracy theorists focus on reports created by the FBI and the CIA, they neglect the arguably more important investigations undertaken by American intelligence agencies on the ground in occupied Germany. Indeed, the American Military Intelligence Division (ID EUCOM) and the CIC detachments it instructed in Germany undertook their own investigation into these matters after the publication of Trevor-Roper's report. However, the evidence surrounding these investigations is very fragmented in comparison with that available concerning the British investigations. Therefore, what follows is only a partial reconstruction.

Although the evidence is incomplete, it is clear that in 1947, the European Command Intelligence Center (ECIC) of the United States Army in Germany was 'directed to compile all documentary evidence on death of Hitler in order to spike rumours that he is still alive'.[49] This investigation was likely sparked by the Baumgart story, as a cutting from *Stars and Stripes* dated 6 October 1947 detailing Baumgart's tale was filed alongside the investigations in question.[50] Officials at the American Intelligence Division began by asking other intelligence agencies what evidence they held concerning Hitler's death. Most significantly, they asked their British counterparts in Herford why they believed firmly that Hitler was dead. The British ID's response was that its 'attitude' was based on Trevor-Roper's investigations, and, as evidence, cited facts published in *The Last Days of Hitler*.[51]

'After three months of research', the ECIC produced a report entitled 'Is Hitler Dead?'[52] This acknowledged that rumours about Hitler's end had been 'rampant' during the past two years and that the one 'definite proof' of Hitler's death, his body, was 'lacking'.[53] It further stated that 'many agencies' had been collecting evidence of Hitler's death but that no attempt at collation had yet been made, aside from that achieved in Trevor-Roper's book.[54] Interestingly, the report noted that Trevor-Roper's book 'apparently failed to satisfy many interested persons since this officer was assigned the task of further research on the question of Hitler's death'.[55] Nevertheless, having analysed the evidence collected by Trevor-Roper, the report concluded that 'Hitler committed suicide ... the body was burned in the garden adjacent to the bunker and the ashes disposed of secretly'.[56] Clearly, no evidence was found which indicated that any survival rumours could be true or that Trevor-Roper had reached erroneous conclusions. However, a few days later, American intelligence obtained information from Fox Mathews, a former ECIC agent, suggesting that the Soviets had forced dentists to identify Hitler's teeth.[57] Consequently, the investigations continued, now focused on establishing the facts behind this story and on the forensic evidence in general.

At this stage American intelligence officers were warned that one of their own could be peddling survival rumours. Indeed, Heimlich, a former lieutenant colonel in the US Army, was suspected of planning to disseminate misinformation for financial gain.[58] As a result, the American Intelligence Division, in its mission to 'put to a stop once and for all rumors that Hitler is alive', sought to find Heimlich and question him under oath about his knowledge of Hitler's last days.[59] Such was the concern over Heimlich that Lieutenant General C. R. Huebner even informed the American military governor, General Lucius D. Clay, about the issue. According to Huebner, Heimlich had 'made statements to the press that Hitler is not dead' but when confronted about his comments, argued that he was misquoted.[60]

On 11 March 1948, 'Mr. William Friel Heimlich appeared before the Inspector, Colonel Harold R. Booth, at OMGUS Headquarters, Berlin, Germany'.[61] The story he told was fascinating. In May 1945, Heimlich was 'Executive Officer' of the top-secret G-2 Division at Berlin District Headquarters. Prior to the Anglo-American occupation of Berlin, Heimlich, along with Colonel Rufus A. Bratton and E. A. Howard of the British Army, was called to SHAEF headquarters. Here, the men were handed a 'sketch of the bunker' which showed 'where Adolf Hitler was buried' (this sketch is published for the first time in Chapter Six). They were then instructed that their first mission in Berlin would be to investigate 'the circumstances surrounding the death of Adolf Hitler'. Further evidence derived from 'guards at the Reich chancellery' would be forwarded to them when they arrived. This evidence again demonstrates that Anglo-American intelligence agents were investigating Hitler's death prior to Hugh Trevor-Roper's involvement.

Upon arriving in Berlin, Heimlich's team visited the bunker and collected more eyewitness testimonies. Despite this, Heimlich felt that not much progress had been made in the investigation. However, in December 1945, his team 'finally obtained permission from the Soviet authorities to excavate the bomb crater where Hitler was allegedly buried'. Consequently, a four-man team, armed with the sketch supplied by SHAEF, excavated the area surrounding Hitler's bunker. Their most exciting discovery was a 'silk hat, water soaked, with the initials "A.H." inscribed therein'. The outcome of Heimlich's dig will be discussed further in the following chapters. For now, what is important to note is that when asked his opinion on Hitler's whereabouts, Heimlich stated under oath: 'In my opinion, Hitler is dead.'

In September 1948, ID EUCOM discontinued its detailed investigation into Hitler's suicide and rumours of his survival.[62] The most 'conclusive proof' of Hitler's death they had discovered was confirmation via several interrogations that dental assistant Käthe Heusermann and dental technician Fritz Echtmann had been shown Hitler's teeth by the Soviets and had confirmed their authenticity.[63] However, officials at the American ID decided not to publish evidence of their investigations. They felt that in the absence of any concrete forensic evidence in American hands (i.e. 'identifiable portions of Hitler's body'), further publication based primarily on eyewitness testimony would only increase public speculation.[64] Still, all the conclusions drawn and all the evidence collected by the American ID throughout its investigations suggested that Hitler was dead, even if they did not wish to publicly say so.

Although the American ID concluded its detailed investigations without adding much to what Trevor-Roper had already discovered, American intelligence agents were encouraged to continue forwarding 'any pertinent information' they came across during their routine intelligence work.[65] As a result, historians have been furnished with even more evidence to disprove rumours of Hitler's survival. For example, in late 1948, the CIC conducted several interviews with one Max Schachtner, 'a lifelong friend of Fritz Braun, father of Eva Braun'.[66] Even though Eva's father believed his daughter and her husband to be dead, Max had 'come to the conclusion that Adolf Hitler and Eva Braun are still alive and together presumably in Argentine'.[67] Max formed these opinions based on 'personal observations and current public reports'.[68] Most notably, a suspected former Luftwaffe pilot allegedly told Max that 'he had seen Adolf Hitler at an airbase in Denmark after his alleged suicide'.[69] However, this case was closed after 'the exploitation of all leads ... proved negative'.[70] The following year, a report indicating 'that Adolf Hitler is now running a coffee room in Amsterdam' received little comment from the Intelligence Division.[71] Hitler at this stage could undoubtedly have written one of the most comprehensive travel guides of the twentieth century. But, of course, all available evidence suggests that such rumours were nonsense.

V: Hitler Everywhere? The Importance of Context

As the above analysis demonstrates, the great majority of Hitler survival rumours contained in recently declassified FBI files stem from questionable sources. It is only by ignoring the unreliability of the authors of these stories and by linking them together, ignoring factual inaccuracies and the opinion of the intelligence agents actually investigating the rumours, that conspiracy theorists manage to construct elaborate stories of Hitler's escape.

On the first episode of the popular television series *Hunting Hitler*, CIA veteran Bob Baer claims: 'In these files there are thousands of leads.'[72] But it is precisely this rich variety of contradictory stories of Hitler's survival that render the arguments of conspiracy theorists all the more unconvincing. Although 'hundreds of FBI documents place Hitler in Argentina', as the narrator of *Hunting Hitler* exclaims, conspiracy theorists often choose to focus solely on these reports, ignoring the fact that such rumours were filed alongside stories of Hitler's escape to Canada, Japan and America by individuals with motives comparable to those who claimed that the Führer was in Argentina.[73] As this book has demonstrated so far, some rumour spreaders were mentally ill, others wanted money and some were journalists looking to publish sensationalist stories; some (like Carmen Mory) may have wanted to divert attention away from their own war crimes, to escape justice or to evade capture, while for some others, the story of Hitler's escape may have been a cry for help or a means of seeking attention. None of them, however, as the FBI discovered, had any tangible evidence of Hitler's escape.

This same lack of contextual analysis is also employed by conspiracy theorists referencing declassified CIA files concerning rumours of Hitler's survival. For example, conspiracy theorists conveniently ignore the fact that in the 1940s and '50s American intelligence agencies often collected, and were sometimes duped by, fabricated intelligence. According to Tim Weiner's (albeit exaggerated) account, the amount of fake intelligence collected by the CIA in post-war Germany and Austria rendered its stations 'factories of fake intelligence'.[74] Dodgy informants were selling dodgy intelligence, and although most of this concerned the Soviet Union, this was likely also to have been the case with some Hitler survival rumours. Sources trying to sell information on Hitler's escape, like those hawking intelligence on the Soviets, may have been 'talented liars' producing a 'patchwork of frauds'.[75] Perhaps the grainy photograph showing 'Hitler' alive in the 1950s is an example of such financially motivated fake intelligence.

Although conspiracy theorists use poor methods to arrive at unreliable conclusions, they do still pose some interesting questions. For example: 'If Adolf Hitler killed himself in Berlin ... why were the world's spy services still looking for him into the middle of the 1950s?'[76] Again, appropriate historical context, so often neglected by conspiracy theorists, is important in answering this question.

It is difficult to decipher the precise meaning of many FBI documents because they are more heavily censored and incomplete than the British files concerning Hitler's death. Still, it is clear that the FBI did not think rumours of Hitler's survival in Argentina were very credible. J. Edgar Hoover himself described a rumour claiming that Hitler was staying at a Brazilian Hotel in 1947 (portrayed as fact in *Grey Wolf*) as 'a rather fantastic story'.[77] Nevertheless, Hitler survival rumours still seemed to be a matter of personal interest for Hoover – who, incidentally, was also 'deeply interested in "flying saucers"'.[78] But aside from any personal interest in often amusing stories, why did the FBI dedicate valuable time to investigating such reports? A contextual knowledge of the changes occurring in the American intelligence 'community' after World War II, so often lacking in conspiracy theories, is essential in answering this question.

The FBI kept detailed logs of some survival rumours in order to prevent duplicate inquiries being made into false stories told repeatedly by the same individuals. Investigating rumours thoroughly when they first surfaced could prevent time being wasted in the future. It was also a good way for the FBI to keep a close watch on people who might be unstable or who could cause further trouble in the future. As was also the case with British intelligence, it was often not so much the rumours of Hitler's escape that attracted the interest of the FBI but the people reporting such rumours and the individuals connected with them. Hoover tactfully responded to most of the reported Hitler rumours, no matter how absurd, with a kind letter of thanks and sometimes a request that the informant keep the FBI apprised of any further similar information. A typical response from Hoover to someone who reported a sighting of Hitler in Argentina in November 1945 read:

Your interest and courtesy in making this information available are greatly appreciated and you may be assured that it will receive appropriate attention.

In the event you have any additional information which you believe should be furnished to this Bureau, please feel free to contact the Special Agent in Charge of our Birmingham Office...

Sincerely yours, John Edgar Hoover Director.[79]

There are two possible reasons why Hoover did this, aside from personal interest. First, it was a good way to keep the general public onside. This was undoubtedly an important consideration for Hoover as the FBI in the immediate post-war era suffered negative press involving unflattering comparisons with the Gestapo.[80] At a time when the future of American intelligence agencies was uncertain following the end of their wartime duties, an unhappy public with the ability to influence the decisions of politicians was not good news for Hoover. Responding positively in the way he did also helped ensure a steady flow of information into FBI offices – information, of course, being a key tool of intelligence agencies, especially of those that were in competition with others, as the FBI was with the CIA.[81]

Nowadays, many readers likely think of the FBI as a solely domestic intelligence agency. But this was not always the case. During the Second World War, by engaging in anti-Nazi intelligence operations, the bureau had amassed for itself what Professor Rhodri Jeffreys-Jones describes in his history of the FBI as a 'Latin American empire', and Hoover wanted to keep that empire intact.[82] Although the 1947 National Security Act legally ended the FBI's power to operate outside America and formally established the CIA, evidence suggests that some FBI agents continued to operate outside the country.[83] Therefore, using his contacts in Argentina and the surrounding countries to investigate rumours of Hitler's survival may have been another convenient way for Hoover to cling on to the FBI's overseas influence. Remarkably, as will be discussed further in Chapter Five, I have found firm evidence that Hoover was given presidential permission to investigate rumours of Martin Bormann's survival in 'South America' one year after the National Security Act legally curtailed FBI involvement in this area.[84] Rumours of Bormann's and Hitler's survival were often interlinked and it is very likely that the preservation of FBI overseas influence was a prime motivator behind the bureau's inquiries into rumours of Hitler's survival. Nevertheless, there are other possible reasons as to why Hoover continued to commit time and resources to investigating such rumours even after the publication of Hugh Trevor-Roper's report.

The FBI under Hoover was in competition not only with the CIA but also, to some extent, with British intelligence. To make matters worse, the director was, as Christopher Hitchens states, 'rather Anglophobic'.[85] He distrusted British intelligence and held the belief 'widely shared in America, that London had manipulated the United States during World War I'.[86] A distrust of British intelligence does indeed appear to have been quite widespread. Evidence of it can even be found in the FBI files concerning Hitler survival rumours. For example, on 3 November 1945, a letter sent to Hoover claiming that Hitler was in Argentina ended with the assertion: 'Do not believe the British lie that Hitler is dead I am a full blooded American and think this should be investigated at once, Your Friend, (name censored).'[87]

Whilst Hoover's willingness to entertain public doubts about Hitler's death and investigate rumours of his survival can to some extent be explained by his own personal interest, by his dislike of British intelligence, by the advantage of having multiple informants, by the need to keep the public happy with the FBI and by his desire to preserve his 'Latin American fiefdom', he was not alone in disliking the British.[88] As was highlighted earlier, other American intelligence officers, such as Heimlich, challenged the British conclusions on Hitler's death, and some members of the American public doubted Hitler was dead largely because the investigations had been conducted by the British. Furthermore, Captain George T. Gabelia, a member of Heimlich's Berlin intelligence team, believed that Trevor-Roper's report contained 'very little actual concrete evidence' and that it 'was put out to satisfy British opinion back home'.[89] Moreover, as was discussed earlier in this chapter, the American Intelligence Division initially expressed doubts about *The Last Days of Hitler*, although its parallel investigation unsurprisingly concluded that Trevor-Roper's findings were accurate. But was there any substance behind this distrust of British intelligence? Conspiracy theorists obviously doubt their conclusions and motives. Some go as far as to claim that political motivations overshadowed the need to establish the truth about Hitler's death.[90] This is a more serious argument which requires further analysis. It is legitimate to question the role of MI6 and of influential intelligence officers such as Dick White, as well as the quality and seemingly late timing of the British investigations, why Trevor-Roper was chosen to lead them, and the basis of Soviet accusations of Hitler's escape, without resorting to unfounded assertions. Such questions will be addressed in the following chapter.

The motive behind his report was an intelligence agenda, set by MI6: to counteract the effects of the Soviet insistence that Hitler was still alive and being protected by ... British intelligence. With all of that in hand, and admitted as such in writing by its author, how is it possible to come to any other conclusion than the report was a work of fiction — a cover story — camouflaged as fact?

—Peter Levenda on Hugh Trevor-Roper's investigations, 2012[1]

Political Motivations? British, American and Soviet Conduct

I: Why Trevor-Roper? Investigating the British Investigations

The way in which the British investigations into Hitler's death were conducted has been criticised by various authors. Conspiracy theorists such as Peter Levenda have argued that political motivations overshadowed the need to discover the truth about Hitler's death and that the investigations were rushed to counter Soviet claims of Hitler's survival in the British Zone of Germany.[2] Gerrard Williams argues that the Allies allowed Hitler to escape in return for providing Nazi intelligence to use against the Soviets in the coming Cold War.[3] James O'Donnell criticised Allied interrogators for lacking objectivity and asking the wrong questions.[4] In this chapter, the aims and conduct of British intelligence agents and their co-operation with the Americans and the Soviets during the Hitler investigations will be analysed in order to determine whether there is any truth to such accusations of poor British conduct and political motivations.

Although large-scale British investigations into Hitler's death did not begin until Trevor-Roper was appointed by Dick White to undertake them in September 1945, British intelligence was gathering evidence concerning Hitler's death prior to Trevor-Roper's involvement. During these initial investigations, pressure was mounting for the Western Allies to release an official statement about Hitler's death. Indeed, the FBI collected newspaper clippings bearing headlines such as 'London is Silent on Hitler Rumour'.[5] The London *Evening News* suggested that 'a full investigation by Scotland Yard and American G men' should be undertaken to solve the 'mystery'.[6] It was the Soviet accusation that Hitler was hiding in the British Zone that inspired White, then head of the Counter Intelligence Bureau (CIB) in the British Zone of Germany, to ask Trevor-Roper to initiate his thorough investigation into Hitler's death.[7]

It is important at this point to dispel a few aspersions that some conspiracy theorists have cast about Trevor-Roper's suitability to lead these investigations. For example, during a Sky News interview in 2011, Gerrard Williams claimed, 'I have no idea why Hugh Trevor-Roper was actually chosen by the Secret Services to do the death of Hitler.'[8] If Mr Williams had studied the evidence properly, he would have realised that Trevor-Roper was a highly regarded and very talented MI6 officer.[9] Prior to the Second World War, Trevor-Roper had taught himself German, read Hitler's autobiography, *Mein Kampf*, and criticised other intelligence officers for not doing so.[10] During the war, he single-handedly broke a German Abwehr cipher whilst musing in the bath 'during an air raid'.[11] In 1943, Dick White claimed he knew of 'no single officer, either in MI5 or MI6, who possesses a more comprehensive knowledge of the Abwehr organisation'.[12] By 1945, Trevor-Roper was an expert on the German Intelligence Services (who would surely have been behind any attempt to help Hitler escape the bunker) and on Nazi ideology through various interrogations.[13] The future Lord Dacre was undoubtedly the most qualified intelligence officer to investigate the Führer's death. Having read his impressive final intelligence report on the German Intelligence Services, White knew this.[14] If any doubt still remains, historians can study the actual letters which resulted in Hugh Trevor-Roper's appointment to lead these investigations.

In a letter to Thomas 'Tar' Robertson asking whether Trevor-Roper could be made available to lead the Hitler investigations, White refers to a 'considerable amount of comment in the press' speculating 'whether or not Hitler is still living'.[15] He describes Trevor-Roper as a 'first-rate chap' who has 'kept the closest tabs on the matter' and is already familiar with reports on various Nazis relevant to the Hitler case. This further demonstrates that conspiracy theorists who claim that Trevor-Roper was unsuitable to lead the investigations are incorrect.

II: Preventing a Hitler Myth: Rumours, Motivations and Context

The letters between White and Robertson that officially began Trevor-Roper's investigations also provide an important insight into the motivations behind British intelligence. Three key motivations provided the impetus for these detailed investigations. First, White stated that undertaking a detailed investigation would be useful for 'quadripartite' discussions with the Soviets, who had expressed the desire to 'review the evidence on the subject with the other occupational powers'. White's wish to review evidence with the Soviets is instructive for section V ('Appeasing the Soviets?') of this chapter, for, as will be demonstrated, the desire to maintain co-operation with the Soviets on wider political issues was hindered by Soviet accusations of Hitler's survival in the British Zone. Indeed, as Sean Greenwood points out, at this time, many British officials sought to maintain co-operation with the Soviets.[16]

Second, the desire to prevent the formation of a 'Hitler myth' is mentioned in Trevor-Roper's book and throughout his investigations as a key motivation.[17] The idea of Hitler still living, or of him dying a 'heroic' death, was certainly a hindrance to the Anglo-American denazification and democratisation programmes in occupied Germany that were under way at the time. This provides another reason as to why rumours of Hitler's survival were investigated into the 1950s. For example, in August 1945, British 21 Army Group intelligence reports noted the following rumours:

a) That Hitler has spoken on Tokio radio
b) That a Werwolf broadcast has stated: "We are ready; Hitler is with us."[18]

Clearly, rumours of Hitler's survival were being used to inspire last-ditch Nazi resistance movements such as Werwolf. As the 21 Army Group report continued:

In the R.B Detmold there seems to be a certain amount of Nazi inspired unrest. Swastikas were found painted on a wall at Osterweg near Halle. In Bielefeld a notice was put up outside the Rathus predicting the return of the Fuhrer and threatening all Germans who collaborate with the Allies.[19]

Just over a week later, 21 Army Group noted rumours that 'Hitler is in Ireland' and 'in Japan with a few selected experts and V-weapon plans'.[20] At a time when 'young military motor cycle messengers' were getting their 'heads cut off' by Nazi fanatics who placed 'wire across the road which you couldn't see', it's easy to understand why British intelligence monitored rumours of Hitler's survival and sought evidence to disprove them, especially when they were being used to inspire such violence.[21] In the summer of 1945, some individuals were even tried by Military Government Courts for spreading rumours 'calculated to excite or alarm the people or to undermine morale of Allied Forces'.[22] As late as November 1945, rumours concerning Hitler's whereabouts continued to help keep nostalgia for Nazism alive. As an American censorship report revealed, a resident of Herbrechtingen was pondering: 'Where might Adolf Hitler be? Believe me, I have often thought about that. For I – that is, we all had it good. It was a noble time.'[23]

But even after the violent Werwolf-style resistance 'petered out', Hitler survival rumours were still being used to inspire Nazi underground movements.[24] In February 1947, people were reportedly 'saying every day in Bremen that German youths should proceed to Spain, in order to rejoin Hitler and the German Forces there, who were already provided with tanks and aeroplanes'.[25] Two years later, a man was arrested for handing out 'leaflets in Cologne's main railway station'.[26] The leaflets were 'printed with a swastika on the top'.[27] They read, 'Our Fuehrer lives and will return soon with unheard of power. Oppose our persecutors and wait. Hail Hitler.'[28] The man claimed he had been working for a woman who was 'hiring agents' to spread this propaganda.

That Anglo-American intelligence spent much time investigating and disproving rumours concerning Hitler was not unusual. Indeed, most Anglo-American general intelligence reports during the occupation of Germany contained sections outlining various rumours that were circulating among the population. Studying them could provide intelligence officers with vital information on how the occupiers were perceived, on the effectiveness of certain policies and on the propaganda of subversive groups. When viewed in this context (which conspiracy theorists neglect), it is clear that there was nothing conspiratorial at all in the desire to prevent the formation of a 'Hitler myth' – a desire that partially inspired the Hitler investigations.

Third, White claims that the investigations would be of 'historical interest', a motivation which is referred to throughout the investigations. Although political considerations (namely, the desire to disprove Soviet accusations and prevent the formation of a Hitler myth) did provide the impetus for the initiation of Trevor-Roper's investigations, this does not mean that political motivations affected the objectivity of the evidence or the conclusions he produced. To prove this, detailed analysis of the investigations must be conducted.

In 1946, Trevor-Roper's book was referred to the Joint Intelligence Committee (JIC; a powerful intelligence co-ordinating body attended by the heads of all the key British intelligence services and the Foreign Office) in order to determine the desirability of its publication and ensure that any material contained within would not jeopardise the secrecy of the intelligence services.[29] White suggested to the JIC that its publication was desirable as it may prevent the creation of a 'Hitler Myth', which was 'the object' of 'the original Press release' (this refers to Trevor-Roper's initial intelligence report on the Führer's death given to the Quadripartite Intelligence Committee [QIC] and the press in modified form on 1 November 1945).[30] The desire to prevent the formation of a 'Hitler Myth' was reiterated at a JIC meeting on 14 June 1946.[31] It was also suggested that the book had 'propaganda value' and may be translated into German 'for dissemination as propaganda'. This view was strongly supported by the Foreign Office. At face value, this would appear to confirm Levenda's argument that the British investigations were obstructed by political motivations. However, Trevor-Roper told the JIC that 'the book is intended as history rather than propaganda; I think the facts are true as given; and I have been more concerned to understand the events and their causes and relations, than to push a point of view'.[32] This shows that Trevor-Roper was not influenced by political considerations but intended to establish historical truth, which he believed he achieved through his conclusions about Hitler's death.

Trevor-Roper further stated that 'the truth is the best ... form of propaganda'.[33] By this, he was implying that the truth of how Hitler died – by committing suicide while old men and young boys continued to fight for him – would be enough to dissuade the German people from reviving Nazism or revering Hitler, without any need to embellish the story. This means that Levenda's claim that British intelligence invented the story of Hitler's death for political purposes is incorrect – a view that is supported by further analysis of Trevor-Roper's investigations.

That Trevor-Roper genuinely believed the conclusions put forth in his intelligence report were true is further supported by a handwritten note preserved in the private papers of Major-General John Sydney 'Tubby' Lethbridge, Chief of the British Intelligence Division in Germany. Although the note is of unclear origin, its attachment to a report on Hitler's death, its mention of lecturing and its humorous style suggests that it may have been written by Trevor-Roper himself. It confidently reads:

Lecture several times – only one student has told me that she still believes Hitler to be alive. I offered to wager Lady R. £100 that he was dead. She compromised on 5/-. If any Lady or Gentleman feels as Lady R. felt on the matter, I will gladly take their money, (on even terms) and I will ask Mr. Bertie Bang to make a note of your bets.[34]

Clearly, Lethbridge and, assuming he did indeed write this note, Trevor-Roper were confident that their conclusions on Hitler's suicide were true.

Although Trevor-Roper did not consider his investigations or conclusions to be influenced by political considerations, the Foreign Office did not share this view. As Greenwood points out, in 1945 most Foreign Office officials believed the main threat to Britain's security was the revival of an aggressive Germany and therefore desired good relations with the Soviets.[35] On the other hand, Greenwood further argues that British military intelligence perceived the Soviets to be the main threat to Britain's future security.[36] Such disagreements were evident in some aspects of the Hitler investigations, particularly regarding the publication of Hitler's wills.

III: Triumph of the Wills

In November 1945, during a 'routine search', copies of Hitler's personal and political testaments were found 'sewn in the lining' of Heinz Lorenz's clothes.[37] Lorenz, Hitler's deputy chief press secretary, had been arrested by the British for using 'false papers'.[38] He revealed that there were in fact three copies of these documents.[39] The other sets had been given to Willi Johannmeier (Hitler's Heeresadjutant) and Wilhelm Zander (Martin Bormann's adjutant) in the bunker.[40] Lorenz was instructed to take his documents to the Nazi Party Archives in Munich, while Johannmeier was told to give his to Field Marshal Schörner (his army group in Czechoslovakia was one of the last to surrender) and Zander to take his to Großadmiral Karl Dönitz, the last Führer of the Third Reich.[41] Johannmeier was apprehended at his parents' house by British intelligence but stubbornly refused to disclose any knowledge of the wills under interrogation.[42] Trevor-Roper, having just submitted his report on Hitler's death and returned to Oxford, received news of these discoveries and promptly returned to Germany.[43] His mission was to locate Zander, who lived in Munich, and to find his copy of Hitler's wills.

On 26 December 1945, Trevor-Roper visited 303 CIC Detachment Headquarters to inform his allies that 'Zander ... was living in the Tegernsee area under the alias of Friedrich Wilhelm Paustin'.[44] It is still not clear how Trevor-Roper obtained this information, but considering the fact that Zander's lying wife had even convinced his own family that he was dead, it is obvious that Trevor-Roper was highly skilled at intelligence work.[45] The CIC easily located 'Paustin's' home.[46] Trevor-Roper, accompanied by CIC Special Agent Ernst J. Mueller and two German policemen, then raided the house.[47] Unfortunately, Zander was 'not at home'.[48] However, the agents learned from Zander's employer that he had just left to visit his girlfriend 'in Vilshofen, near Passau'.[49] Accordingly, Trevor-Roper set off to find Zander in Vilshofen but instructed the CIC to 'make an effort to locate the documents'.[50] On 28 December, the 'sister-in-law' of Zander's girlfriend reported to the Tegernsee police that Zander had 'stored a suitcase in her home sometime in June'.[51] The CIC 'immediately picked up the suitcase' and found it contained Hitler's wills, his marriage certificate and other documents from the bunker.[52] At 3 am on the same day, Trevor-Roper tracked down and arrested Zander in 'the little village of Aidenbach near Passau'.[53] Confronted with this evidence, Johannmeier finally admitted, but only after further hours of interrogation, that he had also hidden a copy of Hitler's political testament.[54] It was recovered from the garden of his house, where he had buried it in a bottle.[55] What happened next has been subject to various interpretations.

The discovery of Hitler's wills sparked a lengthy dispute between the Foreign Office and British military intelligence as to whether they should be published. In a brief submitted to the JIC, the Foreign Office argued for 'complete suppression [of the wills] if feasible, in order to deny Hitler this posthumous weapon which might assist the renaissance of a nationalist Germany in twenty years time'.[56] On the other hand, Major-General 'Tubby' Lethbridge, head of the Intelligence Group of the British

Control Commission for Germany (IG),* argued for 'publication now', as the story could be leaked at a future date when 'the German people might be more receptive to a Hitler mystique than they are today'.[57] However, whilst the Foreign Office was arguing for suppression, the wills were released to the press by General Truscott (Commanding General of the Third United States Army, Munich). Adam Sisman argues that this was part of a deliberate tactic by Trevor-Roper, who wanted the documents to be published and who, knowing that the Foreign Office favoured their suppression, captured the wills in the American Zone, knowing that they would be published as an American scoop.[58] However, this interpretation, as will be shown, is incorrect.

Despite the publication of the wills, the Foreign Office continued to argue that 'the less public notice the documents receive in Germany, inside or outside, so much the better'.[59] Indeed, the Foreign Office attempted to co-ordinate policy with the Americans, who agreed that although the wills had already been published, tight restriction of facsimiles and suppression of the original copies should now be implemented.[60] The Foreign Office was concerned that the wills could become 'objects of great sentimental and political value' to many Germans.[61] British Foreign Secretary Ernest Bevin feared that 'even facsimiles might become objects of veneration and these could be multiplied in Germany if a single facsimile

---

* The Intelligence Group (IG) changed its name to the Intelligence Division (ID) in the summer of 1946. Lethbridge headed both organisations, which were very similar.

copy got into the wrong hands'.[62] He even contemplated destroying the originals.[63] British intelligence, on the other hand, took the complete opposite approach.

Major-General Gerald Templer believed the wills were 'not such bad documents' and 'apart from the ravings against international Jewry, fairly dignified'.[64] Templer believed they should be published. Lethbridge agreed, adding, 'I feel no real harm will come of it' as two other copies were yet to be found and could be published at a less advantageous moment when the Germans were not 'down and out'.[65] The danger of this occurring was highlighted by a threatening anonymous letter received by Hinrich Kopf (Oberpräsident of Hanover) in December 1945. The letter stated that 'Bormann brought us the testament of our beloved Führer' and argued that 'the Anglo-American thieves stole from us the Atom-Bomb'; its author threatened to hang Kopf and other 'traitors' from lamp posts and claimed that Hitler's will dictated the future action necessary to establish 'the National Socialist Great German Reich'.[66] Trevor-Roper concluded that the author had not read the will and 'invented its contents' and the story of its delivery 'in order to give apparent authority to a threatening letter'.[67] This, Trevor-Roper argued, showed 'the advantage of publishing the real document!' Major Peter Edward Ramsbotham of the IG confirmed that British intelligence was indeed hoping to publish the wills.[68] Consequently, a draft press handout was prepared, giving a detailed analysis of their contents.[69]

When the wills were leaked by Truscott, the atmosphere in the War Office appeared to be one of confusion. Indeed, British intelligence had agreed with the United

States Forces European Theatre (USFET) that the wills would be classified as Top Secret pending further instructions. However, the 'story broke when [the] British Rep [presumably Trevor-Roper] had returned to USFET who were unable to explain why their instructions to Third U.S. Army had been disregarded'.[70] Nevertheless, the IG also gave a handout along with copies of the wills to the press when the American story broke.[71] This was perhaps due to Anglo-American intelligence rivalry: British intelligence did not want America to take all the credit for its discovery. One *Daily Telegraph* article somewhat confirms this interpretation in stating that 'following the announcement' that 'Hitler's wills' had been 'seized by United States Intelligence Officers, it was revealed tonight that British Intelligence were *already* in possession of a copy of the two testaments' (emphasis added).[72] Clearly, British intelligence agents wanted it to be publicly known that they had discovered the wills before the Americans. This came as a surprise to some American intelligence officers who, prior to the British press release, had 'no other knowledge of the existence of any copy' other than those discovered in the American Zone.[73] Although the release of information to the press about the British documents may have addressed the British intelligence agents' concern with prestige, it undermined Bevin's arguments. Indeed, the US State Department indicated that it was 'not impressed by Brit argument in view of publication of texts'.[74] The Foreign Office had evidently not been consulted about whether British information on the wills could be published, and it contacted British intelligence in Germany in an attempt to suppress publication of the documents.[75] Lethbridge was irritated by the Foreign Office being so 'touchy' and reluctantly ordered that all outstanding copies due to be distributed should be frozen.[76] Fortunately for some intelligence officers, this did not prevent many copies being distributed as souvenirs.[77] President Truman himself distributed copies of the wills for this purpose.[78] Lethbridge even asked the Foreign Office if an original copy of the will could be exhibited at the Carlton Hotel.[79] The Foreign Office, probably incensed by the lateness of this consultation, rejected the proposal in line with its policy of suppression.[80] Nevertheless, despite initial opposition from the Foreign Office at meetings of the JIC, the position of the IG eventually triumphed, as the wills were published in Trevor-Roper's book.[81]

Major internal disagreements between British officials regarding Hitler's death, however, were rare. Throughout the investigations, evidence (discussed further in Chapter Six) was shared between MI5, MI6, the ID, Government Communications Headquarters (GCHQ), the War Office and the Foreign Office. Disputes between the Foreign Office regarding the use of propaganda and the political suppression of evidence, as made clear by Trevor-Roper's statements to the JIC, did not affect the overall objectivity and conclusions of the investigations. Trevor-Roper's objectivity even triumphed over the staunch Foreign Office position regarding Hitler's wills. However, it is now essential to analyse the nature of Anglo-American co-operation, as this may shed further light on why historians such as O'Donnell believe that Allied interrogators asked the wrong questions, as well as on the extent to which Anglo-American intelligence rivalry may have hindered the investigations.

IV: Anglo-American Solidarity

Recent conspiracy theories have focused on FBI files in their analysis of American investigations into Hitler's death. However, far more interesting are the conclusions and opinions of American military intelligence officers. These agents were on the ground in Germany and liaised most frequently with British intelligence during their investigations into Hitler's death. Unsurprisingly, CIC activities during the Hitler investigations have been largely ignored by conspiracy theorists in favour of Hoover's tales of dollars and doughnuts. But whilst Hoover's motives for investigating Hitler's death are not explicitly recorded, American agents more directly involved with events in Germany clearly stated their intentions.

American military intelligence records demonstrate that America shared the same motives as Britain for aiding Trevor-Roper's investigations into Hitler's death. Indeed, American motives are clearly stated in numerous detailed reports sent to British intelligence of American interrogations of Hitler's doctors and dentists, in which one learns that the Americans hoped to obtain:

a) Data useful for the identification of Hitler or his remains;
b) Further material for the debunking of numerous Hitler Myths;
c) The knowledge needed to expose those frauds who in later years may claim to be Hitler, or who may claim to have seen him or talked to him;
d) Research material for the historian, the doctor and the scientist interested in Hitler.[82]

Clearly, American and British intelligence, as stated in Chapter Two, intended historians to use the evidence they had collected in their investigations to debunk future rumours of Hitler's survival. The use of the word 'frauds' demonstrates that American intelligence genuinely believed that rumours of Hitler's survival were false and that no conspiratorial motives encompassed their investigations, as some authors have argued. Moreover, although not explicitly stated here, the American concern with 'Hitler Myths' and future 'frauds' suggests that American military intelligence was also concerned with underground Nazi movements. Indeed, according to Thomas White, the American naval captain Musmanno's investigations into Hitler's death were inspired by the desire 'to prevent the Nazi guerrilla [sic] from using rumors of his escape to rally resistance'.[83]

Reports concerning Hitler's medical information such as those cited above and American assistance in general were considered to be of great importance to Trevor-Roper's investigations, as the congratulatory letters that were sent following the successful locating of Hitler's wills demonstrate. For example, Brigadier Haylor thanked Colonel Sands of USFET for 'the splendid co-operation and assistance' he gave to British intelligence officers during the Hitler investigations.[84] Haylor claimed that Trevor-Roper 'never failed to receive the fullest degree of co-operation and assistance' from the CIC and that it was thanks to American assistance that the investigations were 'concluded within a surprisingly short space of time'. American assistance was indeed valuable as it enabled British intelligence to operate over a much larger area and maintain surveillance on individuals for longer periods of time, and it increased the chances of capturing key eyewitnesses by the extension of manpower into the American Zone of Germany.[85] Trevor-Roper repeats this positive interpretation of Anglo-American co-operation in *The Last Days of Hitler*.[86] However, evidence in recently declassified documents suggests that this co-operation had not taken place without some major difficulties.

In a letter to Brian Melland, head of the Historical Section of the Cabinet Office, Trevor-Roper expressed views that contradict the dominant narrative in the historiography regarding Anglo-American co-operation during the investigations into Hitler's death. The views he expressed may shed further light on why O'Donnell believes the Allies asked the wrong questions. After commenting on textual discrepancies between the American- and British-held copies of Hitler's will (discussed further in Chapter Six), Trevor-Roper explained: 'I never saw the original which is now in American hands. There is a long history behind this, which, for reasons of Anglo-American solidarity, I have never published.'[87] Trevor-Roper went on to claim:

General Truscott ... was clearly displeased by the fact that a British officer had discovered these documents in his area and determined to claim the entire credit for his own forces. He therefore behaved in a very curious way. First, he had the documents ... shut away in a safe and I was not allowed to see them. Then, in direct contradiction to the assurances given to me that nothing would be published till the British and American texts had been compared, immediately after I had left, sent for the American press and published the whole discovery as a brilliant coup by the U.S. 6th Army. This naturally led to some indignation in the British zone, and somebody in a high place (presumably Truscott), in order to defend his action, evidentially made unspecific charges against me which resulted in my never visiting the American zone again.[88]

This challenges the dominant narrative of the Anglo-American intelligence operation to locate Hitler's wills, which is frequently presented as a triumph of intelligence co-operation, and also the narrative given in Trevor-Roper's biography, which implies Trevor-Roper intended to have the wills published by capturing them in the American Zone.[89] It also demonstrates the rivalry between the British and American intelligence services, outlined by historians such as Stephen Dorril, who argues that they were in competition with each other to become the top intelligence service in Germany.[90] Such competitiveness had serious implications for the Hitler investigations, as Trevor-Roper explained in further correspondence with Melland. When Melland asked him if he could contact Gerda Christian (Hitler's secretary) to obtain information on the discrepancies in Hitler's wills, Trevor-Roper explained:

[Christian was] located later when it was no longer possible for me to go into the U.S. zone ... she was therefore interrogated by the U.S. authorities on a brief supplied by me. This, of course, was not very satisfactory, as the interrogators did not have the necessary background to pursue such topics as might emerge during interrogation, or to detect possible errors or lies at the time. Indeed, this fact was a handicap in respect of all prisoners captured after the end of 1945. The most serious case was that of Axmann ... the one man who claimed to have seen Bormann dead, was interrogated on my brief only, by a U.S. interrogator without any background knowledge.[91]

The inability to interrogate certain witnesses caused some embarrassment for Trevor-Roper. For example, Hanna Reitsch (the famous Luftwaffe pilot who visited Hitler in the bunker) wrote a letter to *Die Welt* in October 1947 denying that she had ever spoken to Trevor-Roper and completely disowning the account attributed to her in Trevor-Roper's book.[92] This has been used by conspiracy theorists to demonstrate the supposed unreliability of Trevor-Roper's investigations.[93] At the time, indeed, it caused some German readers of Trevor-Roper's book to doubt his conclusions.[94] However, Trevor-Roper published a reply to Reitsch's letter explaining that she was interrogated by an American interrogator on a brief supplied by him.[95] Moreover, he pointed out that she was seeking to distance herself from the interrogation as it emphasised her closeness to Hitler, which was hindering her attempts to obtain employment. Furthermore, Reitsch had claimed that her account was crucially important to Trevor-Roper's book, a statement that Trevor-Roper correctly argued was not true, as will be shown in Chapter Six.

Another issue caused by the Americans' refusal to allow Trevor-Roper to interrogate witnesses was that information was shared very slowly. Indeed, throughout the investigations, British intelligence officers complained about USFET taking too long to deliver answers to interrogation briefs. On one occasion, Trevor-Roper asked MI5 to 'ginger up' USFET because 'they gradually get callous to prods, so one has to prod harder each time I find!'[96]

Trevor-Roper's unpublished account concerning 'Anglo-American solidarity' appears to be reliable, as it was written in confidence to Melland, who was Trevor-Roper's cousin.[97] This picture is further confirmed by the initial confusion that existed when the wills were published, and it provides the only explanation available to historians as to why Trevor-Roper did not interrogate some eyewitnesses directly. This new evidence is of significant historical value as it gives Trevor-Roper's perspective on why some authors may feel the Allies asked the wrong questions. In Melland's words, this reason appears to have been American 'childishness'.[98] However, although inconvenient and a 'handicap', American interrogation reports still provided useful evidence in determining Hitler's fate, as will be shown in Chapter Six. Despite some tensions, the joint Anglo-American investigations into Hitler's death managed to uncover a remarkable amount of evidence in a small space of time. By far a larger hindrance to the Hitler investigations than the Anglo-American intelligence rivalry (which was about who collected and supplied the evidence more than it was about the evidence itself) was Soviet conduct, to which the focus of this chapter now turns.

V: Appeasing the Soviets? British Intelligence and Soviet Conduct

On 23 May 1945, the JIC presented a report on 'relations with the Russians' to the War Cabinet. It argued that

Britain should be 'more tough' with the Soviets and that 'nothing should be given to the Russians gratuitously'.[99] Further, 'no Russian request should normally be granted unless some request of ours to which we attach importance is granted in connection with it'. It rightly predicted that 'with the end of the war in Germany', political events would have an 'even greater effect upon the attitude of the Russian military authorities'. Overall, it argued that Britain should 'drive a hard bargain' and impose a 'strict principle of reciprocity' when negotiating with the Soviets. This evidence supports Richard J. Aldrich's argument that the military and intelligence services' post-war planning was conditioned by prejudices inherited from inter-war espionage activities against the Bolsheviks.[100] The attitude of British intelligence towards the Soviets during the Hitler investigations is therefore surprising.

Documentary evidence suggests that in-depth British investigations into Hitler's death did not begin until September 1945 because British officials were waiting for evidence to be provided by the Soviets. Indeed, on 30 May 1945, MI6 received a report from 'our American friends' detailing Hitler's dental information (obtained from the American interrogation of Dr Hugo Blaschke, Hitler's dentist).[101] This information was forwarded to the War Office and MI14 (thus illustrating the co-operation between British intelligence services). MI14, knowing that 'the Russians have apparently been trying to identify Hitler's body from his dental records', suggested that the information should be given to the Soviets as 'it may be of assistance to them in settling an issue of equal interest to all the Allies'.[102] It is unclear if this information was given to the Soviets as objections were raised due to it originating from an American 'secret source'.[103] However, the willingness to provide evidence to the Soviets despite earlier JIC recommendations demonstrates a more open-minded attitude towards them during the Hitler investigations, and a belief that they would provide evidence to the Allies once their investigations were complete. This belief may have led to the enthusiasm expressed by the British about an 'ingenious' suggestion given to Aneurin Bevan by Graham Hodgson (head of the X-ray department of the British Red Cross) that X-rays of Hitler's skull could be used to compare the 'skull in Berlin' supposedly found by the Soviets and thus certify the identity of Hitler.[104] This message was passed from the Foreign Office to the War Office (further demonstrating inter-service co-operation) with great alacrity, thus arguably showing that British intelligence officers expected the Soviets to allow them access to forensic evidence at some point.

British and American officials waited for Soviet confirmation of Hitler's death as contradictory reports were collected by MI14 and the Foreign Office regarding whether Hitler was alive or whether the Soviets had discovered his corpse and confirmed his method of death. On 6 June 1945 Soviet officers, including a staff officer to Marshal Georgy Zhukov, the influential and important military commander of the Soviet Zone (famous for his exploits during World War II), informed British newspapers that Hitler's body had been found and that doctors had confirmed he had died from poison.[105] On the same day, Stalin told Harry Hopkins that Hitler was still alive.[106] Then, Zhukov announced on 9 June that Hitler's body had not been found and that he could have flown away at the last moment.[107] At the Potsdam Conference in July, Stalin reiterated that Hitler could have escaped to Spain or Argentina.[108]

The damage done by such statements was clear to British officials. Newspapers collected by the Foreign Office said that many people in Berlin believed Hitler was still alive.[109] One censorship report showed that some Germans doubted Hitler was dead because 'the Russians swear by all that is holy that he is still alive'.[110] Soviet behaviour even made one Foreign Office official doubt Hitler's death, as he stated that 'the Russians are, up to now, very dubious as to the exact cause of Hitler's death, if he is dead'.[111] A SHAEF report on Hitler's death noted that 'it is impossible to give any authoritative account of Hitler's last days as evidence is still accumulating ... much of the evidence, too, is in Russian hands'.[112] Yet, British intelligence still believed Hitler was dead, despite Soviet scepticism, as was shown in Chapter Two. Nevertheless, one Foreign Office official worried: 'can we say we believe Hitler to be dead without annoying the Russians, whose press seem to be always suggesting the contrary?'[113] This concern for the possible deterioration of Anglo-Soviet relations lends credence to Greenwood's argument that maintaining good relations with the Soviets was a key objective of the Foreign Office. However, the Soviet accusation that Hitler was living in the British Zone must have convinced British officials that the Soviets could not be trusted to provide an objective account of Hitler's death and that it would put too much strain on Anglo-Soviet relations for British intelligence to wait for a conclusive Soviet statement any longer.[114] Therefore, Trevor-Roper's investigations were launched, but they were not tainted by anti-Soviet prejudice.

From the outset of Trevor-Roper's investigations, the Soviets informed Dick White that they had 'no satisfactory evidence' that Hitler was dead and expressed the desire to share information on Hitler's death with the other occupational powers, and White agreed to share British evidence with them.[115] Therefore, throughout Trevor-Roper's investigations, the Soviets were consulted about British evidence at the QIC, an intelligence-sharing organisation with representatives from all the occupying powers in Berlin. Despite Soviet accusations that Britain was hiding Hitler and the JIC's recommendation of strict reciprocity, British intelligence continued to pass evidence to the Soviets.[116] The British also continued to show interest in searching for X-rays of Hitler's skull.[117] This demanstrates that prior to the tabling of Trevor-Roper's conclusions at the QIC on 1 November 1945, British intelligence still expected to gain eventual access to forensic evidence, despite the earlier Soviet accusations. However, when Trevor-Roper's report (which formed the basis of his book) was tabled, the Soviets simply stated that it was 'very interesting'.[118] Another QIC meeting was held on 10 November, during which British intelligence asked the Soviets if they held and could make available for interrogation key eyewitnesses such as Heinz Linge (Hitler's valet) and if they would declare any other evidence they possessed on Hitler's death.[119] By 30 November, 'no reaction' had been received from the Soviets.[120]

Surprisingly, in December 1945, American intelligence officers, including Heimlich, convinced the Soviet General Sidnev to allow British, American and French representatives to dig in the Reichschancellery garden.[121] However, only one day's digging was carried out 'because on the next day the Russians, for a reason which has never been explained, prevented the entrance of the party'. On 2 January 1946, numerous newspapers in Berlin, including 'Russian controlled' papers, reported that Hitler's body had been identified by his dentist 'without the possibility of doubt'.[122] The IG complained that 'clearly the Russians can have told us nothing' and demanded a statement from them. Attempts were made to telephone numerous Russian officers, but British intelligence received such evasive responses as 'we have no official information'.[123] The Soviets eventually stopped answering the phone. The IG was particularly angry because 'each Ally undertook to supply any forthcoming information' on Hitler's death 'at once to other representatives' and 'the Russians have promised that they would let us know if any further information' about Hitler's death 'came to their notice'.[124] At the next QIC meeting, the Soviets were asked about the story, but simply stated that 'they had no information of this story and that the report must be the imagination of a newspaper reporter'.[125] The Soviets 'guaranteed' to inform the QIC of any further information they obtained relating to Hitler's death and ironically argued that 'rumours should be the subject of official denial in the Press'.[126]

Despite the rumours of Hitler's survival, the accusation that Hitler was living in the British Zone and the fact that the Soviets were clearly withholding information from British intelligence, the latter continued to supply evidence to the Soviets. For example, in June 1946, the Soviets asked the IG to give them copies of an interrogation report 'rendered from Hitler's former adjutant, von Below'.[127] One British intelligence officer asked his superiors to 'kindly' consider this request from our 'Russian Allies', and the IG showed a desire to reply to the request 'reasonably quickly' and, indeed, did so.[128] The JIC report of May 1945 was therefore disregarded. This arguably demonstrates a remarkable objectivity on the part of British intelligence during the Hitler investigations. Despite wider Cold War tensions, British intelligence officers were willing to co-operate with the Soviets, even when evidence was not forthcoming from Moscow and they were being consistently ignored.

No documentary evidence has yet been produced to explain why the Soviets repeatedly stated that Hitler was alive, despite possessing large quantities of evidence to the contrary.[129] The Foreign Office could not explain why 'Russia has been ... putting out reports that Hitler is alive, for some obscure reason of their own', and it was 'unclear what motive' the Soviets had in 'spreading lies'.[130] Historical speculation has therefore been widespread. Most historians argue that Stalin's political aims provided the motive for the spreading of such rumours. Indeed, by claiming Hitler was alive, Stalin could strengthen his claims to territory in Germany during disagreements with Britain by suggesting that it would be safer for the Soviets to remain in disputed areas; undermine his perceived political opponents, such as Zhukov, who had earlier claimed that Hitler was dead; attack his political enemies by claiming that Hitler was in Spain or Argentina; and provide an external threat that was advantageous to totalitarian governmental systems like Stalin's.[131] Other historians have argued that Stalin preserved Hitler as the common enemy in order to maintain the wartime alliance, or that he genuinely believed Hitler had escaped.[132] However, as will be discussed in Chapter Six, the 2009 DNA results lend weight to one particular interpretation of the Soviets' conduct – namely, that they were unhappy with the quality of their investigations and did not want their evidence to be scrutinised by the West.[133]

The British investigations into Hitler's death were of great political significance as a result of being conducted amid a torrent of Soviet accusations.[134] However, they were not conducted with political bias, but rather with remarkable objectivity, even towards the Soviets. Any attempts by the Foreign Office to turn Trevor-Roper's findings into propaganda were refuted by intelligence officers, including Trevor-Roper himself, as recently declassified MI5 documents have revealed. Survival rumours and, as will be seen in the following chapters, alternative versions of Hitler's death were not ignored in an effort to reach a rushed, preconceived conclusion to counter Soviet claims of Hitler's survival. They were instead investigated thoroughly by British intelligence and all found to be false. Despite some issues of rivalry between the British and American intelligence services, which hindered the collection of evidence, there is nothing to suggest that the data obtained during the British investigations was tainted by political motivations. The objectivity with which British intelligence officers conducted their investigations into Hitler's death suggests that if the evidence had pointed to Hitler's escape or murder, then Trevor-Roper would have concluded accordingly – but it did not. However, the evidence concerning the disappearance of other Nazis alleged by conspiracy theorists to have helped Hitler escape was not as straightforward.

01 The block shaped bunker exit from which Hitler received his final salute – and from where the rag that set his corpse alight was thrown.

02 The 'Führerbunker' sign which today marks the location of Hitler's bunker. Underneath this unassuming car park, Hitler committed suicide.

haben die Ehe einzugehen, erkläre ich die Ehe vor dem Gesetz
rechtmäßig für geschlossen.

Berlin, am 29 April 1945

Vorgelesen und unterschrieben:

1.) Ehemann:
2.) Ehefrau:
3.) Zeuge zu 1:
4.) Zeuge zu 2:
5.)

als Standesbeamter

03 Signatures on Hitler and Eva's marriage certificate. Note that
Eva mistakenly goes to write 'Braun' but crosses out the B.

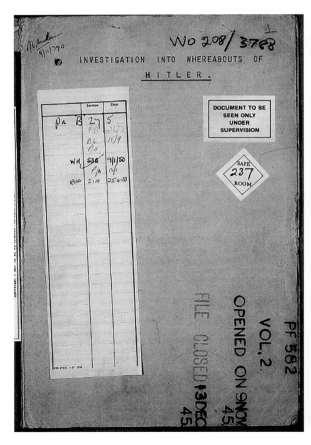

04 Several volumes of War Office files help to disprove
conspiracy theories.

NEWS CHRONICLE.

Cutting dated............5 JUL 1945............194

THE BODY OUTSIDE HITLER'S SHELTER WAS NOT HIS

From IAN BEVAN, News Chronicle War Correspondent

BERLIN, Wednesday.

THE Russian officer who led the first forces into the Reich Chancellery and who found the charred body of a man lying on the ground near the entrance to Hitler's air-raid shelter told me to-day : "It was not Hitler ; it was a very poor double."

In a detailed inspection of the air-raid shelter I was able to confirm detail after detail of the story of Hitler's death which British Intelligence officers heard a few weeks ago from Hermann Kernau, who claimed to have been one of the police guards at the shelter.

Up to a point I believe that Kernau was telling the truth, and that he did see the body burning outside the shelter. He may have thought it was Hitler. But the final detail—the all-important identification—I could not confirm.

Not evidence

I can only report that the Russian officer, Major Feodor Platonov, has no doubt that the body he found was not Hitler's.

Russian intelligence officers do not accept anything found at the Reich Chancellery as positive evi-

DAILY TELEGRAPH.

5 JUL 1945

Cutting dated............

BODY RUSSIANS FOUND WAS NOT HITLER'S

'A DOUBLE' : NO TRACE OF EVA BRAUN

From DENIS MARTIN

BERLIN, Wednesday.

The charred body found by Russian officers in the shelter beneath the Reich Chancellery was not that of Hitler. A member of Marshal Zhukov's staff declared this to me categorically to-day as he showed me round the fantastic structure.

"It was the body of a double, and a rather poor one at that," said the officer. "We were so convinced that it was not Hitler's that the experts who examined it ordered its immediate reinterment in the garden."

No trace was found, the officer added, of a body resembling that of Eva Braun, Hitler's supposed wife, who was reported to have died with him.

The account of Hitler's death in the shelter, and the burning of the body, as told by the German policeman Kernau at 21st Army Group H.Q. recently, fits in perfectly with the evidence on view here.

SUSPICIOUS EVIDENCE

There are even five petrol cans, all marked with the S.S. sign, like those referred to in the German version. Corroboration is so overwhelming as to be almost suspicious.

Whatever the truth about Hitler and Eva Braun, declared the Russian officer, he had no doubt that other bodies he saw in the shelter were those of Goebbels, his wife and children.

This is what I saw in the shelter : At the bottom of four flights of concrete spiral stairways was a small ante-room bearing evidence of hurried flight by the S.S. guards after a desperate fight.

Hand-grenade handles, steel helmets, army blankets and rubbish of all sorts lay on the floor, ankle deep in black, greasy water.

Through the first door I entered the rooms occupied by Hitler and Eva Braun. A woman's hat-box, a weighing machine and a feminine touch in the decoration of the beautifully-appointed bathroom were the only traces of her presence.

Her bed had a lamp and a telephone beside it. Luxurious cushions and pieces of curtain lay in a sodden mass on the floor.

Hitler's room, still decorated with oil paintings, was in a state of wild disorder. German encyclopædias were scattered everywhere.

A tin box, apparently treasured by Hitler, contained documents relating to the battles in the West, and a soiled and tattered Reuter despatch from Gen. Patton's front, dated April 11, it said.

The next 24 hours will probably bring news of the greatest importance from this front. German is falling like skittles."

Someone, possibly Hitler, had drawn a line with a thick blue pencil down the margin.

Across a central hall I came to Goebbels's apartments.

The Russian officer said to me : "I was the first down here after the capture of the Chancellery. Goebbels was dead on the floor, shot through the head. Frau Goebbels and the children were dead in the next room, all poisoned."

In the first room I saw the bunks, obviously

DAILY HERALD.

Cutting dated............5 JUL 1945

Hitler Still Alive Says Moscow

"Herald" Reporter

Berlin, Wednesday.

NO one with whom I have talked in Berlin believes that Hitler is dead.

They all think he "got away."

The story which the German policeman, Herman Karnau, recently told to British Intelligence officers about the death of Hitler was true in every detail except one—it was not the body of Hitler.

I found this out to-day after touring the bunker or underground headquarters beneath the Reichs Chancellery garden when the Russian major who was the first Red Army man to enter it, told me : "I saw the body lying in the garden. It was a double—and not even a good double."

As the emergency exit to the bunker I saw the five cans containing the petrol which Karnau said had been poured over Hitler's body before it was set alight.

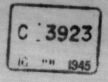

C 3923

1945

---

05 Newspaper clippings concerning Hitler's survival collected by the Foreign Office.

FTG:MJB

CONFIDENTIAL
BY SPECIAL MESSENGER

Date: September 6, 1945

To: Assistant Chief of Staff, G-2
War Department
Washington, D. C.
Attention: Reading Panel
Military Intelligence Service

From: John Edgar Hoover - Director, Federal Bureau of Investigation

Subject: REPORT THAT ADOLF HITLER IS IN ARGENTINA

It will be recalled that ████████████████ had furnished information that Adolf Hitler was in Argentina located on a ranch 675 miles west of Florianopolis, Brazil and 450 miles north, northwest of Buenos Aires. ████████████ decline to furnish the identity of the individual from whom he had received the report as to Hitler's whereabouts.

It has now been learned that the source of ████████ information was ████████████████ of Orlando, Florida. ████████████ is a 97 year old spiritualist, leader of a spiritualist cult and a spiritualist prophet.

One of ████████████████████████████████

To date no serious indication has been received that Adolf Hitler is in Argentina.

cc: Director of Naval Intelligence
Navy Department
Washington, D. C.

06 J. Edgar Hoover refutes rumours of Hitler's survival in Argentina.

LADbible
31 Oct at 23:04 · 🌐

There's also photographic evidence.

CIA Files Reveal They 'Found' Hitler Alive In Colombia In 1954

⚡ LADbible

08 During the Potsdam Conference Stalin claimed Hitler could have escaped to Spain or Argentina.

09 The Moscow skull. In 2009, DNA tests proved that this skull, once thought to be Hitler's is female.

10 Hugh Trevor-Roper in 1950 after leading the British investigations into Hitler's death.

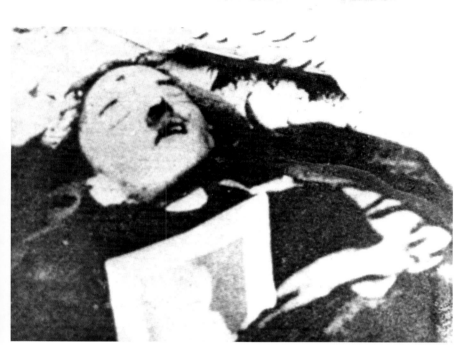

11 A 'poor double' found by the Soviets.

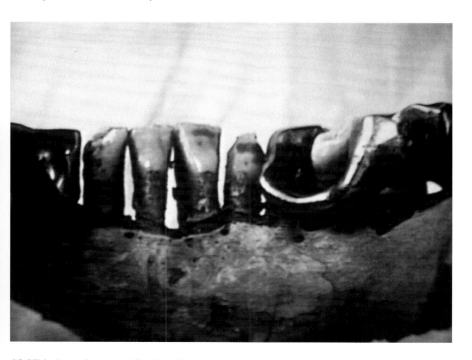

12 Hitler's teeth are archived in Moscow.

Box with Hitler's corpse

Box with Eva Braun's corpse

13 According to Lev Bezymenski the mush photographed in these boxes is all that was left of Adolf Hitler and Eva Braun.

14 The sofa on which Adolf and Eva Hitler committed suicide photographed in July 1945 by *Life* correspondent Bill Vandivert. Note the bloodstains on the armrest which match where Axmann saw Hitler's body slumped over.

15 Adolf and Eva sit beside each other in happier days for the Nazis.

16 British Prime Minister Winston Churchill enjoying his visit to the bunker.

17 Looters' paradise. The Reichschancellery in ruins.

Hitler's Air-raid bunker in the groun
of the Reich Chancellery (Soviet Secto
Flooded to a depth of 40 feet on oro'
of Russian Commandantura, 1945.
- The top of the ventilating syste
can be seen - the bunker itself
was very deep underground.

The trench in front of the
bunker where two bodies, supposedly
those of Hitler & Eva Braun, were
found burned amid a litter of
petrol jerricans.

The conical bunker by the side
of the entrance to the main bunker
which was used by Hitler's S.S.
bodyguard, - The bodies of Goebbel
his wife & children, & other high-
ranking Nazis (all suicides) were
found in the main bunker.

18 Captain Eric Mundy of the British Intelligence Corps photographed
the Führerbunker between 1945–1947. His incorrect captions reflect the
confusion caused by the Soviets.

19 Vandivert captured several eerie photographs inside Hitler's bunker.

20 Unsecured crime scene: souvenir hunters even tore fabric from furniture in the bunker.

21 Long before the bunker, Hitler greets Hanna Reitsch, overlooked by Hermann Göring (centre) and Nicolaus von Below (left).

22 After the battle: the East–West Axis where Reitsch landed her Fiesler Storch before her last meeting with Hitler.

23 The 'normal' face of evil. Joseph and Magda Goebbels pose with their children.

24 Near the end: the Führer and Artur Axmann greet members of the Hitler Youth in the Reichschancellery Garden.

25 Hitler and his friend, Albert Speer.

26 The last government of the Third Reich. Albert Speer, Karl Dönitz and Alfred Jodl.

27 J. Edgar Hoover with President Truman. In 1948, Truman gave Hoover's FBI permission to investigate rumours of Martin Bormann's survival in Argentina.

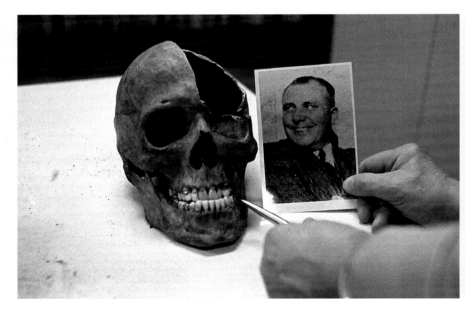

28 Martin Bormann's skull compared to a picture of him when alive.

*On the 14th at about mid-day a car arrived,
and not long afterwards K.H.K. was fetched by
W. into a small room which had bare walls and
contained a few chairs, a desk, a globe protected
by a transparent box, and a large table piled with
maps. Bormann was there.*

—Karl Heinz Kaerner, in an interview
with R. J. T. Griffin, British Embassy,
Paris, 1949[1]

Helping Hitler Escape? The Hunt for Hitler's Henchmen

I: Bormann is the Key?

The Anglo-American investigations into the circumstances of Hitler's death and rumours of his survival often overlapped with similar investigations into the deaths or disappearances of other notable Nazis who accompanied Hitler in his suicide bunker. Unsurprisingly, most conspiracy theorists who argue that Hitler escaped to Argentina also claim that other high-ranking Nazis helped him to escape and lived in exile with him.[2] Some even claimed that certain Nazi 'big fish' who went missing at the end of the war held the key to discovering the true fate of Hitler. For example, according to a newspaper extract collected by the FBI with the headline 'Bormann May Be Key', 'Allied authorities are inclined to believe that Bormann is the key to the mystery. If Hitler is alive, Bormann is likely to be with him, or to know his whereabouts.'[3] Consequently, before the evidence which convinced British intelligence of Hitler's death can be considered, the arguments of conspiracy theorists have rendered it necessary to consider the intelligence investigations into the fate of Hitler's henchmen, who were also surrounded by an abundance of rumours. Once again, it will be demonstrated through contextual analysis and through consideration of the opinions of intelligence officers that far from providing added weight to rumours of Hitler's survival, the fate of his fellow Nazis bolsters the evidence of the Führer's suicide.

Martin Bormann is rightly considered by many historians to have been the second most powerful man in Hitler's Third Reich. At least this was the case towards the end of the Nazi regime. He was tried *in absentia* at the Nuremberg trials, which took place at the same time that Hugh Trevor-Roper was searching for evidence of Hitler's last days. The decision to try Bormann *in absentia* also fuelled rumours of his survival, and, combined with the statements of other Nazis at similar trials, helped circulate the same rumours about Hitler. Eyewitnesses to Bormann's death, interrogated by Anglo-American intelligence in 1946, did not agree on how or where the Reichsleiter met his end. According to Hitler's chauffeur Kempka, his breakout group (number five) left the bunker area via Wilhelmsplatz, taking a 'U-Bahn tunnel to Bahnhof Friedrichstrasse'.[4] Having crossed Weidendammer Bridge following an unsuccessful attempt to do so, Kempka came to an anti-tank barrier, where he met Bormann and Dr Stumpfegger, among others, including Werner Naumann (Goebbels's Minister of state), whose escape and reappearance features later in this chapter. Naumann, Bormann, Kempka and Stumpfegger 'formed around' a tank, which attempted to proceed down Friedrichstrasse through the heavy Russian fire.[5] However, the tank suffered a direct hit 'from the right'.[6] Kempka saw Bormann and Naumann 'thrown off their feet' by an explosion so powerful that he assumed they could not have survived it. Kempka himself was 'thrown to the right' by the explosion, was temporarily blinded and lost consciousness. He did not see any dead bodies when he recovered. A sketch illustrating this attack (see Figure 1) was attached to Kempka's interrogation report.

Axmann was also injured by the tank explosion. However, he told his interrogator that he managed to meet up with Bormann, Naumann and Stumpfegger after the attack.[7] They were not seriously injured and continued their escape together. The group separated at 'Lehrter Bahnhof', Bormann and Stumpfegger going one way, Axmann and Naumann another. However, Axmann was forced to turn back when he met 'strong Russian patrols and sentries'. On his return, 'behind the Invalidenstrasse bridge … he saw Bormann and Stumpfegger with arms and legs stretched out, lying on their backs'. He did not have time to check the bodies but assumed they had been shot 'in their backs' because they looked unwounded. A sketch showing the location of Bormann's body as

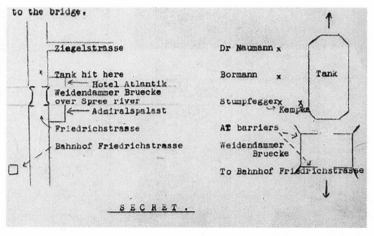

FIGURE 1 Sketch showing the Friedrichstrasse tank attack as recalled by Erich Kempka. TNA, WO 208/3789.

described by Axmann was also attached to his interrogation (see Figure 2). In 1946 Bormann was sentenced to death by hanging *in absentia*.[8] No corpse had been found. As Trevor-Roper pointed out, Axmann's claims were 'unsupported by any other testimony'.[9] He could have been lying to cover up Bormann's escape.

Perhaps inevitably, rumours began flooding into intelligence offices in Britain, America and Germany detailing sightings of 'the Brown Eminence'. In December 1945, American intelligence officers in Germany were already discussing a growing 'Martin Bormann legend'.[10] Bormann had allegedly been sighted in Northern Italy, 'attempting to enter Switzerland'.[11] Almost one year after the dramatic events in Hitler's bunker had concluded, some intelligence reports 'indicated that Martin Bormann is now in the interior of Argentina and that he has in his possession the Testament of Hitler'.[12] Characteristically, British intelligence agents, who were not fans of Nazi

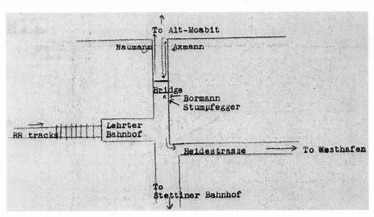

FIGURE 2 Sketch showing the location of Bormann's corpse as recalled by Artur Axmann. TNA, WO 208/3789.

legends, decided to try to solve this mystery by conducting thorough investigations.

In late October 1946, Brigadier S. N. Shoosmith, Deputy Chief of the British Intelligence Division (ID) in occupied Germany, telephoned MI5 in London, asking to speak with Dick White.[13] Although the 'line was extremely bad', the gist was that the ID had received information indicating that Bormann 'may possibly be alive'.[14] Although at this stage some Anglo-American intelligence officers believed Bormann could have outlived his Führer, one thing is certain: the Allies did not help him escape. On the contrary, they tried to catch him. Indeed, Guy Liddell wrote to Stewart Menzies, the head of MI6, informing him that according to Shoosmith, 'B.A.O.R. have received reliable reports that Martin Bormann is living Schaffhausen area of Switzerland. We consider this information merits investigation and that it could be more easily and expeditiously carried out by London than ourselves.'[15] Consequently, MI6 agreed to lead the British hunt for Martin Bormann.[16] In doing so, 'the Friends', as MI6 is sometimes referred to in government circles, would join many other international intelligence services also searching for the Führer's deputy.

The origins of the MI6 investigations demonstrate that the British approached the possibility of Bormann's survival with an open mind, as they began by looking into seemingly reliable reports claiming that Bormann was alive. However, it did not take long before the Secret Intelligence Service (SIS) found that unreliable individuals with similar motivations to those fuelling rumours of Hitler's survival were responsible for most of the fuss about the Führer's deputy. Throughout 1946–1947, MI5 collected newspaper cuttings detailing elaborate stories of Bormann's survival and his whereabouts, each as fantastic and unlikely as similar rumours about Hitler, which were also under investigation at the time.[17] For example, in December 1946, an Egyptian newspaper claimed that 'Hitler's deputy, was living in the Middle East. No other details were given.'[18] Such reports were passed on to MI6 'for what it is worth'.[19] Unsurprisingly, upon investigation, these reports seldom proved to be worth much. As usual, some reports originated from individuals who appeared to be 'mentally unbalanced', others from irresponsible reporters seeking to create sensation.[20] However, as was also the case with the Hitler investigations, not all reports of Bormann sightings were dismissed out of hand, some being subjected to more thorough investigation. For example, in March 1947, having received various reports that Bormann may be hiding in Italy en route to Argentina, the American CIC 'requested that local police agencies be alerted, and if any information is received regarding Bormann it be transmitted immediately to this office'.[21] Some reports even suggested that Bormann could be 'living incommunicado in the Argentine Embassy in Rome'![22] Nevertheless, by mid-1947, having been inundated by both Hitler and Bormann survival rumours from unreliable sources claiming that both men were in several places – all over the world – at once, some intelligence officers developed a scepticism, which is shared by myself.

This change of attitude is effectively revealed by the following account. In May 1947, an enthusiastic British Special Branch agent, based in Colombo, Ceylon (modern-day Sri Lanka) wrote to MI5 requesting an up-to-date photograph and description of Bormann so that he could 'keep a lookout'.[23] This request, although by the agent's own admission 'a long chance', had been inspired by 'a news cutting which appeared in the local Press'.[24] The MI5 officer, Mr Courtenay Young, charged with replying to the agent seemed uncertain as to whether British intelligence believed Bormann to be alive or not, and stated that 'any suggestions as to how I should answer this letter would be gratefully received'.[25] A Miss Gunn, (unknowingly) delivering a damning blow to recent conspiracy theorists, fired off the following waspish response in the style of Hugh Trevor-Roper himself:

> I think Perera might be commended for his enthusiasm, but it might also be broken to him gently that the late but peripatetic Herr Bormann is currently being seen in Switzerland (the most persistent locale), Bolivia, Italy, Norway and Brazil – in the last country, sitting in state on a high mountain beside his pallid Fuehrer. The Egyptian story is not being pursued by the Press, which is doubtless waiting to break the silly season scoop: that he has been seen riding the Loch Ness Monster. That ought to fetch some dollars. Or something.[26]

The actual response sent to Ceylon by the Director-General of MI5, Sir Percy Sillitoe, was also revealing: 'Bormann is almost certainly dead ... [although] he has been reported in Switzerland, Bolivia, Italy, Norway and Brazil. Most of these reports derive from the Press and probably came from irresponsible persons.'[27] The very multitude of contradictory survival rumours, rather than adding weight to theories of Hitler's survival, as conspiracy theorists suggest they do, made British intelligence even more certain that Bormann, and Hitler, died in 1945. They had reached the correct conclusions. But until more decisive evidence became available, the rumours continued. Even though Miss Gunn's witty response was published widely throughout British newspapers in 2009, when the MI5 folder was declassified, this did not deter the publication of *Grey Wolf*, putting forward arguably the most successful conspiracy theory to date, two years later.[28]

By June 1947, MI5 was now almost certain that Bormann was dead, but MI6 had apparently not yet finished its investigations. Consequently, MI5 continued to pass on reports of Bormann's survival to MI6.[29] Moreover, the ID on the ground in Germany continued to take an interest in rumours of Bormann's survival, most likely due to the possibility that they might reveal underground Nazi organisations, which the ID was determined to stamp out and to which such rumours were often linked.[30] On 28 June, Captain Hodges of the ID requested that MI5 check the truth of a story in the *Evening Standard* claiming that numerous important Nazis had testified that Bormann was a Soviet spy, 'and is now in Russian hands'.[31] One MI5 officer believed that 'the "Standard" story seems to be an early manifestation of silly seasonitis', but still suggested that its reliability should be checked.[32] The official response, sent to ID HQ in Herford, expanded on the nature of this silly-season disease. 'The Press stories as to the fate and whereabouts of Bormann offer a variety of sensational turns as the silly season reaches its height. In recent weeks he has been variously, and glibly, reported to be in Switzerland, Bolivia, Argentina, Italy, Norway, Brazil and Egypt. We have no confirmation of the Russian story, but are making enquiries and will let you know the result.'[33] The sinister Russian story was actually supported by General Reinhard Gehlen, the head of West Germany's Secret Intelligence Service and former head of Hitler's Fremde Heere Ost (Foreign Armies East) intelligence organisation.[34] Nevertheless, Gehlen likely had his own ideological motives for suggesting that the Soviets were harbouring Bormann, given that the many stories of Bormann's escape to Russia have now been convincingly disproved, as the evidence discussed later in this chapter will demonstrate.[35]

'Silly seasonitis' was a particularly infectious ailment in the summer of 1947. As one perceptive MI5 officer, Norman Himsworth, noted, 'it is the ambition of every newspaper reporter who steps upon German soil to discover the whereabouts of Martin Bormann, or, should this prove impossible, at least "discover" some evidence which would justify his writing a story on this subject'.[36] Bormann stories evidently sold papers. Consequently, individuals who had earlier attempted to profit from stories of Adolf and Eva in Argentina later peddled rumours of Bormann's escape.[37] Later that year, the CIC in Milan reported to Washington 'a circulating rumor in Verona that Martin Bormann is at present in Lugano, Switzerland'.[38] Bormann, of course, had 'undergone a plastic facial operation which has completely changed his physical appearance'.[39] Not only did Hitler and Bormann appear to have become key supporters of the global travel industry after the war, it seems they were also keeping many plastic surgeons in business!

MI6 were now beginning to tire of these investigations. After looking into a survival rumour suggesting that Bormann was on his way to Sweden and finding no concrete evidence to support it, one officer from the Secret Intelligence

Service quipped to Mrs Quin of MI5 that '[i]t was about time Martin Bormann should arrive in Sweden!'[40] Predictably, Bormann never turned up in Sweden, but rumours claiming that he was living in Ecuador or Argentina continued to be filed by the FBI and the CIA the following year.[41] Although by May 1948 MI6 was fairly certain of Bormann's death, serious doubts were raised in the American intelligence community that month. Indeed, Judge Robert 'Justice' Jackson received a telephone call from one John F. Griffiths, previously employed by the American Embassy in Argentina, claiming to have information suggesting that Bormann was living in Argentina.[42] Concerned by the seeming reliability of this report, Justice Jackson discussed the matter with President Truman, who advised Jackson to discuss it with Hoover, head of the FBI.[43] The latter informed Jackson that the FBI no longer had 'any coverage in foreign countries and that this came under ... CIA's jurisdiction'.[44] A few days later, Jackson assured Special Agent Francis E. Crosby 'that he and President Truman ... would both prefer that the FBI conduct any inquiry looking to a location of Bormann in preference to any other agency'.[45] The peculiarities of the case, combined with the desire for utmost secrecy, would apparently avoid CIA criticism. Hoover, with his desire to maintain FBI influence in Argentina, must have been delighted to read Jackson's message. He must also have been pleased to learn that 'President Truman is keenly interested in Griffiths' report'.[46] Consequently, a memorandum was prepared outlining the reasons for, and tasks involved in, a preliminary investigation. It was hoped that such a memorandum would receive presidential approval 'in order to cut off any criticism any agency interested in Bormann might otherwise make'.[47]

Whilst this memorandum was being prepared, a security leak led to the FBI receiving information that British intelligence had intercepted clandestine radio traffic indicating that Bormann was alive.[48] Consequently, the bureau discreetly asked the American legal attaché at the British Embassy in London to obtain the opinion of British intelligence concerning whether or not Bormann was dead.[49] MI5 responded first. Miss Chenhalls informed the embassy that '[t]here is at present no final answer to the query raised in your letter' but '[t]his office is of the opinion that this highly important Nazi character is no longer alive'.[50] After reiterating the ever-growing list of unlikely places where Bormann had been sighted (Ceylon now added) and questioning the reliability of the Russian rumour, Miss Chenhalls couldn't resist mentioning one particular report that 'suggested that he might be found sitting in state on a high mountain in Brazil beside his pallid Fuhrer!'[51] MI5 was clearly fairly certain, to the point of being able to make jokes about it, that Bormann was dead, but wise enough to keep an open mind regarding the slight possibility that he could be alive until more definitive evidence was obtained. They would also have done this in the case of Hitler had the evidence suggested that he too could possibly have lived beyond 1945, but as will be demonstrated in Chapter Six, it did not. MI6 concurred: 'Your letter dated 28 May 1948 asks whether Martin Bormann is considered to be alive or dead. We have no specific information on this point and can only say that all Allied Intelligence agencies have searched for him in vain.'[52]

Despite receiving this information, American intelligence officers decided to continue their investigations. It is important to look at their reasons for doing so. The FBI, like modern conspiracy theorists, did at first consider the possibility that the British were lying. However, they found it 'difficult under the circumstances to conceive a set of facts which would prompt the British to give the Bureau a direct lie in this case, and their belief that he is dead is stated in unequivocal language'.[53] The clandestine messages intercepted by British intelligence, contrary to the narrative in *Grey Wolf*, where they are used to bolster tales of Hitler and Bormann's post-war exploits, 'do not, in the British view, indicate that Bormann is alive'.[54] The FBI even informed Jackson that further investigation of the Griffiths story was unlikely 'to disprove the British belief'.[55] Consequently, Jackson informed President Truman in his memorandum: 'Circumstantial evidence indicates that Bormann probably is dead.'[56] Nevertheless, he went on to warn him that 'publicity might be given to the fact that this information was laid before United States officials who did nothing and therefore are charged to be, in effect, protecting him. This claim would have propaganda value to Russia.'[57] Clearly, American intelligence wished to avoid the creation of conspiracy theories such as that put forward in *Grey Wolf* which allege that Bormann escaped with American knowledge and approval. It also wished to avoid further Soviet accusations along these lines. Consequently, President Truman granted the FBI permission to undertake a 'preliminary investigation'.[58] Jackson 'felt strongly that no Agency, other than the FBI, had any business handling the inquiry'.[59] The authority of the CIA had been undermined by the President favouring the FBI. Hoover's personal interest in Nazi survival rumours had paid off.

Throughout July and August of 1948, Special Agent Crosby conducted investigations in Argentina and

Uruguay.[60] However, 'no information whatever which could be regarded as illuminative, much less conclusive on the reliability of the report was developed'.[61] The behaviour of Griffiths' source was suspicious and he was unable to produce 'any verifiable fact'.[62] Moreover, Griffiths was in close contact with a 'renegade newspaperman, notorious for his light regard for the truth'.[63] Furthermore, 'One of the first requests Griffiths made of Crosby was that he do everything he could, when the case broke, to make it possible for Griffiths to sell a news story, or possibly a feature story on the capture of Bormann'.[64] As a result, Crosby returned home and the President was informed that a full-scale inquiry would not be necessary.[65] Griffiths, it seemed, like many other rumour spreaders, had been motivated by the desire to disseminate sensational newspaper stories. But this was not his only motivation, nor was it the end of the matter.

In September 1948, Hoover was informed that 'Argentine President, Juan Peron' had accused Griffiths of being 'the principal conspirator in a plot to assassinate him'.[66] This story had been reported in American and Argentinian newspapers. State Department officials, who had been kept in the dark about the FBI's secret Argentine adventure, were furious. According to the Argentinian Ambassador, reports claimed that Crosby had botched his mission. Apparently, 'due to the FBI agent not being very discreet, his mission became known, whereupon the Nazis in Argentina concocted the idea of "using Peron as somewhat of a sucker" and producing an assassination plot ... to start anti-United States feelings'.[67] Hoover vigorously defended Crosby's conduct, arguing that any compromise of this mission must have come from Griffiths.[68] Moreover, the FBI argued that Nazis could not have concocted such a plot 'because no such group of Nazis existed as was alleged by Griffiths'.[69] Historians may never know exactly how or why this assassination story came about. Nevertheless, the FBI, in hindsight, now attached more importance to a certain motivation of Griffiths which should have made them suspicious from the outset: Griffiths had wanted to 'embarrass the Argentine Government' by exposing the fact that it was harbouring top Nazis.[70] He was a strong opponent of Perón's regime and had in fact been expelled from his position at the American Embassy in 1946 due to his indiscretions during Perón's presidential campaign.[71] This gives historians yet another reason for the constant sightings of Hitler, Eva and Bormann in Argentina — it was useful propaganda for opponents of Perón.[72]

Whilst Special Agent Crosby was in Argentina, MI6 was continuing its own investigations into the interlinked rumours of Hitler's and Bormann's survival. On 28 July 1948, Aubrey Halford, a Foreign Office official who maintained regular contact with MI6, received a letter designated 'Top Secret' from Fred Warner, then based at the Palais des Nations in Geneva.[73] The latter had been 'approached by a Swiss national called Rolf Eberhard', who was 'almost certainly known to your [i.e. Halford's] friends'.[74] During a recent holiday to Italy, Eberhard had been approached by SS 'General Dolman [*sic*]', then hiding from Allied capture.[75] Dollmann, Warner claimed, had 'informed Eberhard that Martin Bormann is still alive. He says that he is in contact with him and can reveal where he can be caught.'[76] More alarmingly, according to Warner, Dollmann had reported during this conversation that Bormann was 'in touch with the Russians and is negotiating to place at their disposal the considerable network of the S.S. which has remained underground'.[77] Warner disseminated this survival rumour to the Foreign Office with a healthy dose of scepticism and the usual emphasis on the suspicious motives of Dollmann (noting, 'He may hope to get something for himself') – doubts that were shared by MI6.[78] He stated, 'Eberhard thinks that Dolman may conceivably be lying but he very much doubts it and hopes that we will be willing to look into the matter, even though we have apparently satisfied ourselves that B. is dead.'[79] Warner concluded his letter by emphasising his ignorance and gullibility concerning such matters, but still requested that Halford 'have a friend or two in Switzerland' look into the matter – 'Even if it looks phoney'.[80] Although MI6 were satisfied that Bormann was most likely dead, they did indeed revisit the matter, demonstrating again their objectivity and willingness to draw conclusions based on evidence, not on preconceived ideas. The conclusions they reached are revealing.

In August 1948, an MI6 officer (described as 'an agent of your friends') interviewed Eberhard.[81] This agent managed to gain information from Eberhard that enabled him to locate Dollmann, whom he interviewed in September. Once again, the comments of MI6 provide convincing evidence to disprove theories of Bormann's survival, as they do those of Hitler. MI6 found that '[t]he evidence that Bormann is living is not convincing' and, moreover, that 'Dollmann's statement' rested 'solely' on hearsay.[82] Consequently, SIS believed that 'Dollmann's statement about Bormann is totally unsubstantiated and similar to a number of rumours which have been current since the war'.[83] Of Dollmann's motive, the friends were 'inclined to think that he is merely trying to secure his own position, so that he may no longer remain in hiding'.[84] Evidently, some Nazis sought to use rumours of Hitler's and/or Bormann's survival to gain favour with Anglo-American intelligence services and distract attention away from their own war crimes. The concluding remarks of MI6 in this particular investigation provide further convincing rebuttals to conspiracy theorists who claim that Anglo-American intelligence knew of, or even allowed, the escape of Hitler and Bormann: 'Since the end of the war your friends have received many reports from all over the world purporting to give Bormann's whereabouts. These reports have usually been vague and, when not too incredible, have been conscientiously investigated, but without result.'[85] MI6 anticipated that similar rumours would be reported in the future, but reassuringly stated that 'there is no reason to think that any nucleus of German nationalism opposed to our interests is centred round Bormann'.[86] However, MI6, although perhaps 90 per cent certain that Bormann was dead, was not against investigating future rumours if the evidence surrounding them was more reliable, and it expressed a willingness to 'locate or apprehend him' should this be the case.[87] Clearly, British intelligence agencies were not part of any conspiracy to allow Bormann and Hitler to escape; if they had been, they would not have wasted time investigating such survival rumours or attempting to locate and apprehend a man whose whereabouts they knew and whose freedom they had aided. Moreover, the Foreign Office remained particularly interested in investigating rumours alleging that Bormann was in 'Soviet hands' (this is unsurprising, considering that the Cold War was heating up in Germany with the Berlin Blockade crisis during this period).[88]

Despite British intelligence officers' near certainty that Bormann and Hitler were dead, survival rumours continued to amuse, irritate and waste the time of intelligence services throughout the world, as MI6 had predicted they would. However, fortunately for historians, not all rumours were dismissed, and those that were investigated provide further evidence to disprove conspiracy theories today. As was demonstrated by newspaper silly season in Britain, rumours of Bormann's escape sometimes overlapped with those of Hitler's, as they do in many recently published conspiracy theories. For example, on 21 July 1949, a man sporting 'a close clipped black Hitlerian mustache with streaks of grey', a 'neatly pressed' suit and 'ancient vintage' overcoat entered the American Embassy in Uruguay.[89] Captain Lazo Toledo had come to 'relate a story which might be of interest' to American officials.[90] He told his story 'in a calm dead-pan manner without any change of expression. Nor did the tone of his voice change during the conversation. He did not smile once during the interview nor did his gaze falter whenever I looked him straight in the eye.'[91] In this manner, Toledo informed the embassy of 'the well-known but unverified story of a German submarine landing off Patagonia and disembarking Hitler and Martin Bormann'.[92] As usual, little credence was given to this story, which embassy officials by now seemed tired of hearing. Indeed, the reason this survival rumour was filed and preserved by the CIA was again related to the motives of the individual who supplied it, as well as to intelligence concerning others implicated within the report, rather than to the story of Hitler and Bormann's escape itself. As Toledo's interviewer noted, 'the only point of interest in the conversation' was when Toledo said he had mentioned this story 'only to one other person, namely, John F. Griffiths'.[93] The latter was 'an American citizen who was accused in September 1948 by the Argentine Government of having been implicated in an attempt to assassinate President and Mrs. Peron'.[94] Whilst Toledo's manner during interview may have been unnerving, the American official on the receiving end of his gaze was probably not surprised by his somewhat intimidating style of conversation owing to his existing knowledge of Toledo. Indeed, the American officer had noted that, according to reliable sources, Toledo was 'an Agent of the Argentine Government'.[95] 'Whether or not Lazo Toledo had some ulterior purpose in naming Griffiths' was never established, but, considering the earlier FBI investigation, it is likely that he did.[96] This 'Renewed Attempt to Peddle the Old Story of the Presence in Argentina of Adolph Hitler and Martin Bormann', as the embassy put it, may have been part of an Argentinian espionage effort to 'Penetrate the Embassy, Montevideo'.[97] The Allies, it seems, were right to be concerned that rumours and the resulting conspiracies they inspire could have seriously negative consequences.

One year later, MI5 was still being forced to deal with Hitler and Bormann survival rumours. In May 1950, an MI5 officer filed a newspaper clipping from the *Evening Standard* with the following alarming headline in bold print: 'Hitler Lives, Say Nazis'.[98] The owner of a 'pro-Nazi' German magazine, Karl Heinz Kaerner, had allegedly interviewed Bormann 'in Spanish Morocco last summer'.[99] During this interview, Bormann is supposed to have revealed that 'Hitler is alive in a Tibetan monastery'.[100] Rumours of Bormann's survival were being used, as they still are by conspiracy theorists today, to support theories of Hitler's survival. As the newspaper summarised, 'The fate of Martin Bormann has remained a mystery for five years. He alone among the Nazi leaders was unaccounted for after the fall of Germany. He was said to have been killed by a shell on a bridge... But nobody found his body ... there have been rumours of his being seen in various countries, but they have never been confirmed.'[101]

British intelligence had already investigated this story and anticipated its publication. Once again, Kaerner's motives and those of the investigating intelligence agents are revealing. What initially drew the attention of MI5 to this particular rumour was not so much its claims of Hitler's and Bormann's survival, which were now considered to be sensational and fantastic, but rather the possibility that such stories might have been being used to aid Nazi underground organisations in Germany, the existence of which the ID was very interested in, for obvious reasons. Kaerner had first reported this story to R. J. T. Griffin of the British Embassy in Paris in August 1949. On this occasion, he had related a very elaborate story, spanning six pages, describing in some detail how Bormann 'was alive and directing a Nazi organisation with wide ramifications'.[102] Despite the detailed nature of the story, Griffin was unconvinced. In his words, 'the chief reason for being sceptical about what he says seems to me to be not the tallness of the story – for other things quite as odd have happened – but the suspicion that some such organisation may in fact exist and may be using K. H. K. as a stooge – with the object, perhaps, of fanning into a blaze the rising fire of nationalism in Western Germany by the inspiring "news" of Bormann being alive and flourishing'.[103] 'Hayter's friends' (MI6) were consulted about this rumour but felt that the story was so obviously untrue that no harm could come from publishing it, despite having some initial reservations.[104] The Foreign Office and MI5, having yet again investigated the possible existence of a Bormann-led or -inspired Nazi organisation, agreed that the story was 'undoubtedly pure fabrication'.[105] Kaerner, then, had two motives for disseminating the idea that Hitler and Bormann survived the Second World War. First, it suited his own ideological agenda. Second, as he admitted himself, he wanted to 'publish this story in order to get the money which he very much needed'.[106] Stories of Hitler's and Bormann's survival sold publications, as they still do today, no matter how questionable the evidence on which they were based.

In Germany, American intelligence was continuing their parallel investigation into Bormann's fate. Indeed, the CIC had been 'keeping a close watch on the acquaintances and postal communications' of Bormann's son, but 'nothing of interest' had been 'uncovered so far'.[107] However, in August 1950, the CIA received a report of an interview with a soldier who was 'stationed in Hitler's HQs during the last days of WWII'.[108] He had been captured by the Soviets, was released around 1946–1947, and had worked on his family farm near Linz, Austria since then. According to a seemingly reliable source, the soldier 'together with Martin Bormann made a break-through of Soviet lines at which time, according to Subject, Bormann was shot down from a German Tank and was killed'.[109] But this account still did not explain Axmann's conflicting story of seeing Bormann alive, a short while after the tank incident. Amidst the circulation of such truths and half-truths, Anglo-American intelligence continued to receive reports of Bormann's escape. On 24 October, an MI6 officer telephoned MI5 to enquire about a British newspaper article claiming that Bormann was now ironically known as 'the Grey Eminence because of the robes worn by the monks at his monastery hide-out in Spain'.[110] Unsurprisingly, having consulted its ever-growing file on Bormann, MI5 reassured the Secret Intelligence Service that this story was 'probably just as fictitious' as all the others.[111]

Not to be outdone by the numerous 'Hitler in America' stories investigated by the FBI, some sensation seekers in London disseminated similar hoaxes about Bormann. For example, on 14 August 1951, Arthur Veysey, the American representative of the *Chicago Tribune* based in London's Fleet Street, received a mysterious telephone call from a man claiming to be Martin Bormann.[112] Veysey met this man later in the day.[113] The American Embassy informed the Metropolitan Police Special Branch of this story.[114] As a result, two policemen – a police inspector and a sergeant – interviewed Veysey.[115] In their report, they said that they told him 'frankly that we thought the whole thing was a hoax' but he remained 'convinced that guy was Bormann'.[116] The men from Special Branch were right to be sceptical. As they noted, in January, an assistant editor of the *New York Times* 'had had his "leg pulled"' by a similar false sighting of Bormann in London.[117] After further investigation, Chief Inspector Hughes managed to come face to face with 'the man who said he was Borman [*sic*]'.[118] Predictably, 'At a glance it was obvious he was not.'[119] He was in fact a Mr 'Harry Adcock' who had previously been convicted for obtaining money 'by means of a trick' – namely, pretending 'to an Evening Standard reporter that he had had a part in the theft of the Duke of Windsor's jewels'.[120] Clearly, money was again a motivator behind this rumour. However, there was also a sad reality behind Adcock's quest for riches through sensation, as there was behind the accounts of some of those who claimed to have seen Hitler in America. Mr Adcock was 'a man of good background who ... [had] come down in the world'.[121] He had been wounded at Gallipoli in the First World War and destroyed his later teaching career through heavy drinking, resulting in his being 'reduced to casual work as a waiter or dishwasher'.[122] He was also admitted to hospital after suffering a nervous breakdown.[123] Perhaps he was a victim of what is now known as post-traumatic stress disorder, and was trying to escape the horror of what he had experienced during the Great War. Chief Inspector Hughes concluded this case by cautioning Adcock and informing Veysey that he had been 'easily hoaxed'.[124]

Throughout the early to mid-1950s, Anglo-American intelligence agents continued to receive and investigate stories of Hitler's and Bormann's survival, not one of which provided any reliable evidence to substantiate their extraordinary claims. As B. G. Atkinson commented in January 1952, most of these newspaper stories were 'wild'.[125] A week after Atkinson made his comments, the CIA filed a report of an individual who offered to 'tell where Martin Bormann was living in Argentina' – for 'ten thousand pesos', of course.[126] Just as the rumours themselves became repetitive, so too did the motives of their spreaders. Commenting in February 1952 on a rumour that Bormann was a monk living in Rome, the CIA stated that it believed that such claims were reminiscent of 'similar publicity stunts mounted by Italian Neo-Fascists in order to attract press attention in period 46–49'.[127] Rumours of survival, then, could help keep what was left of Fascism alive, and also generate cash.

By 1955, in the words of Hoover, 'intensive investigations' had 'been made by allied intelligence services to determine his [i.e. Bormann's] whereabouts'.[128] If, as conspiracy theorists have argued, Anglo-American intelligence helped Hitler and Bormann escape, then such investigations would not have been necessary. Hugh Trevor-Roper, like many Anglo-American intelligence officers in the 1940s, believed it was possible that Bormann could still be alive.[129] This is important for two reasons. First, it further demonstrates that Trevor-Roper did not allow ideological considerations to cloud his conclusions on Hitler's death. Indeed, if this had been the case, it would have been more advantageous for Trevor-Roper to have stated with certainty that Bormann was also dead, thus depriving the Soviets of another Nazi whom they could accuse the Western Allies of hiding or about whom neo-Nazis could construct a legend. Second, it reveals that Trevor-Roper would not reach firm conclusions if he did not feel the evidence available was sufficient to enable him to draw them. At the time, Trevor-Roper and other intelligence officers did not hold all the evidence now available to historians concerning Bormann's fate. Still, as Hitler and Bormann continued to be reported to have been sighted all over the world in unlikely locations by individuals with a variety of questionable motives, MI5 and MI6 grew more sceptical. Consequently, in 1952, the ID informed MI5 that the rumour claiming 'that Bormann is in Russia is one that has had widespread currency in the press at various times but we know of no evidence which would lead us to that conclusion'.[130] As with rumours of Hitler's survival, Anglo-American intelligence officers' interest in investigating rumours of Bormann's survival often had more to do with those reporting the rumours, with internal power struggles among the various intelligence agencies, or with the chance they offered of uncovering underground organisations involving other Nazis, than with Bormann himself. In the 1950s and '60s, the evidence that was then available did not enable Anglo-American intelligence to draw firm conclusions on how Bormann died, but the lack of evidence to support any of the many rumours of survival they investigated enabled them to state with near certainty that he never escaped Berlin. But the story of the hunt for Bormann does not end here.

In December 1972 two skeletons were accidently uncovered by the Invalidenstrasse Bridge near Lehrter Bahnhof during construction work.[131] This, of course, is the spot where Axmann reported that he saw the dead bodies of Bormann and Stumpfegger in 1945. In 1976, Reidar Sognnaes published an incredibly detailed forensic analysis comparing records produced by Bormann's dentist, Dr Blaschke, with the uncovered skull. He convincingly concluded that the skeleton belonged to Bormann.[132] But even this was not the end of the matter. Conspiracy theories continued to evolve and some notable American publishers paid considerable amounts of money for books conveying survival rumours.[133]

The continuing speculation about Bormann's alleged survival even after the positive identification of his remains in the 1970s inspired a team of scientists to settle the matter once and for all.[134] Fortunately, it also encouraged the Bormann family to consent to DNA analysis.[135]

Consequently, K. Anslinger et al. compared a DNA sample provided by an '83-year-old female cousin of Bormann' with a sample taken from Martin Bormann's bones.[136] The DNA sequences matched.[137] As these sequences were not found in 1,500 other DNA samples, the scientists were able to conclude that the DNA was indicative of the Bormann family.[138] In other words, the bones found in 1972 belonged to Martin Bormann.

Despite this evidence, conspiratorial publications such as *Grey Wolf*, published in 2011, continue to insist that Bormann helped Hitler to escape to Argentina with Allied approval. Unsurprisingly, conspiracy theorists use DNA and forensic analysis selectively. For example, when the 2009 DNA results revealed that 'Hitler's skull' in Moscow belonged to a woman, numerous conspiracy theorists used this as evidence to bolster their tales of Hitler's escape. However, despite the positive identification of Bormann's remains by numerous scientists, some conspiracy theorists, by either ignoring the scientific analysis of his remains or suggesting that this was part of a cover-up, continued to insist that Bormann escaped.[139] Their faith in the scientific method and the evidence it produces extends only as far as it supports their theories. Fortunately, however, good historians are trained to form their opinions on the basis of evidence, not to mould evidence around preconceived conclusions. Ironically, conspiracy theorists are guilty of the same flawed methods of evidence selection that they wrongly accuse Trevor-Roper of employing. The remains found in 1972 have been scientifically proven to belong to Bormann. His grinning skull provides a haunting smile for historians to gaze at in perpetuity.

II: The Hunt for Heinrich 'Gestapo' Müller

On 1 May 1945, Heinrich 'Gestapo' Müller, Hitler's murderous chief of the Gestapo (hence the unofficial middle name), was standing in the ruins of the Reichschancellery as the leftovers of the Nazi regime scrambled to assemble groups that would attempt to break out through the Russian lines that evening.[140] According to eyewitnesses, he had no intention of leaving. Like his late Führer, Müller declared that he did not wish to be captured by the Russians, and expressed his willingness to 'fall' with 'the regime'.[141] Horst Kittler, when leaving with a breakout group, claimed he saw Müller 'waving goodbye'.[142] If Müller had been involved in some sort of elaborate plan to help Hitler escape, it seems inconceivable that he should have been sighted making these comments and gestures, a day after Hitler's suicide, in the chaos of the breakout groups, facing the same danger as everybody else. He was, as the CIA put it, 'caught in the Berlin trap'.[143] However, nobody witnessed his death and his body has never been found or reliably identified.[144] Hence, no historian can state with certainty what happened to Müller after May 1945. However, it can be proved with the available evidence that Müller did not help Hitler escape, despite numerous erroneous attempts to suggest otherwise, as well as to suggest that this was done with the knowledge of Anglo-American intelligence.

There is plenty of factual (and, interestingly, puzzling) material about Heinrich Müller's end that one could discuss without resorting to elaborate tales of Hitler's escape. For example, in the early 1960s, newspapers, inspired by the recent capture in Argentina of Müller's erstwhile colleague, the Holocaust enthusiast Adolf Eichmann, by Israeli intelligence agents, were publishing numerous stories about Müller's alleged escape.[145] Consequently, American and German intelligence agents made renewed efforts to solve the mystery. On 25 September 1963, a grave bearing Müller's name, which had been lovingly tended by his mistress, was dug up.[146] It contained the skeletons of three different men, none of whom, due to their age and other characteristics, could have been Müller.[147] Even CIA investigators were confused by what they called this 'comedy of errors'.[148] The minutiae of the Müller case could be the subject of a totally separate book and need not be delved into in too much detail here. What is important is that, having investigated contradictory claims that Müller had been recruited by the Soviet intelligence services, had committed suicide in 1945 or had been killed in action, the CIA humbly concluded in 1970 that 'the only thing that is clear is that it is unclear as to what fate befell Mueller at the end of the war'.[149] As with the Hitler and Bormann investigations, the CIA's confusion was compounded by individuals with questionable motives giving false information. For example, one Herr Harz claimed 'he had a recruitment pitch made to him by the RIS [Russian Intelligence Service] with the help of Mueller who he recognised working for the KGB. However, in his 1958 efforts to peddle his wares to the USA he makes no mention of this startling and important matter – in all probability because at that time he had not thought it up...'[150]

Predictably, some conspiracy theorists have thrived on this uncertainty. In the early 1990s Gregory Douglas claimed to have uncovered documentary material proving that Müller worked for American intelligence after the war and revealed details about Hitler's escape from the bunker under interrogation.[151] However, as Joachimsthaler points out, numerous factual errors throughout Douglas's works (such as the fact that he cites planes that had been destroyed as having aided Hitler's escape) prove that his story of Hitler's fate was 'obviously fictitious'.[152] Despite this, in 2005, Ron T. Hansig published *Hitler's Escape*, which draws predominantly on Douglas's fictitious account to claim that Müller helped Hitler escape from Berlin via helicopter (!) on his way to Barcelona.[153] The CIA's excellent and revealing summary of the events surrounding the search for Müller could be easily applied to those surrounding Hitler's last days, too:

> Publicity hounds, amateur sleuths, writers, fabricators, and provocateurs in the employ of interested parties, spread rumours and confuse matters still further. Moreover, as events recede into the background of history what was (or seemed to be) self-evident to contemporaries becomes mysterious and confusing. Records disappear, memories change, and those who study the events tend to evaluate them in the modern instead of contemporary context. The search for Mueller provides a good illustration of these phenomena.[154]

Although some conspiracy theorists have tried to link the murky fate of Müller to theories of Hitler's escape, I could find no information in the large CIA files documenting the post-war hunt for Müller linking the Gestapo chief to survival rumours concerning his former master. Indeed, unlike the Bormann rumours, this is one survival rumour whose link to Hitler's alleged escape seems to have been invented by conspiracy theorists themselves; it therefore has absolutely no basis in historical fact whatsoever. On the contrary, as Timothy Naftali, Norman J. W. Goda, Richard Breitman and Robert Wolfe discovered whilst researching these documents, they provide further evidence to disprove theories of Anglo-American knowledge of Müller's alleged escape. Indeed, the fact that American intelligence agents were still investigating and compiling reports on the unknown whereabouts of Müller in the 1960s demonstrates that '[t]he Central Intelligence Agency and its predecessors did not know Müller's whereabouts at any point after the war. In other words, United States intelligence agencies were never in contact with "Gestapo" Müller.'[155] If American intelligence had captured or even recruited Müller, as some authors have theorised, then such investigations would not make sense, and FBI correspondence with the CIA concerning Müller further supports these conclusions.[156] Thanks to an (albeit comparatively small) MI5 personality file on Müller, declassified in 2007, the same can also be said for British intelligence. As Captain Hodges of the ID stated in 1949, 'Various investigations have been made from time to time since 1946 with a view to tracing Mueller's whereabouts, if alive, but without success.'[157]

The fact that there are thousands of files created by Anglo-American intelligence agencies investigating Müller and Hitler's whereabouts can also be used as a further argument against the theories of Hitler's escape; their huge number helps to demonstrate that Anglo-American intelligence agents did not allow Hitler or any of his henchmen to escape from the bunker in 1945. If they had done, they wouldn't have wasted years searching for evidence of their fates.

III: The Mass Suicide

It is convenient for conspiracy theorists to focus on the fate of the Nazis from the Führerbunker who – not unusually, given the circumstances – disappeared, or whose bodies were never found at the end of the war.[158] In doing so, they ignore the fact that many other top Nazis who were close to Hitler and present during his last days, such as Joseph Goebbels, chose to commit suicide. Many, including Goebbels, did this because they were inspired and encouraged by the knowledge that their Führer had also done so. As mentioned earlier in this book, it is inconceivable that Magda Goebbels would have killed her children with the reluctant consent of her husband had either of them believed Hitler would outlive them.

When discussing Hitler's death, it is again important to emphasise the need to maintain a sense of context. Suicide was not an unusual form of death for Hitler and Eva to have chosen, and due to the circumstances, it was one that many other Nazis chose to take as well. For example, Heinrich Himmler, head of the SS, chose to bite down on a cyanide capsule whilst undergoing a medical examination in British captivity.[159] He had been 'arrested at a check point on a bridge near Bremervorde', wearing an eyepatch and carrying forged papers under the name Heinrich Hitzinger.[160] Himmler had hoped to have a meeting with Field Marshal Bernard Montgomery to help determine Germany's future.[161] The moment a British doctor's fingers poked at his mouth he must have realised that he would be treated as an undignified war criminal, not a statesman. His unrealistic objective had failed to come to anything. Revealingly, he gave a 'shake of his head' before biting down on his cyanide capsule.[162] In taking his own life in this way, he preserved a slight semblance of control and authority by denying the Allies the chance to determine the time and method of his death. But despite photographic evidence and the existence of a death mask, even this suicide has been the subject of lengthy conspiracy theories (discussed further in the following section).

Reichsmarschall Hermann Göring, of Luftwaffe fame, also cheated the hangman by committing suicide at Nuremberg in 1946.[163] Interestingly, a British Intelligence Division report from Germany at the time tellingly stated that 'the news of his suicide gave rise to many rumours. Some said he had escaped, others that he was being taken to England to be used in the next war, others that he had really been dead for some considerable time.'[164] Obviously, Göring's dead body was identified and photographed beyond certainty, so modern conspiracy theorists have wisely not elaborated on these rumours. Again, what is important about this is the context. Rumours about the deaths of important Nazis, often motivated by the various factors discussed earlier in this book, as well as suicide itself, were not unusual in occupied Germany. As one report from 1946 preserved by the CIA states, 'various reports and rumours ... circulated after the German collapse on the subject of the final fate of the top Nazis in Berlin'.[165] If rumours could be stirred about the likes of Göring, whose death was beyond doubt, is it any wonder that stories of Bormann sightings circulated as they did in the web of intrigue that was the multi-zonal Cold War hub of post-1945 Germany? This, of course, doesn't make the rumours of Hitler's escape any more credible than those of Göring's, inspired as they often were by people with the same questionable motives. Or, perhaps, more sadly, by a tendency to distrust authority, fostered by years of Goebbels' propaganda.[166] As one British Regional Intelligence Office report observed in November 1946, 'there is almost a complete lack of trust in all "official" explanations and the good intentions of Military Government are universally doubted'.[167] This tendency was in fact a key concern of the Allies in their mission to create a democratic Germany and another reason why rumours were of such interest to British and American intelligence agencies.

In 1945, the Nazi world was coming to an end and thousands of fanatics chose death rather than the humiliation of trial or the prospect of living in a world without National Socialism.[168] Hitler, like many other Nazis, did not want to be publicly displayed and ridiculed. He confirmed that this was the case with various statements made in the bunker as reported by numerous eyewitnesses.[169] He feared that, if captured, he would be paraded in a 'monkey cage' before Moscow.[170] Hitler believed there was honour in choosing suicide over surrender and expected his commanding officers to make this gruesome choice too.[171] Some, to Hitler's delight, did what was morbidly expected of them.[172] For example, Field Marshal Walter Model shot himself on 21 April 1945 when his Army Group B lost the battle for the Ruhr.[173] Unsurprisingly, then, committing suicide rather than surrendering following a defeat in battle was glorified by Nazi propaganda.[174]

When Hitler made his bid for world mastery, it wasn't with the idea that he could try again another time if it failed. It was all or nothing.[175] Total war. Many Nazi fanatics knew this. Consequently, Richard Beisel argues that the mass suicide which accompanied the end of the Third

Reich was so widespread that 'Germany was committing suicide'.[176] Indeed, Hitler's desire to escape Russian retribution was evidently shared by many German people. For example, the Soviets captured some villages only to find that the majority of their inhabitants had committed suicide.[177] This, it must be stated, was not solely the result of Nazi ideological fanaticism but was often inspired by a very real fear of rape.[178] Sometimes it was a mixture of both.[179] Nevertheless, the key point is that Hitler and Eva's desire to avoid the nasty consequences of Russian capture by suicide was not an unusual decision to have taken in April 1945.

Members of the Hitler Youth shot their comrades and themselves when their defensive positions were overrun, homeowners jumped to their deaths in despair at losing everything, husbands and wives committed suicide together, mothers and fathers killed daughters and sons before killing themselves.[180] People shot, drowned, hung themselves and jumped for a variety of personal reasons. This was, as Beisel puts it, 'an orgy of collective suicide'.[181] There was in fact something suicidal in Nazi ideology, and in Hitler's thinking itself, that has been referred to by many authors.[182] Hitler viewed war as an essential part of life, forcing superior races to remain tough.[183] The logical end point to this is that eventually a superior race will conqueror all others through war but will then surely have to turn on itself to remain at its full potential. In the end, the Nazis would have to make war on themselves, which is of course exactly what they ended up doing to some extent in the last days of the regime, as mass state-sanctioned murder accompanied mass suicide.[184] Whilst some Nazis undoubtedly committed suicide out of despair that their ideology had been proved wrong (i.e. the Germans had been shown not to be racially superior), others may have done so out of a commitment to that same twisted racial ideology (i.e. having proved to be inferior to the Soviets, the Germans deserved total annihilation).[185] But it was not all about nihilism; as Christian Goeschel argues, some Nazis felt that choosing suicide let them remain in control of their own fate despite the chaos erupting around them.[186] Clearly the reasons why many Germans chose suicide rather than capture or surrender were complex and multicausal. On a personal level, Hitler had threatened to commit suicide before the Second World War, and Eva had attempted to do so on several occasions.[187] Hitler's suicide, in this context, was not at all unusual. On the contrary, it was to be expected. But as is well known, not all Nazis chose to kill themselves. Some did in fact escape from Berlin successfully. Could they have helped Hitler to escape with them?

IV: 'Why Not Hitler?' Real Escapes from the Bunker

In 1946, British and American guns once again exchanged fire with Nazis 'at scattered points in Western Germany'.[188] Operation Nursery was under way. This operation involved the capturing of Artur Axmann, a high-ranking Nazi and witness to Hitler's funeral who certainly did escape from the Führerbunker. He was not the only one. Hitler's companion from the Führerbunker and appointed successor to Dr Joseph Goebbels, Werner Naumann, was later arrested by British intelligence for trying to revive Nazism in Germany in the 1950s.[189] Surely such important figures would have been privy to knowledge of Hitler's escape? If they had been, why would they have had to break out of the bunker in extreme danger and attempt to set up their own neo-Nazi-style movements? Considering Hitler's hostile reaction to the attempts by other Nazis, such as Hermann Göring, to take over leadership of the Nazi Party in the final days, it would have been completely inconsistent with what are known to have been his opinions for Hitler to have allowed groups practising variants of Nazism, headed by the likes of Axmann and Naumann, to emerge.

Still, some conspiracy theorists attempt to use the Anglo-American investigations into such post-war Nazi plots to bolster their stories of Hitler's escape. A common method is for them to take the codenames of intelligence operations that, in the absence of any research into their origins, may sound conspiratorial, and attempt to find some significance in them that is simply untrue. For example, Peter Levenda suggests that Operation Nursery was designed by British intelligence to feed the general public a nursery tale about Hitler's death to cover up the 'fact' that he escaped the bunker.[190] In reality, Operation Nursery was a well-documented Anglo-American intelligence operation which involved the arrest of Axmann and other members of the Hitler Youth who, using a transportation company as their cover, were trying to revive Nazism in Germany.[191] As the operation was aimed at arresting Hitler youths, rather than for the reason suggested by Levenda, Nursery, as Wellington Long points out, was in fact an 'apt code name'.[192]

Similarly, conspiracy theorists who claim that Himmler was murdered by British intelligence or that a double committed suicide in his place deliberately mislead readers by discussing intelligence operations. For example, Hugh Thomas in *SS-1: The Unlikely Death of Heinrich Himmler* confusingly suggests that Operation Globetrotter was a secret British intelligence operation investigating rumours of Himmler's survival that was undertaken within the larger Operation Selection Board without American knowledge.[193] By searching for Himmler under the guise of a larger anti-Nazi intelligence operation, Thomas argues, British intelligence was able to hide its hunt for Himmler from the Americans whilst also benefiting from American co-operation. However, he later suggests that the secret hunt for Himmler was disguised by a secret operation being conducted within Globetrotter rather than by Operation Selection Board acting as a cover for Globetrotter.[194]

Having analysed several British Intelligence Division reports, it is clear that Operation Globetrotter was not kept hidden from the Americans, nor was the possibility of Himmler's survival considered throughout the operation. On the contrary, reports updating the Americans on the progress of Operation Globetrotter were routinely disseminated to American authorities.[195] Moreover, internal British ID reports on Globetrotter, not circulated to the Americans, make no mention of Himmler's survival.[196] As correspondence between British and American liaison officers demonstrates, British intelligence were not trying to hide Globetrotter personalities' connections to Himmler from their American counterparts.[197] The search for and arrest of individuals linked to Himmler was openly discussed throughout the operation, but this was mostly in connection with missing loot and subversive activity, rather than rumours of Himmler's survival.[198]

Furthermore, a future attempt to rediscover the location of Himmler's unmarked grave was inspired not by doubts that Himmler was really dead, but by the fear that a 'raid on Himmler's grave, on the model of that on Mussolini's', was being plotted by Nazi supporters.[199] As the pencil note next to Himmler's photograph in the War Office file containing Globetrotter correspondence makes clear, British intelligence were certain that Himmler was 'dead'.[200]

Analysis of British ID reports reveals that Operation Globetrotter concerned several Nazi groups, none of them under Himmler's leadership, and the most alarming of which sought 'to bring former SS and HJ leaders into an organisation which, in the event of an east/west war, could trade its services to either side'.[201] Thomas, unsurprisingly, makes no mention of such files and relies mainly on unverifiable personal conversations to support his conspiratorial claims. Interestingly, Operation Globetrotter did involve investigation of the 'Organization "ODESSA"'.[202] Clearly, Anglo-American intelligence agencies investigated organisations suspected of facilitating the escape of wanted Nazis to countries such as Argentina, especially when they may have had links to subversive activities in Germany. As was demonstrated in Chapter Two, this partly explains why British intelligence officers investigated rumours of Hitler's survival. They did not doubt that Hitler was dead, but thought that investigating certain stories of his survival could help them find other Nazis who 'might have escaped from Germany'.[203] In 1960, the capture in Argentina of Adolf Eichmann, a key orchestrator of the Holocaust, briefly reignited interest in stories of Hitler's and Bormann's escape.[204] If Eichmann managed to escape to Argentina, 'some asked, why not

Hitler?'[205] Several answers to that question have already been provided by this book, and further answers are given in the following chapter. In addition, it should be noted that Nazi escapes to South America have been the subject of lengthy publications, none of which have found any evidence that Adolf Hitler was among the escapees.[206] If there was anything even hinting that Hitler scurried out of the bunker down a ratline, somebody would surely have unearthed it by now. Unsurprisingly, authors such as Guy Walters who have researched these matters in detail have found little to foster belief in the claims of conspiracy theorists.[207]

Operation Selection Board has also been studied in some depth by historians, including myself. No hint of Himmler's or Hitler's survival can be found within the many files documenting this operation, which rounded up several groups intending to restore Nazi rule in Germany.[208] It should at this stage be pointed out that if one were to believe all of Thomas's conclusions, then the last days of not only Himmler but also Hitler and Hess would have to be reconsidered. Thomas is a good example of conspiracy theorists spotting conspiracy everywhere. As David Aaronovitch points out, this apparently helps make an 'individual theory … seem less improbable'.[209] Clearly, stories of Himmler's and Bormann's escape have been used in an attempt to bolster the credibility of conspiracy theories concerning Hitler's suicide, and vice versa. Such theories therefore deserve further refutation.

Thomas is not the only author to attempt to rewrite the accepted story of Himmler's suicide. In 2005, Martin Allen claimed to have discovered documents proving that Himmler was murdered on the orders of Churchill to prevent America gaining knowledge about secret negotiations conducted with Himmler during the war.[210] Again, it is important to highlight the fact that conspiracy theorists frequently contradict each other's arguments. Thomas implies that the photographed corpse of Himmler was a double, whilst Allen claims that it was in fact the murdered Himmler. Both cannot be true. Unsurprisingly now, but shockingly at the time, forensic analysis determined that the documents cited by Allen were forgeries.[211] But forged documents were not the only tools Allen used to convey his conspiracy theory. He also made confusing and misleading use of codenames and operations to encourage his readers to find conspiracies where there were none.[212]

Similarly, some conspiracy theorists, including Thomas, like to overwhelm their readers with seemingly relevant pages of context before stating their conspiratorial conclusions. This gives the reader the illusion that an immense amount of study has been undertaken by the author or authors before reaching reasoned conclusions based on evidence. However, it is debatable whether those interested in Hitler's or Himmler's death need to read almost one hundred pages of background on the intricacies surrounding Nazi economics at the end of the war before getting to the subject at hand. Because of this, some conspiracy theorists, including the authors of *Grey Wolf*, can be accused of causing death by selective context rather than the more commonly known 'death by footnote' method of clouding woolly thinking described by David Aaronovitch.[213] If new facts are to be revealed and corrections made to the accepted story of Himmler's suicide, these are likely to come from the release of MI6 documents, if they are ever released, not from Thomas's confusing and misleading tales derived from personal conversations. Until such a time, historians should visit the Museum of Military Medicine at Keogh Barracks in Aldershot, where I was kindly shown Himmler's death mask, his post-mortem, photographs of his corpse and detailed contemporary accounts of his suicide copied from documents at the National Archives.

Operation Selection Board was not the last major anti-Nazi operation undertaken by British intelligence, nor was Artur Axmann the last Nazi from the bunker to be apprehended. In January 1953, the world was surprised by the arrest of Werner Naumann and his Nazi circle, which was plotting to use a legitimate German political party, the FDP, as a vehicle for reintroducing a Nazi style of rule to Germany.[214] When Naumann was arrested, he had nothing to say of Hitler's alleged escape but, rather, confirmed his suicide.[215] Due to the increased Cold War focus on anti-communist rather than anti-Nazi intelligence activities at this time, British intelligence was seemingly short on experienced interrogators with a detailed knowledge of Nazi matters in Germany.[216] Importantly, amidst the Foreign Office considerations concerning who should interrogate Naumann and his gang, the name of one man kept cropping up. They tried to bring back Hugh Trevor-Roper.[217] Despite the fact that he had long since returned to his lecturing duties at Oxford, his name was still one of the first that influential officials could think of when considering who was best suited to interrogate neo-Nazis. What had he done to achieve such a status? He had directed an extremely effective intelligence investigation that provided convincing evidence of Hitler's suicide, as the following chapter will demonstrate.

You may say it's a man's duty to shoot himself,
just as in the old days generals fell on their
swords, when they saw that the game was up.
—Adolf Hitler, 1943[1]

6

The Evidence Still Stands

I: Positive and Consistent Evidence

Although the narrative of Hitler's last days has been disseminated in many publications, the historiography lacks a detailed analysis of how British intelligence selected their evidence and determined the reliable from the fictitious before concluding that Hitler shot himself and Eva Braun took poison on 30 April 1945. Conspiracy theorists argue that Hugh Trevor-Roper used unreliable eyewitness testimonies, and they have criticised his report (delivered to the QIC on 1 November 1945) and his book as rushed, suggesting instead that Hitler was murdered or escaped the bunker.[2] In order to fully assess these claims, it is essential to analyse the evidence collected by all sources of British intelligence, determine the reliability of the evidence historians have to claim that Hitler died on 30 April 1945, how he died and assess the significance of the 2009 DNA results.

Throughout May 1945 British officials began collecting intelligence relating to Hitler's end. This included signals intelligence (SIGINT) from the Japanese Ambassador at Bad Gastein, who informed Tokyo on 30 April 1945 that 'the Fuehrer was determined to link his fate with Berlin, and if Berlin fell, he would not survive', and Hitler's last request for battle information, intercepted from the Führerbunker on 29 April 1945.[3] Additionally, the Foreign Office noted that Admiral Dönitz (Hitler's nominated successor) had broadcast a message on Hamburg Radio on 1 May 1945 stating that Hitler died 'at his command post ... fighting to the last breath against Bolshevism' (this is discussed further in section II of this chapter).[4] Churchill was kept informed of such developments but was apparently in no mood to speculate about the 'manner of Hitler's death'.[5] Replying to a minute from Sir Orme Sargent on the subject with a characteristically short but (with hindsight) puzzling sentence, Churchill advised the Foreign Office to 'let it rip for a day or two'.[6] Towards the end of the month the War Office began to receive interrogation reports from captured Nazis such as Johanna Wolf (Hitler's secretary), who was 'convinced' Hitler had 'committed suicide'.[7] The most important interrogation was that of Hermann Karnau, who was a guard on duty outside the bunker at the time of Hitler's cremation. He claimed to have been ordered by an SS officer to leave the vicinity of the Reichschancellery 'for a time' and did so. When he returned to the garden he saw the bodies of Hitler and Eva on fire 'two metres from the emergency exit'.[8] He was interrogated several times and 'cross-examined carefully' until his interrogators were satisfied that he was 'speaking the truth'.[9]

Karnau drew an image of the location where he claimed Hitler and Eva were buried which has never previously been published (see Figure 3). This location closely matches those given in similar diagrams in Soviet documents.[10] Captain George T. Gabelia, a member of Heimlich's bunker excavation team, recalls that the 'rather sketchy map' they used when digging for Hitler's remains was 'drawn by a German SS national by the name of Karnak'.[11] It is likely

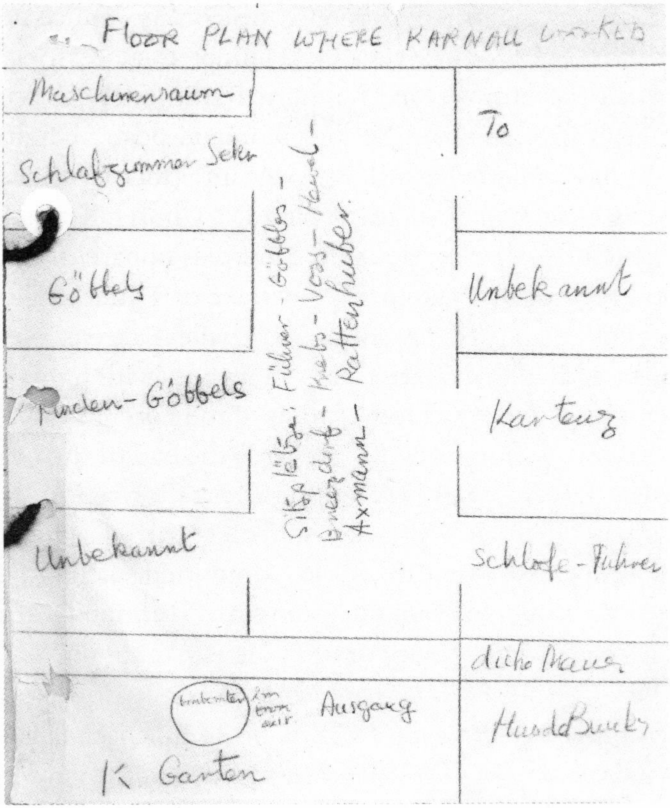

FIGURE 3 Drawing by Hermann Karnau shows the location of Hitler and Eva's burial next to the word 'Ausgang'. TNA, KV 4/354.

that Captain Gabelia was referring to Karnau's sketch. On 20 July 1945, British intelligence obtained a statement from Kurt Samuel, who said a friend had informed him that a member of 'Hitler's personal guard' named Mansfeld claimed that 'Hitler had committed suicide on 30 April' and that he had witnessed Hitler and Eva's bodies being carried into the garden and burnt.[12] In July 1945, a SHAEF report entitled 'Hitler's Last Days' was produced, bringing together the testimonies and statements of Albert

Speer (Reichsminister of Armaments), Karnau, SIGINT and the Soviets to conclude that 'it seems probable that, from all we know of Hitler's last days, he chose to die in Berlin'.[13] However, the report left Hitler's manner of death undetermined due to the large number of alternative accounts that had been put forward. Indeed, it found that the evidence at this point was 'sometimes contradictory and incomplete and depends often on hearsay and conjecture'.[14] It was left mainly to Trevor-Roper to determine what was reliable and what was fictitious.

Trevor-Roper built on evidence collected by investigators before him, including a survival rumour reported by MI6 in July 1945 to MI14 (again showing inter-service co-operation).[15] It is impossible to assess the full role of MI6 in the Hitler investigations. However, the fragments that remain demonstrate that numerous sections of British intelligence were investigating Hitler's death before Trevor-Roper's involvement, and this partially explains the prompt completion of his report, which drew mainly on evidence obtained from interrogations conducted over the winter of 1945. Karnau was re-interrogated in September and retold his story almost identically.[16] His testimony was supported by the interrogation of another Reichschancellery guard, Hilco Poppen, who stated that Karnau told him on 1 May 1945: '"Hitler ist tot"', '"Sie liegen (Hitler and Eva Braun) im Garten, und Brennen."'[17] He also claimed that Hitler was buried in a bomb crater in the garden, which he drew on a diagram closely matching the one drawn earlier by Karnau (see Figure 4). Poppen was re-interrogated in October 1945 and, like Karnau, repeated his story almost identically. His interrogator, Captain Ingham, considered that 'he has

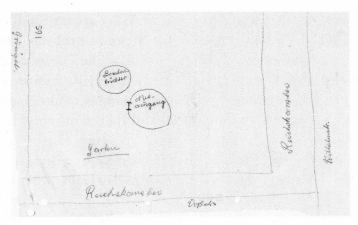

FIGURE 4   Rough sketch by Hilco Poppen showing the location of
Hitler and Eva's burial. TNA, WO 208/3787.

given the information to the best of his ability' and that 'as
far as he is informed, the statements are true'.[18]

Hugh Trevor-Roper's interrogation of Kempka (Hitler's
chauffer) confirmed the testimonies of Karnau and Poppen.[19]
Kempka claimed that Otto Günsche (Hitler's adjutant/
bodyguard) telephoned him on 30 April and requested that
200 litres of petrol be sent to the Führerbunker. Kempka
complied and later made his way over to the Führerbunker,
where Günsche told him that Hitler was dead and had shot
himself in the mouth. Kempka then saw Hitler and Eva's
bodies being carried out of Hitler's room and helped carry
them into the garden with Günsche and Linge. They then
poured petrol over the bodies and quickly retreated to the
bunker exit due to heavy Russian artillery fire. Günsche
lit a 'rag' and threw it on the bodies 'and they burst into
flames'. They each gave a final Hitler salute and returned
to the bunker. Despite 'some discrepancies', Trevor-Roper
noted that Kempka's account 'generally agrees' with that of
Mansfeld, who also stated that Hitler's body was brought

up first into the garden in a blanket with his legs protruding, followed by Eva, who was uncovered. Trevor-Roper had clearly received a copy of the American interrogation of Erich Mansfeld conducted on 30 July 1945 at the Bremen Interrogation Centre and used information obtained therein to compare facts obtained from the interrogation of Kempka.[20]

Attached to Mansfeld's interrogation is a sketch of Hitler's bunker that has never previously been published, showing where the burning and the burial of the bodies took place and the concrete guard tower in which Mansfeld worked (see Figure 5). Mansfeld stated that 'he saw thru an observation slit in the tower a huge column of black smoke … minutes later, when the smoke had partly cleared, he could see two burning bodies, about 2 meters to the left of the emergency exit… From time to time somebody poured additional gasoline on the burning bodies.'[21] He later investigated the corpses and could still recognise Eva, but the 'other body was almost completely burned and no longer recognizable'.[22] While in the 'guard room', Mansfeld heard 'SS Gruppenfuhrer Rattenhuber' order 'one of the SS Oberscharfuhrers … to request three men to bury the bodies'.[23] The next time Mansfeld was ordered to guard the emergency exit 'the bodies were nowhere to be seen'.[24] Mansfeld noticed that 'a shell crater, 4 to 5 meters in front of the emergency exit door, had been partly covered'.[25] He believed that what was left of Mr and Mrs Hitler lay within.[26] After cross-examining him three times, his CIC interrogator thought that 'Mansfeld's final story is the truth, as he has been brought to the point where he talks freely and accurately'.[27]

Trevor-Roper combined this evidence with recollections of Hitler's statements and behaviour given by numerous

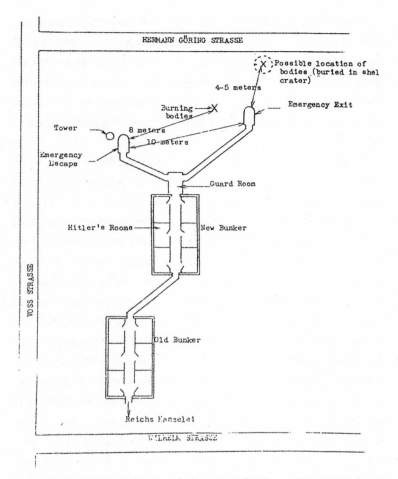

FIGURE 5 Diagram showing the location of Hitler and Eva's burning and burial as recalled by Erich Mansfeld. NARA II, RG 263, UD 2, Box 4, Folder 2, 16967345.

eyewitnesses who were present in the bunker throughout April 1945 and with information on his physical health from records and interrogations of his doctors to produce a detailed psychological analysis of Hitler's decision to commit suicide. For example, Hanna Reitsch, whose testimony was considered 'reliable' by her interrogator, believed 'the tactical situation and Hitler's own physical condition made any thoughts of his escape inconceivable'.[28] Indeed, Reitsch and other witnesses noted how Hitler frequently proclaimed his wish to shoot himself in Berlin and have his body burned rather than be captured 'alive or dead' by the Russians, and how Goebbels spoke about 'setting an example that would long blaze as a holy thing from the pages of history' by dying in Berlin.[29]

Trevor-Roper never claimed his intelligence report was definitive; indeed, he explicitly states that the 'evidence is not complete; but it is positive, circumstantial, consistent and independent', as opposed to rumours of Hitler's survival, which had all been investigated and found to be 'baseless'.[30] He admitted that 'the only conclusive evidence' would be 'the discovery, and certain identification, of the body ... in absence of this the only positive evidence' is provided by eyewitness accounts. Another reason his report was submitted promptly was because (as explained in Chapter Four) British intelligence had arranged to pool evidence with the Soviets at the QIC, and this was the first major attempt to do so – and an unsuccessful one at that. In concluding that it was 'quite impossible' that eyewitnesses had invented a 'cover story' or that Eva Braun could have been 'fobbed off with the corpse of a double' as the eyewitnesses were each questioned under 'detailed and persistent cross-examination', Trevor-Roper was responding to speculation in the press that 'circumstantial evidence' from 'lesser fry could well be an attempt to cover Hitler's trail'.[31] It was in fact Trevor-Roper's reliance on 'lesser fry' that made his conclusions more believable, as their evidence was independent of each other and circumstantial. Indeed, Karnau stumbled upon

Hitler's cremation by accident; he was not supposed to have witnessed it. Karnau saw the petrol ordered by Günsche delivered to the bunker and a later witness confirmed that he overheard the telephone conversation between Günsche and Kempka regarding petrol.[32]

Shortly after the publication of Trevor-Roper's report, Hitler's wills and marriage certificate were discovered. The wills explicitly stated that Hitler and Braun had chosen to die in Berlin and thus confirmed Trevor-Roper's conclusions. Hitler's marriage was verified by numerous eyewitnesses, such as von Varo, who claimed that the marriage 'was openly discussed by everyone', and the secretaries who attended the wedding reception, and by Hitler's wills, which mention the marriage directly.[33] As Robert P. Patterson, the Secretary of State for War, informed President Truman, 'Hitler's final anti-Semitic tirade, his frantic attempt to maintain a semblance of German government, and what amounts to a suicide pact between himself and Eva Braun vividly illustrate the closing hours of the Nazi regime.'[34] Trevor-Roper had the signatures on the wills authenticated by an MI5 handwriting expert who, from years of experience, was in 'no doubt' that the 'signatures' were 'genuine', and also by von Below, who signed Hitler's personal will.[35] In March 1946, the 'FBI Laboratory' conducted a separate detailed analysis of the American copies of Hitler's wills and his marriage certificate.[36] The tests indicated that the documents were authentic.[37] Melland had the British copies authenticated again by forensic scientists in 1966.[38] Indeed, Melland had planned to transfer the wills from the Foreign Office to display at the Imperial War Museum, and in the process noticed textual discrepancies between the British- and the American-held copies.[39] These discrepancies were minor grammatical errors which did not affect 'the sense of the contents' and they were eventually attributed to the 'frenzied atmosphere' in the bunker.[40] More importantly, Melland discovered that the Soviets held a fourth copy of the wills, a fact that was unknown to Trevor-Roper.[41] Its existence was confirmed in Marshal Chuikov's memoirs and by the historian John Erickson, who was shown the wills by Chuikov.[42] Trevor-Roper, Erickson and Melland concluded that the fourth copy was taken by General Krebs to Chuikov during truce negotiations on 30 April 1945 after Hitler's suicide.[43] However, they were unable to discover who typed it, and it is not mentioned in any publications about Hitler's death. Melland attempted to contact the Soviets to compare the copies but was ignored.[44] It is clear, therefore, that the Russians are withholding more evidence than has previously been assumed. This documentary evidence was bolstered by further interrogation reports.

One criticism of Trevor-Roper's book voiced by German readers in 1948 was that 'we are unable to test the sources'.[45] Fortunately, we are in a better position today, as the recently declassified MI5 files contain a detailed summary of the main sources used by Trevor-Roper as submitted to the JIC.[46] In addition, a timetable of events produced by Captain Searle of the IG and modified by Trevor-Roper shows that the latter used the testimonies of several eyewitnesses for each key date to substantiate his conclusions, thus refuting Reitsch's claim that her testimony was crucial to his thesis.[47] Since Trevor-Roper was prohibited from the American Zone after the Truscott incident, later interrogations were conducted by American interrogators on briefs prepared by him. Such briefs asked precise, detailed and extensive questions that were usually answered in full in the resulting interrogation reports.[48] Trevor-Roper is therefore arguably too critical of American interrogators. Indeed, USFET produced several detailed reports on Artur Axmann (head of the Hitler Youth), who claimed to have entered Hitler's room after his suicide and to have seen both Hitler and Eva dead on their sofa.[49] Hitler shot himself in the right temple, 'as Axmann saw most of the blood on Hitler's right temple and on the right side of the face', and Eva had taken poison.[50] His interrogator, Leo Barton, drew a diagram of the position of the bodies from the viewpoint of Axmann (see Figure 6).

Barton concluded that Axmann was 'able to distinguish actual observations from conjecture' and 'was not shaken by objections or doubts raised by the interrogator', and remarked that 'the Russians must have been able to verify the truth and accuracy of his story'. It was mainly Kempka and Axmann who convinced Trevor-Roper that Hitler had shot himself and Eva had taken poison. This conclusion was also supported by the testimonies of Hitler's secretary Junge and Bormann's secretary Krueger, who were both told by Günsche (then a Russian prisoner of war [PW])

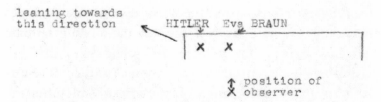

FIGURE 6 Diagram showing the position of Hitler and Eva's corpses on the sofa as viewed by Axmann. TNA, WO 208/3790.

that Hitler had shot himself whereas Eva had taken poison, and by that of Christian, who heard the same from Linge (also a Russian PW).[51] However, in order to reach this conclusion, the problem of eyewitness discrepancies had to be dealt with.

Eyewitness discrepancies in Trevor-Roper's investigations have been used by conspiracy theorists to present his account as an 'intrinsically flawed ... forgery' and to bolster claims of Hitler's escape.[52] Cooper has outlined in detail many discrepancies between the statements of Günsche, Kempka and Linge, given over a wide range of time, regarding the position of the bodies, which body was carried out first, who entered the suicide room first and at what time to argue that they show that this was an 'SS charade' that provides proof that Hitler did not die in the bunker.[53] However, Trevor-Roper took many discrepancies into account. For example, Karnau believed Hitler was cremated on 1 May, whereas Axmann claimed the date was 29 April and Kempka 30 April. Kempka was re-interrogated in January 1946 due to these discrepancies and repeated his story identically; his interrogator concluded that he had told a 'straight story'.[54] Consequently, Trevor-Roper used captured documents (such as a telegram sent from Goebbels to Dönitz on 1 May 1945 informing him that Hitler had died the previous day) combined with the testimonies of those last to see Hitler to confirm that Hitler died on 30 April 1945.[55] Discrepancies relating to time were attributed to 'the turmoil of the last days'.

Joachimsthaler provides a detailed and convincing explanation for discrepancies in the accounts of numerous eyewitnesses, including Linge and Günsche (who were released from Soviet captivity in the 1950s). Indeed, he argues that due to the urgency of the situation, the witnesses may not have made 'precise observations', instead only noting the positions of the bodies subconsciously, and therefore that they would have experienced 'flash-back' recall, with the result that months of interrogations were necessary for a coherent observation constructed from these flashbacks to surface.[56] Historians may never be able to definitively explain all of the discrepancies. Nevertheless, as Petrova and Watson point out, eyewitness discrepancies are common in court cases, with some witnesses remaining certain of what they saw even when proved wrong.[57] In addition, C. A. J. Coady suggests that conspiracy theories themselves are particularly unbelievable when they rely on the assertion that an improbably large number of people are lying, as this brings testimony itself, on which much of history is based, into disrepute.[58] Most importantly, as Joachimsthaler points out, all the witnesses who saw Hitler's body *in situ* agree that he shot himself, due to the blood on and around his corpse, whereas Eva's corpse was not bloody but smelled of bitter almonds, indicating cyanide poisoning.[59] However, one major discrepancy is that various eyewitnesses claimed that Hitler had poisoned himself; this requires further analysis.

II: Alternative Versions of Hitler's Death

The announcement on 1 May 1945 that Hitler had died 'fighting to his last breath' sparked a flurry of comments from the Foreign Office. The general worry was that 'German propaganda will play up the manner of Hitler's death with a view to establishing the Hitler legend'; therefore, 'we must do all in our power to play it down'.[60]

On 24 April, Himmler had stated during secret peace negotiations with Count Bernadotte that Hitler was so ill that he would likely be dead within two days.[61] The Foreign Office considered this a good 'weapon' with which to counteract Dönitz's story of Hitler's heroic death, which they correctly believed was formulated 'in an effort to secure maximum resistance by the German'.[62] Consequently, Eisenhower authorised a press statement describing Himmler's comments in order to 'destroy the Hitler martyr myth'.[63] However, this statement gave rise to claims that Hitler was murdered by his doctors on the orders of Himmler, a conclusion supported by some American intelligence officers.[64] Far from ignoring conflicting eyewitness testimony, as conspiracy theorists claim, British intelligence investigated these alternative versions of Hitler's death.

On 7 May 1945, Churchill received SIGINT from numerous ambassadors stating that Hitler had died in a variety of ways. For example, the Brazilian Ambassador claimed that 'Hitler, Goering and Goebbels were assassinated' during a struggle between Himmler and the military.[65] At the end of the month, the Foreign Office collected newspaper cuttings asserting 'that according to evidence discovered by the Russians, Hitler was probably killed by an injection given by his physician Dr. Morrell'.[66] From May to September 1945, British intelligence investigated rumours that Hitler was assassinated on the orders of Himmler in 1944 and buried in a crypt at Obersalzberg.[67] In October 1945 Bernadotte asserted: 'it is my absolute conviction that Hitler is dead and that Himmler killed him'.[68] Conspiracy theorists accuse Trevor-Roper of overlooking this statement.[69] Furthermore, several of the eyewitnesses interrogated by British intelligence, including Karnau, claimed that Hitler had poisoned himself.[70] Similarly, Willi Otto Mueller believed that Dr Stumpfegger had poisoned Hitler with an injection.[71] According to the American interrogation of Mansfeld, this was also 'rumored among the guards'.[72]

During Trevor-Roper's investigations, eyewitnesses were questioned on the possibility of Himmler having murdered Hitler. Werner Grothmann (Himmler's aide-de-camp) 'did not believe that Himmler ever contemplated murdering Hitler; he regarded such a suggestion as fantastic; Himmler always professed complete loyalty to Hitler'.[73] Other close associates of Himmler agreed with this statement. Trevor-Roper thus established that Bernadotte was mistaken.[74] He found the statements of those who claimed that Hitler had poisoned himself, or that he was poisoned by his doctors, to be based on hearsay. Indeed, Karnau, when re-interrogated, admitted that 'the poison story ... is mere hearsay based on old stories that the Fuehrer would take poison before being captured by the Russians'.[75] Many witnesses, including Karnau, had simply assumed that Hitler poisoned himself as they believed that Dr Stumpfegger had poisoned Hitler's dog Blondi.[76] Crucially for Trevor-Roper, the eyewitnesses who saw Hitler dead on his sofa claimed he had shot himself and informed his immediate entourage of the fact. Clearly, as Ian Kershaw argues, the conclusions of conspiracy theorists such as Thomas that Hitler was murdered 'belong in fairyland'.[77] Nevertheless, the Soviets, having carried out an autopsy, claimed that Hitler was poisoned. However, the Soviet autopsy, like the skull claimed to be Hitler's, is questionable.

III: The Skull Changes Everything?

As the first chapters of this book recounted, Hitler has been said to have fled to Ireland, Egypt and Hamburg. Therefore, one must question why most conspiracy theories claim Hitler escaped to Argentina. Their logic is quite simple: he must have fled there, because other Nazis did. However, if this logic was applied to other survival rumours, the outcome would be ridiculous. For instance, one Nazi was apprehended in May 1945 disguised as a monk, so does this mean that survival rumours of Hitler dressed as a monk should be taken more seriously?[78] Clearly not. Yet, this is the level of speculation that conspiracy theorists employ in an effort to convince their readers to draw history-changing conclusions. A similar lack of relationship between evidence and conclusion exists when conspiracy theorists use the 2009 DNA results as evidence of Hitler's escape.[79] Their basic line of argument is this: Stalin said Hitler escaped to Argentina, other Nazis escaped there, the skull in Moscow thought to be Hitler's belongs to a woman, the Soviets did not find Hitler's body, so therefore Hitler must have escaped. Yet, if one analyses the Soviet investigations in more detail, interesting questions are raised and matters become more complex, but nothing suggests that Hitler escaped from the bunker.

Petrova and Watson's analysis of Soviet documents came close to plausibly explaining the 2009 DNA results. As the documents revealed, the first corpse claimed to be Hitler's found by the Soviets at the bunker was in fact a very poor lookalike. Historians disagree as to whether this was Gustav Weler (Hitler's doppelgänger) or a corpse deliberately dressed up by SMERSH to look like Hitler.[80]

Nevertheless, because the Soviets thought this corpse was Hitler, two bodies found in a bomb crater near the bunker exit were reburied.[81] This was an embarrassing start to the investigations for the SMERSH unit, which had been ordered to find Hitler's body. Even more embarrassing was the way in which evidence in the bunker was disregarded. Indeed, the first Soviets to enter the Führerbunker were a group of women from the medical corps who stole Eva Braun's lingerie.[82] No wonder the CIA, whose knack for coining phrases has been demonstrated elsewhere in this book, would later refer to the 'souvenir-hungry Soviets'.[83]

It was not until July 1945 that the Russians allowed Anglo-American troops to enter Berlin, and many, as can be imagined, then immediately sought to investigate the site of Hitler's end. Even Churchill himself couldn't resist visiting the spot where his arch-enemy had met his grisly end, and he was pictured gesturing to onlooking Russian guards on one of Hitler's chairs outside the bunker exit, looking towards the ground where the Hitlers' bodies were burned.[84] John Rhys of the Control Commission Planning and Intelligence Section entered the bunker with 'a US Intelligence unit' and remembers seeing Hitler's 'bloodstained velvet sofa and carpet where he had evidently slumped over when he had shot himself in the head'.[85] Byford-Jones was later shown a room full of Hitler's personal belongings looted from the bunker by Soviet guards.[86] British intelligence officers also belatedly engaged in this souvenir hunting, collecting papers signed by Hitler, Iron Crosses and other memorabilia from the ruins of the Reichschancellery, which loomed over the bunker.[87] Even the Chief of the British Intelligence Group couldn't resist taking a postcard from the top drawer of Hitler's desk, hand signed by the Führer himself.[88] According to Rhys, one could smuggle such souvenirs past the Russian guards under one's clothes.[89] The vicinity around the Führerbunker was clearly not properly secured, because on 10 September 1945, British Lieutenant-Colonel McCowen broke into it and found Hitler's engagement diary, kept by his valet Linge, still there. It was then used by Trevor-Roper to validate certain times and dates.[90] That vital evidence such as this could have still been left in the bunker for five months after Hitler's death demonstrates how poor Soviet evidence gathering was. As Heimlich rightly reflected on his visits to the bunker, 'By the time we were able to make a detailed study of the bunker, literally hundreds of morbidly curious, including newspapermen, had been there before we were... I never saw those blood stains in the Reich chancellery bunker and if I had we would have submitted them to proper chemical analyses... All of the fabrics have been torn off the furniture when we arrived.'[91] But although Heimlich was right to criticise the Soviets for their poor evidence gathering, he, like many conspiracy theorists, jumped to unsubstantiated conclusions.

When it was discovered that the lookalike corpse was not Hitler, SMERSH had the two bodies (which Soviet documents claim are Hitler and Eva) near the bunker exit re-exhumed and sent for autopsy, the conclusion of which was that they died from poisoning.[92] However, as Petrova and Watson point out, there are significant issues with the SMERSH investigation.[93] For instance, the autopsy did not include dissection of the organs of the alleged Hitler and Eva corpses to determine for certain whether they died from poisoning, yet the corpses of the Goebbels family were subjected to such dissection.[94] Even Hitler's dog, Blondi, was dissected![95] Furthermore, as Heimlich observed at the time, if the Soviets had found Hitler's body, they surely 'would have taken pictures of ... [it] and produced other evidence as they did in the case of other high Nazi officials'.[96] The low-quality Soviet photographs published in Bezymenski's book claiming to depict Hitler and Eva's corpses look more like piles of mush than human bodies. By contrast, the several photographs depicting the Goebbels family corpses from several angles are much clearer.

Stalin himself was probably unsatisfied by the initial SMERSH conclusions, because he authorised a second commission into Hitler's death, this time by the NKVD (the Soviet Secret Service), in 1946.[97] Petrova and Watson argue that Stalin might have ordered this second investigation out of embarrassment and jealousy that the West may have collected more evidence than him, which could also explain why the Soviets refused to share evidence with Trevor-Roper.[98] The Soviets had displayed similar behaviour before, leading the JIC to conclude in April 1945 that 'the Russians' were unlikely to allow western 'intelligence teams' to visit areas under their control as they were conscious 'of their administrative inferiority as compared with the Americans and ourselves' due to their 'rapid advance'.[99]

The second NKVD investigation suggested that Hitler had died by shooting after confirming that bloodstains on Hitler's sofa and on the walls in the bunker were of his blood type and finding a piece of skull damaged by a bullet hole in the bomb crater where the two corpses found by SMERSH were buried.[100] That such evidence could be found a year after the initial investigation shows the poor quality of that investigation. Suspiciously, SMERSH did not allow the bodies alleged to be Hitler and Braun to be re-examined by the NKVD, despite an order from Moscow.[101] This, Petrova and Watson argue, was because SMERSH were embarrassed that they had 'botched' the autopsy, causing them to reach the incorrect conclusion that Hitler had poisoned himself.[102] The Soviets, therefore, according to this argument, maintained an official silence as they did not want to admit their mistakes.[103]

The 2009 DNA tests, which showed the skull fragment belonged to a woman, suggest that the Soviet investigations were in fact more botched than was previously thought. Indeed, Anatoli Prokopenko (director of the State Special Trophy Archive in Moscow) had claimed that the skull fragment was genuinely Hitler's.[104] Bold claims made by historians that the skull proved once and for all Hitler's method of death were refuted by these DNA results. Rather than unearthing evidence indicating that Hitler had escaped, it is more likely that the NKVD had simply recovered a fragment from one of many corpses that were strewn around the Reichschancellery garden as a result of Soviet artillery fire and then thrown into numerous bomb craters.[105] What, then, did happen to Hitler's body?

Due to the high number of eyewitness discrepancies, Trevor-Roper could only conclude that 'like Alaric ... the modern destroyer of mankind is now immune from discovery'.[106] Most historians agree that the Soviets recovered Hitler's teeth; these have been identified by his dentists, confirmed by X-ray comparison and subjected to modern forensic analysis.[107] But, as Fest argues, it is likely that the teeth are all that remained of Hitler.[108] As some eyewitnesses claim, the rest of his body was probably destroyed by artillery fire.[109] According to Bill Vandivert, the *Life* magazine correspondent who visited Hitler's bunker in July 1945 and took several harrowing photographs, the chancellery area was 'shelled to hell'.[110]

How, then, can one explain the Soviet autopsy findings? There are all sorts of possibilities. Perhaps, as Petrova and Watson have suggested, the Soviet soldiers performing the original autopsy were overjoyed on VE day, resulting in mistakes being made.[111] In the probably celebratory atmosphere they might have also enjoyed a giggle by throwing in questionable jibes (such as Hitler only having one testicle).[112] Or maybe, out of fear, they wrote the report they thought Stalin would want to read – that Hitler had died by poisoning (a cowardly death – the same way his dog had died) and was not fully equipped in his lower regions.[113] Or, possibly, they never found Hitler's body but, having been ordered to determine his whereabouts, felt they needed to report to Moscow that he had been found, or else face accusations of incompetence and the consequences of Stalin's displeasure. As a result, the Soviet soldiers picked up whatever mush they could find in front of Hitler's bunker exit, put it in a box and claimed it was the corpses of Adolf and Eva Hitler, when in reality all that was left was little more than teeth, ash and a garbled mess, barely recognisable as a 'body'. This would also explain why these 'corpses' were not dissected – there may have been very little left to dissect. Although these possibilities are just conjecture, they are each more likely and more in agreement with the evidence available than any of the tales of Hitler's escape.

In 2017, Professor Philippe Charlier (co-author of the recent *Internal Medicine* article with Jean-Christophe

Brisard) and his colleagues visited Moscow to examine the 'Hitler' skull fragment along with Hitler's teeth. They have since questioned the reliability of the 2009 DNA results.[114] However, the scientists from the University of Connecticut who carried out these DNA tests seemed very convinced that the skull was female, and so far no further DNA analysis has been undertaken, even by those scientists questioning the original results.[115] If, on further analysis, the skull does turn out to be Hitler's after all, it will surely be game over for the escape theorists. However, if the results again indicate that the skull is female (and I suspect they will), the following conclusion can be drawn.[116]

The unprofessional behaviour of the Soviet intelligence officers and the resulting poor quality of their investigations, the dubious autopsy report riddled with scientific inconsistencies and tainted by ideological motivations, along with the 2009 DNA revelations all lead me to agree with historians such as Joachimsthaler, Fest and Kershaw, who suggest that the Soviets did not find Hitler's body[117] However, this does not mean that Hitler escaped. Thorough cross-examinations of eyewitnesses, documentary evidence in the form of captured telegrams and Hitler's wills and marriage certificate, bloodstains on Hitler's sofa and the positive identification of Hitler's teeth provide ample evidence to refute these escape theories. Indeed, without knowing the final location of Hitler's corpse, Trevor-Roper was able to conclude convincingly that he committed suicide. Ultimately, the 2009 DNA results reveal more about the quality of the Soviet investigations than they do about Hitler's suicide.

The weight of circumstantial evidence set out in Trevor-Roper's book, when added to the state of Hitler's health at the time and the psychological probability that this was the end he would choose, make a sufficiently strong case to convince all but the constitutionally incredulous – or those who have not bothered to study the evidence.
—Alan Bullock[1]

Conclusion

'The Onus is on Hitler'

Through analysis of overlooked, underused and recently declassified Anglo-American intelligence files, this book has shed further light on the mystery surrounding Hitler's death. Having analysed the opinions of American and British intelligence officers concerning various Hitler survival rumours and determined that political motives did not affect their conclusions, it has been established that every major Anglo-American intelligence agency considers the evidence they collected throughout a variety of investigations, proves there to be no basis in fact whatsoever to any conspiracy theories on the subject of Hitler's suicide. Indeed, previously unpublished interrogation reports preserved by MI5 and recently declassified have revealed just how meticulous British intelligence was in cross-examining witnesses, and have demonstrated the objectivity of its conclusions, through Hugh Trevor-Roper's statements to the Joint Intelligence Committee.

By focusing on documents produced by the British and American intelligence services, this book has been able to analyse in detail the motives of those creating and disseminating Hitler survival rumours – a topic that was previously thought to be unexplorable owing to a lack of evidence. These motives ranged from the tragic to the absurd. Neo-Nazis spread rumours to help inspire underground movements, journalists did so in the hope of making money, pranksters to create a sensation, political opponents in an attempt to discredit each other, other individuals to draw attention to personal problems or to distract attention away from their crimes. Some, too, were mentally ill. Through its analysis of intelligence documents, this book has also been able to explore why Anglo-American intelligence agents investigated these rumours, and it has demonstrated that there were no conspiratorial intentions in their investigations. Unsurprisingly, intelligence officers often showed more interest in those who were disseminating rumours of Hitler's and Bormann's survival than they did in the rumours themselves. It can reasonably be assumed that modern-day conspiracy theorists are inspired by at least some of the same motives that inspired their mid-twentieth-century counterparts. Whatever motivates them, it is clear that they either do not know, or bother to learn, how to properly contextualise and analyse historical documents, or that they deliberately mislead the public.[2] As Charles Pigden argues, 'we are rationally entitled to believe in conspiracy theories *if that is what the evidence suggests*' (italics added).[3] Having analysed the evidence surrounding Hitler's last days, including evidence put forth by conspiracy theorists, I hope the reader will agree that there is no sufficient evidence to support the extraordinary claims of conspiracy theorists when it comes to Hitler's suicide. As Ernst Haiger has argued, some conspiracy theories could make interesting historical fiction.[4] But they should not be presented as historical fact.

Historians and journalists needn't trudge around Argentina looking for evidence of Hitler's alleged hiding place. To a certain extent, intelligence officers have already done that for us in the 1940s and 1950s. Each rumour they investigated turned out to be false. Readers interested in the Nazis who actually did escape justice may consult one of the many existing works on this subject. We know that Nazis escaped from Germany after the Second World War to places like Argentina – such escapes have been studied in detail. However, none of the evidence points to Hitler escaping with them. When studying Hitler's suicide, there is enough evidence to keep historians firmly focused on the ground in Germany, where the main focus of this book has remained.

It is rarely possible when studying intelligence files to recreate the personal relationships that existed between intelligence officers.[5] However, the files concerning Hitler's death contain personal correspondence, jokes and compliments. This book has therefore been able to shed further light on the dynamic relationship between numerous Anglo-American intelligence agencies that resulted in both friendships and vendettas. It has also revealed more about the history of the British Intelligence Division, an organisation about which very little is known but the activities of which were crucial to the British investigations concerning Hitler's death.[6] More importantly, the analysis of the contributions of numerous intelligence officers has distanced this book from the 'one-man show' of Hugh Trevor-Roper and enabled the efforts of other officers, which have often gone unsung, to be acknowledged.[7] However, the role of Trevor-Roper must not be understated. His failure in later life to identify the fake 'Hitler diaries' (which Sisman convincingly argues came about through a betrayal of Trevor-Roper's trust) has enabled conspiracy theorists to be overly critical of his early intelligence work.[8] But, as this book has shown, Trevor-Roper was a highly regarded intelligence officer in 1945 who showed a great deal of objectivity in his scrupulous hunt for the truth of how Hitler died. The 'Hitler diaries' fiasco should not reflect badly on his earlier intelligence work.

Although some American intelligence officers initially doubted Trevor-Roper's conclusions, even after the publication of his book, the lengthy parallel investigations they undertook found that Trevor-Roper was in fact correct. This again bolsters the evidence available to historians to disprove conspiracy theories. Indeed, if Anglo-American intelligence agencies had conspired together to help Hitler escape, as these theories allege, such parallel investigations would have been unnecessary. Moreover, the fact that American intelligence carried out its own independent review of the evidence and reached the same conclusions as Trevor-Roper adds further credibility to his work. The evidence analysed in this book therefore suggests that any doubts regarding Trevor-Roper's alleged political motives or the reliability of his conclusions are unwarranted.

It is interesting that conspiracy theorists seldom reference the arguments of other conspiratorial authors, though most attack the credibility of historians such as Trevor-Roper. Perhaps they realise that if one conspiracy is disproved, it could undermine the argument of another, as was demonstrated in Chapter Five. More likely, though, they do not even agree among themselves about when Hitler supposedly escaped, who with or where to. Hence the never-ending stories of Hitler sightings and hideouts throughout the world undermine rather than give credence to theories of Hitler's escape. Many conspiracy theorists ignore this inconvenient fact, as they do the historical context of what was actually occurring on the ground in Germany throughout the years of occupation, and consequently arrive at erroneous conclusions.

Nevertheless, no conclusions about Hitler's death can be definitive, as many Russian archives remain closed. Consequently, although this book has debunked numerous conspiracy theories, it has also raised more questions, such as who typed the fourth copy of Hitler's will? The files of Stalin's secretariat, if they are ever released, may reveal why Stalin decided to suppress evidence and could contradict the conclusions made in this book about Soviet conduct. Moreover, files held at the British National Archives in Kew relating to MI6 activities in Germany throughout 1945 remain closed to the public.[9] The cataloguing of these records suggests that it is intended to declassify them for public scrutiny at some point. When this happens, perhaps these files will reveal more about why MI6 conducted investigations into rumours of Hitler's survival and will supply further evidence to disprove these rumours.

Whilst this book has analysed all the main War Office and FBI files concerning Hitler's death, even this account cannot be considered fully comprehensive. There may well be other files buried within the hundreds of weekly and monthly Anglo-American intelligence reports that could come to light. Hopefully, such documents will be interpreted by historians in the context of those discussed here, and not by conspiracy theorists. Indeed, I hope the synthesis of primary and secondary sources provided in this book will aid future researchers and convince journalists that stories of Hitler's escape are, in fact, very old news.

Clearly, much more remains to be written about Hitler's death and the intelligence activities that took place in post-war Germany. This being the case, even though the evidence outlined in Chapter Six suggests that Hitler shot himself, it would be foolish (as the 2009 DNA results showed) to claim that this is the definitive answer. What is needed in future studies is co-operative scholarship between forensic scientists and historians using archives throughout the world. Perhaps, as Fest argues, due to numerous eyewitness discrepancies, historians may never know Hitler's method of suicide. There is, however, no longer any ideological baggage attached to the conclusion that Hitler shot himself. Indeed, despite Dr Goebbels' attempt to create a myth that would revive Nazism from the ashes of a heroic Wagnerian ending, the lies of conspiracy theorists and the deliberate confusion stirred up by the Soviets, Hitler's actions have shown historians that he died a hypocrite and a coward.

By challenging the criticisms that have been made of Trevor-Roper's investigations, assessing the opinions of Anglo-American intelligence officers concerning rumours of Hitler's survival, analysing the motives of conspiracy theorists and providing a plausible explanation for the 2009 DNA results, I hope to have undermined the conspiracy theories that have dominated public debate and the historiography of Hitler's last days since 2009. That they were able to do this demonstrates that some topics which may appear to belong in the narrow field of amateur historians are too important for academic historians to ignore. Indeed, despite the 2009 DNA results, there is still an overwhelming amount of evidence to suggest that Hitler died in Berlin. Trevor-Roper concluded that Hitler had committed suicide without analysing any corpse, and his conclusions are still convincing today. As one Foreign Office official wrote in October 1945, 'I think the onus is now not on His Majesty's Government to prove that Hitler is dead but on Hitler to prove that he is alive.'[10] The onus has been on Hitler for over seventy years. It is certain beyond all reasonable doubt that he committed suicide on 30 April 1945.

ACKNOWLEDGEMENTS

Arnold Schwarzenegger likes to say that he is not a 'self-made man', as many others have helped him along the way. In a similar vein, no book of this sort can be attributed entirely to the efforts of the author. It has benefited much from the works of several authors mentioned throughout and I am grateful to them all. I must give thanks to Dr Jonathan Colman for supervising my BA (Hons) thesis on which this book is based. My research would be poorer without the benefit of Jonathan's numerous inspiring conversations, patience and immensely valuable assistance during my undergraduate studies and after. Likewise, I cannot thank Dr Billy Frank enough for his encouragement throughout my studies and his belief in my ability to undertake a double dissertation on this topic back in 2015. Billy's support for my research and his friendship has been invaluable since our first conversation. Billy and Dr Robert Poole also have my gratitude for organising a public lecture to promote this book at the University of Central Lancashire in April 2018. Many of my former classmates and students attended this event and whilst I cannot thank them all individually, I trust they know that I greatly appreciate their support. I was questioned *in absentia* at the latter lecture by Dr Caroline Sharples, who I must thank for her useful comments on earlier drafts of some of these chapters and for her inspiring lectures on the Third Reich. Like Caroline, Dr David Stewart has also endured with great patience many discussions with me concerning Hitler's last days despite his own impressive workload. I am thankful to him for always being open to a conversation about British intelligence or the general trials of research whenever I knock on his office door (often unexpectedly). Many other historians at the University of Central Lancashire have been influential in teaching me how to practise history, although my conversations with them have mostly concerned other topics of research, I hope they will appreciate this collective thank you to the entire history department at Livesey House.

I am currently studying at the University of Leeds, where my PhD supervisors, Professor Simon Ball and Dr Elisabeth Leake, have greatly helped to hone my research skills and temper my often-overexcited language (though I must apologise to them for some of my unscientific prose here!). This book would be lacking in much useful evidence were it not for Professor Ball's advice that I consult private papers in the course of my PhD research, many of which are cited here. Professor Simon J. D. Green supervised my master's thesis, and although the latter concerned the Napoleonic legend, our personal conversations often turned to the subject of Hugh Trevor-Roper, which helped keep my interest in his work alive. I would like to thank Professor Green for all his help. Studying at the University of Leeds has enabled me to gain a much wider contextual knowledge of Anglo-American intelligence in occupied Germany, thus sharpening the analysis and arguments conveyed in this book. Consequently, I would like to thank the entire School of History at the University of Leeds, the White Rose College of the Arts and Humanities (WRoCAH) and the Arts and Humanities Research

Council (AHRC) for continuing to fund and support my PhD research. Thanks must also be given to the very hard-working Emma Chippendale, Joanna Philips, Richard Borowski, Hayley Brindle, Caryn Douglas, Clare Meadley and Professor Julian Richards, who have dealt with several of my overseas research trips and responded often to my last-minute questions concerning paperwork, forms and a whole manner of administration tasks which I find bewildering.

My interest in Hitler's last days pre-dates my university education and is largely the product of my general enthusiasm for history, which was kept alive throughout my studies at Deyes High School by several remarkable teachers: Mr Haywood, Mr Shannon and Mr Blackburn. The amount of work they put into preparing engaging lessons is phenomenal, and without their efforts I would never have achieved the GCSE and A-level results which formed the basis of my future career in history. It took a lot to inspire discipline from me at that young age, but these teachers commanded the respect of me and my classmates. They are better historians than I and could write better books than this one.

During my research at the National Archives in Kew I was kindly helped in tracing some files cited in this book by several friendly members of staff who always received my often time-consuming enquiries with patience. Likewise, the security and 'floor-walking' staff corrected my violations of regulations with good humour. Contrastingly, the gentleman searching bags at the door endured my bad jokes day after day. Timothy Cross is an asset to the National Archives. Without his help in drafting a book proposal for this work and discussing its content, the quality of this text could have been poorer and the format unsuitable. Thanks to Salvatore Bellavia at the Liddell Hart Centre for Military Archives in King's College London for arranging and supervising my visit to view the private papers of Major-General Lethbridge. Equal thanks to the staff at the Imperial War Museums, to Dr Patricia McGuire at King's College Archive Centre, Cambridge University and to Rob McIntosh, curator of the Museum of Military Medicine, for enabling me to read and photograph several of the files cited in this book. I am also very grateful to Christoph Laue and the *Verein für Herforder Geschichte* for helping me find the old British Intelligence Division Headquarters.

I would also like to thank all of the staff at the National Archives and Records Administration in College Park, Maryland – in particular, Paul Brown for teaching me how to use the often-bewildering file request system, for pointing me in the right direction of several important documents and for dealing with my over-ambitious pull-slip requests with patience and charm. Likewise, Eric S. Van Slander dealt with similar requests from me with much-appreciated patience. My research in America would not have been possible if Nazgol Ghandnoosh and her family had not allowed my fiancée and I to stay in their lovely apartment. I would like to thank them for being excellent hosts.

Whilst I have been fortunate to visit archives throughout the world in the course of my studies, I am also indebted to several individuals who have shared with me their private recollections of intelligence work and shown me personal documents. In particular, I would like to thank Colonel Miles Templer for kindly showing me his father's private papers, as well as for his gracious hospitality and friendly conversations. Michael Glueck was kind enough to put me in touch with Dr Bruce Haywood, whose conversations with me concerning his time working with the Counter Intelligence Corps in 1940s' Bremerhaven have been more useful to me than he may think. I must also thank A. F. Judge, senior researcher at the Military Intelligence Museum, Shefford, for admirably grappling with my tsunami of correspondence concerning a variety of subjects from conspiracy theories to serious intelligence matters and Christopher Yates of the Intelligence Corps for putting us in touch and also helping me in a variety of ways.

Without the support of Bloomsbury Publishing and Osprey, this book would not have been possible. My sincerest thanks to everyone there for working hard to produce an excellent front cover, for superb promotional materials and for investing in my work as an author. Special thanks to Lisa Thomas, who has dealt with countless lengthy emails from me concerning everything to do with this book from content to covers. Thanks also to my editor, Mandy Woods, who has analysed this book in impressive detail and helped to greatly improve it.

Like many other children of the late twentieth century, modern family life has resulted in me acquiring a forest containing several family trees rather than one great oak. Consequently, the personal influences on my historical work come from several individuals from different 'sides' of my family who all deserve thanks. On my mother's side, 'the Groves', I would like to thank my parents, Denise and Alan. From a young age they taught me discipline, respect and several other virtues without which I could not have been successful in historical research. I still remember our many visits to historical sites, castles and ruins throughout the world, which inspired the wonder that drives my interest in the past. I also regret not reading the many history books they bought me more often. Without their continued support and that of my sister, Sophie, this book would not have been possible. Sophie is wise beyond her years and I would like to thank her for enduring with great patience my absence on many occasions during my studies at times I would like to have shared with her. Her wisdom at the age of 12 is a great check to my hubris! My grandparents Winifred Mylett and Norman Halewood have engaged in many a conversation with me concerning the Second World War and Hitler's last days. Having lived through the end of World War II themselves, they have always kept me going with fascinating stories when the research gets tough. Their wisdom is truly inspiring and I am forever grateful that they are always there to help me with any problem, academic or practical. I don't think my grandad would mind me saying that it is he who has taught me to argue! I owe Nan and Grandad 'Boo Boo' all the thanks in the world, but also a brief apology because this book concerns 'that man' rather than Winston Churchill. I would also like to thank my grandparents Brenda and Mike Wynne for allowing me to stay in their lovely home in Surrey to conduct research at the National Archives on several occasions. Their hospitality and generosity is unending and their wisdom has often forced me to think harder.

On my father's side, 'the Dalys', I would like to thank my dad, Paul. He has endured many a conversation about Hitler with patience and genuine interest and is always willing to talk about the past should I wish to. His enthusiasm for my successes and his encouragement in failure is always appreciated. He reminds me never to be complacent and that only through hard work can good things be achieved. But, as my grandparents John and Sylvia taught me, breaks are essential. Nan and Grandad Daly have likewise endured several conversations about Hitler but have still kindly and eagerly awaited the release of this book, promoting it throughout Liverpool to friends and family. I would like to thank them for their continued belief in my work and for their generous hospitality. I hope my brother Nathan will find inspiration for his studies in these pages and I would like to thank him for his kindness, his willingness to listen, his honesty and for many fun conversations. Thanks are also due to all my aunties, uncles, cousins and friends who have all at some point or another (usually at Christmas parties) engaged in conversation with me about Hitler's death.

Last but by no means least I would like to thank the Parrys and the Reynolds, who make up my fiancée's family. Each and every one of them has made me feel so welcome throughout the years at several family events and I am forever grateful for their continued enthusiasm for my work. But final thanks must go to Jessica Rachel Parry, my fiancée and best friend for ten years. It was Jessica who first listened to my tales of Hitler's bunker as a teenager during our walks around our local town and it was her belief in me that sealed my decision to pursue the topic for my undergraduate dissertation. Jess has endured endless discussions about Hitler and given me many of my best ideas. She has also dealt with the lows of research when stress has brought out the worst in me. But her unwavering loyalty and caring heart always bring me back to my best. I cannot thank Jess enough for risking her employment to travel with me for two months to Washington, DC and photograph files that I have later analysed in this book whilst I was conducting PhD research. I could never have written this book without her. When I am too strident, she tempers, when I am too meek, she inspires, when I am annoyed, she reminds me to think. She has taught me many things. I can never thank her enough. I can only hope that she finds in these pages some justification for the many hours I have spent locked away in the bunker of my office so that we can now emerge victorious to live our lives together as proof of the fact that love conquers all.

BIBLIOGRAPHY

PRIMARY SOURCES
Churchill Archives Centre, British Diplomatic Oral History Programme, Cambridge:
Sir Peter Edward Ramsbotham, interviewed by Malcom McBain (09/01/2001).

FBI Records: The Vault (Digital Archive):
Adolf Hitler, Vols 1–4 (https://vault.fbi.gov/).

Imperial War Museums, London:
Photograph Albums of Captain Eric Mundy.
Private Papers of J. E. Rhys.

King's College Archive Centre, Cambridge University:
Private Papers of Noel Gilroy Annan.

The Liddell Hart Centre for Military Archives, King's College London:
Private Papers of Major-General John Sydney Lethbridge.

The Museum of Military Medicine, Aldershot:
RADC/CF/4/5/Himm.

The National Archives and Records Administration at College Park, Maryland:
Army Staff Records:
RG 319, A1 134B, Box 101, 7356891.
RG 319, NM3 82, Box 1846, 2155420.
RG 319, NM3 82, Box 1847, 2155420.
RG 319, ZZ6, Box 8, 6828925.

Central Intelligence Agency (CIA) Records:
RG 263, A1-27, Box 8, 7283100.
RG 263, UD 2, Box 3, Folder 1, 16966402.
RG 263, UD 2, Box 4, Folder 2, 16967345.
RG 263, UD 2, Box 4, Folder 3, 16967821.
RG 263, ZZ 18, Box 15, Folder 6, 26186820.
RG 263, ZZ 19, Box 29, 19049305.

RG 263, ZZ 20, Box 19, Folder 2, 26299481.
RG 263, ZZ 20, Box 20, 26300439.

Federal Bureau of Investigation (FBI) Records:
RG 65, A1 1360, Box 6, 6136364.
RG 65, A1 136P, Box 38, 6133250.

G-2 Records:
RG 498, UD 308, Box 1380, 5717055.
RG 498, UD 993, Box 4629, 5917790.
RG 498, UD 964, Box 4563, 5891629.

Seized Foreign Records:
RG 242, P 26, Box 1, 12008425.

United States Army, Europe Records:
RG 549, A1 48, Box 734, 563465.
RG 549, A1 48, Box 748, 563465.
RG 549, A1-52, Box 820, 563511.

The National Archives, Kew:
Cabinet Office Records:
CAB 146/438.
CAB 191/1.
CAB 79/33.

Foreign Office Records:
FO 1005/1165.
FO 1005/1700.
FO 1005/1715.
FO 1005/1722.
FO 1050/583.
FO 1093/448.
FO 371/103736.
FO 371/103896.
FO 371/46748.
FO 371/46749.
FO 938/196.

GCHQ Signal Intelligence Passed to the Prime Minister:
HW 1/3760.
HW 5/767.

Security Service (MI5) Records:
KV 4/354.
KV 2/2655.
KV 2/3033.

War Office Records:
WO 204/2349.
WO 208/3781.
WO 208/3787.
WO 208/3788.
WO 208/3789.
WO 208/3790.
WO 208/3791.
WO 208/4431.
WO 208/4475.
WO 311/39.

SECONDARY SOURCES

Articles

Ainsztein, Reuben, 'How Hitler Died: The Soviet Version', *International Affairs*, Vol. 43, No. 2 (1967), pp.307–318.

Anslinger, K., Weichhold, G., Keil, W., Bayer, B. & Eisenmenger, W., 'Identification of the Skeletal Remains of Martin Bormann by mtDNA Analysis', *International Journal of Legal Medicine*, Vol. 114, No. 3 (2001), pp.194–196.

Beisel, David R., 'The German Suicide, 1945', *Journal of Psychohistory*, Vol. 34, No. 4 (2007), pp.302–313.

Bennett, Luke., '*The Bunker*: Metaphor, Materiality and Management', *Culture and Organization*, Vol. 17, No. 2 (2011), pp.155–173.

Biddiscombe, Perry, 'Operation Selection Board: The Growth and Suppression of the Neo Nazi "Deutsche Revolution" 1945–47', *Intelligence and National Security*, Vol. 11, No. 1 (1996), pp.59–77.

Charlier, P., Weil, R., Rainsard, P., Poupon, J. & Brisard, J. C., 'The Remains of Adolf Hitler: A Biomedical Analysis and Definitive Identification', *European Journal of Internal Medicine* (2018), pp.1–3.

Clarke, Steve, 'Conspiracy Theories and Conspiracy Theorizing', *Philosophy of the Social Sciences*, Vol. 32, No. 2 (2002), pp.131–150.

Coady, David, 'Are Conspiracy Theorists Irrational?' *Episteme*, Vol. 4, No. 2 (2007), pp.193–204.

Doyle, D., 'Adolf Hitler's Medical Care', *Royal College of Physicians of Edinburgh* (2005), pp.75–82.

Georgescu, Tudor, 'Hitler's Downfall Revisited', *Totalitarian Movements and Political Religions*, Vol. 7, No. 3 (2006), pp.371–377.

Gilbert, Christopher J., 'Playing with Hitler: Downfall and its Ludic Uptake', *Critical Studies in Media Communication*, Vol. 30, No. 5 (2013), pp.407–424.

Goeschel, Christian, 'Suicide at the End of the Third Reich', *Journal of Contemporary History*, Vol. 41, No. 1 (2006), pp.153–173.

Haiger, Ernst, 'Fiction, Facts, and Forgeries: The "Revelations" of Peter and Martin Allen about the History of the Second World War', *Journal of Intelligence History*, Vol. 6, No. 1 (2006), pp.105–118.

HITLER'S DEATH

Klich, Ignacio, 'Review of Uki Goñi, *The Real Odessa: How Perón Brought the Nazi War Criminals to Argentina* (London: Granta, 2002)', *Journal of Latin American Studies*, Vol. 37, No. 2 (2005), pp.400–402.

Marchetti, Daniela, Boschi, Ilaria, Polacco, Matteo & Rainio, Julia, 'The Death of Adolf Hitler – Forensic Aspects', *Journal of Forensic Sciences*, Vol. 50, No. 5 (2005), pp.1147–1153.

Naftali, Timothy, Goda, Norman J. W., Breitman, Richard & Wolfe, Robert, 'The Mystery of Heinrich Müller: New Materials from the CIA', *Holocaust and Genocide Studies*, Vol. 15, No. 3 (2001), pp.453–467.

Oliver, Eric J. & Wood, Thomas J. 'Conspiracy Theories and the Paranoid Style(s) of Mass Opinion', *American Journal of Political Science*, Vol. 58, No. 4 (2014), pp.952–966.

Pigden, Charles, 'Conspiracy Theories and the Conventional Wisdom', *Episteme*, Vol. 4, No. 2 (2007), pp.219–232.

Sognnaes, Reidar, 'Dental Evidence in the Postmortem Identification of Adolf Hitler, Eva Braun and Martin Bormann', *Legal Medicine Annual* (1976), pp.173–235.

Sognnaes, Reidar, 'Hitler and Bormann Identifications Compared by Postmortem Craniofacial and Dental Characteristics', *American Journal of Forensic Medicine & Pathology*, Vol. 1, No. 2 (1980), pp.105–115.

White, Thomas, 'A Pittsburgh Judge's Path to Nuremberg and Back', *Western Pennsylvania History*, Vol. 98, No. 1 (2015), pp.92–103.

Winter, P. R. J., 'A Higher Form of Intelligence: Hugh Trevor-Roper and Wartime British Secret Service', *Intelligence and National Security*, Vol. 22, No. 6 (2007), pp.847–880.

Books

Aaronovitch, David, *Voodoo Histories: The Role of Conspiracy Theory in Shaping Modern History* (London: Jonathan Cape, 2009).

Aldrich, Richard J. & Cormac, Rory, *The Black Door: Spies, Secret Intelligence and British Prime Ministers* (London: William Collins, 2016).

Aldrich, Richard J., *The Hidden Hand: Britain, America and Cold War Secret Intelligence* (London: John Murray, 2002).

Andrew, Christopher, *For the President's Eyes Only: Secret Intelligence and the American Presidency from Washington to Bush* (London: HarperCollins, 1995).

Andrew, Christopher, *The Defence of the Realm: The Authorized History of MI5* (London: Penguin, 2009).

Beevor, Antony, *Berlin: The Downfall 1945* (London: Penguin, 2003).

Bezymenski, Lev, *The Death of Adolf Hitler: Unknown Documents from Soviet Archives* (London: Michael Joseph, 1968).

Brisard, Jean-Christophe & Parshina, Lana, *The Death of Hitler: The Final Word* (Boston: Da Capo Press, 2018).

Bullock, Alan, *Hitler and Stalin: Parallel Lives* (London: HarperCollins, 1991).

Byford-Jones, W., *Berlin Twilight* (London: Hutchinson, 1947).

Cantwell, John D., *The Second World War: A Guide to Documents in the Public Record Office* (Kew: Public Record Office Publications, 1998).

Churchill, Winston S., *The Second World War, Volume VI: Triumph and Tragedy* (Boston: Houghton Mifflin, 1985).

Cooper, Harry, *Hitler in Argentina* (Hernando, FL: CreateSpace Independent Publishing Platform, 2014).

Dorril, Stephen, *MI6: Fifty Years of Special Operations* (London: Fourth Estate Limited, 2000).

Dunstan, Simon & Williams, Gerrard, *Grey Wolf: The Escape of Adolf Hitler* (New York: Sterling, 2011).

Eberle, Henrik & Uhl, Matthias (eds), *The Hitler Book: The Secret Report by His Two Closest Aides* (London: John Murray, 2005).

Evans, Richard J., *Altered Pasts: Counterfactuals in History* (London: Little Brown, 2014).

Fest, Joachim, *Inside Hitler's Bunker: The Last Days of the Third Reich* (London: Macmillan, 2005).

Frei, Norbert, *Adenauer's Germany and the Nazi Past: The Politics of Amnesty and Integration* (Chichester: Columbia University Press, 2002).

Goñi, Uki, *The Real Odessa: How Perón Brought the Nazi War Criminals to Argentina* (London: Granta, 2002).

Greenwood, Sean, *Britain and the Cold War* (London: Macmillan, 2000).

Hansig, Ron T., *Hitler's Escape* (Twickenham: Athena Press, 2005).

Hitchens, Christopher, *Blood, Class and Empire: The Enduring Anglo-American Relationship* (London: Atlantic, 2006).

Hitler, Adolf, Weinberg, Gerhard L. (ed.), Smith, Krista (trans.), *Hitler's Second Book: The Unpublished Sequel to Mein Kampf* (New York: Enigma Books, 2003).

Hughes, Matthew & Mann, Chris, *Inside Hitler's Germany* (London: Windmill Books, 2012).

Jeffery, Keith, *MI6: The History of the Secret Intelligence Service 1909–1949* (London: Bloomsbury, 2011).

Jeffreys-Jones, Rhodri, *The FBI: A History* (Connecticut: Yale University Press, 2007).

Joachimsthaler, Anton, *The Last Days of Hitler: Legend, Evidence and Truth* (London: Cassell, 2000).

Junge, Traudl, *Until the Final Hour: Hitler's Last Secretary* (London: Orion, 2004).

Kempka, Erich, *I Was Hitler's Chauffeur* (Barnsley: Frontline Books, 2012).

Kershaw, Ian, *Death in the Bunker* (London: Penguin, 2005).

Kershaw, Ian, *Hitler 1936–1945: Nemesis* (London: Penguin, 2000).

Kuby, Erich, *The Russians and Berlin: 1945* (New York: Ballantine Books, 1969).

Levenda, Peter, *Ratline: Soviet Spies, Nazi Priests, and the Disappearance of Adolf Hitler* (Lake Worth, FL: Ibis Press, 2012).

Linge, Heinz, *With Hitler to the End: The Memoir of Hitler's Valet* (Barnsley: Frontline Books, 2009).

Long, Wellington, *The New Nazis of Germany* (Philadelphia: Chilton, 1968).

McCorristine, Shane (ed.), *Interdisciplinary Perspectives on Mortality and its Timings* (London: Palgrave Macmillan, 2017).

McKale, Donald M., *Hitler: The Survival Myth* (New York: Stein and Day, 1983).

Moore, Herbert & Barret, James W. (eds), *Who Killed Hitler?* (New York: Booktab Press, 1947).

Moran, Christopher R. & Murphy, Christopher J. (eds), *Intelligence Studies in Britain and the US: Historiography since 1945* (Edinburgh: Edinburgh University Press, 2013).

Moran, Lord, *Winston Churchill: The Struggle for Survival, 1940–1965* (London: Constable, 1966).

Musmanno, M. A., *Ten Days to Die* (New York: Doubleday, 1950).

O'Donnell, James P., *The Berlin Bunker* (London: J. M. Dent, 1979).

Overy, Richard, *Interrogations: Inside the Minds of the Nazi Elite* (London: Penguin, 2001).

Petrova, Ada & Watson, Peter, *The Death of Hitler: The Final Words from Russia's Secret Archives* (London: Richard Cohen Books, 1995).

Roberts, Frank, *Dealing with Dictators* (London: George Weidenfeld & Nicolson, 1991).

Robertson, K. G. (ed.), *British and American Approaches to Intelligence* (London: Macmillan, 1987).

Roper, Michael, *Records of the War Office and Related Departments 1660–1964* (Kew: Public Record Office Publications, 1998).

Rubinstein, William D., *Shadow Pasts: History's Mysteries* (Harlow: Pearson, Longman, 2008).

Ryan, Cornelius, *The Last Battle* (London: NEL, 1980).

Sayer, Ian & Botting, Douglas, *America's Secret Army: The Untold Story of the Counter Intelligence Corps* (London: Fontana, 1990).

Schroeder, Christa, *He Was My Chief* (Barnsley: Frontline Books, 2012).

Selby, Scott Andrew, *The Axmann Conspiracy: The Nazi Plan for a Fourth Reich and How the U.S. Army Defeated It* (New York: Berkley, 2012).

Seligmann, Matthew, Davison, John & McDonald, John, *In the Shadow of the Swastika: Life in Germany Under the Nazis 1933–1945* (Kent: Spellmount, 2003).

Senn, David R. & Veems, Richard A. (eds), *Manual of Forensic Odontology*, fifth edition (Boca Raton, FL: CRC Press, 2013).

Shirer, William L., *The Rise and Fall of the Third Reich* (New York: Simon & Schuster, 2011).

Sisman, Adam, *Hugh Trevor-Roper: The Biography* (London: Phoenix, 2011).

Strong, Major-General Sir Kenneth, *Intelligence at the Top: The Recollections of an Intelligence Officer* (London: Cassell, 1969).

Thomas, Hugh, *Doppelgängers: The Truth about the Bodies in the Berlin Bunker* (London: Fourth Estate, 1995).

Thomas, Hugh, *SS-1: The Unlikely Death of Heinrich Himmler* (London: Fourth Estate, 2001).

Thomas, Hugh, *The Murder of Rudolf Hess* (London: Hodder & Stoughton, 1979).

Tolland, John, *The Last 100 Days* (London: Phoenix, 1994).

Trevor-Roper, Hugh, *The Last Days of Hitler* (London: Macmillan, 2002).

Trevor-Roper, Hugh, *The Secret World: Behind the Curtain of British Intelligence in World War II and the Cold War* (London: I. B. Tauris, 2014).

Twigge, Stephen, Hampshire, Edward & Macklin, Graham, *British Intelligence: Secrets, Spies and Sources* (Kew: The National Archives, 2008).

Vinogradov, V. K. Pogonyi, J. F. & Teptzov, N. V. (eds), *Hitler's Death: Russia's Last Great Secret from the Files of the KGB* (London: Chaucer Press, 2005).

Von Loringhoven, Bernd Freytag, with d'Alançon, F., *In the Bunker with Hitler: The Last Witness Speaks* (London: Orion, 2006).

BIBLIOGRAPHY

Walters, Guy, *Hunting Evil: How the Nazi War Criminals Escaped and the Hunt to Bring Them to Justice* (London: Bantam, 2009).

Weiner, Tim, *Legacy of Ashes: The History of the CIA* (London: Penguin, 2008).

Whiting, Charles, *The Hunt for Martin Bormann: The Truth* (Barnsley: Leo Cooper, 1996).

Whiting, Charles, *The Search for 'Gestapo' Müller* (Barnsley: Leo Cooper, 2001).

Television

Downfall, dir. Oliver Hirschbiegel (Constantin Film: 16/09/2004).

Hunting Hitler, History Channel, Seasons 1–3 (2015–2018).

Mystery Quest, Hitler's Escape, UK television broadcast (16/09/2009).

Sir David Frost interviews Gerrard Williams, YouTube, https://www.youtube.com/watch?v=03aEr4SqVpM

Sky News television interview with Gerrard Williams (16/10/2011), YouTube, https://www.youtube.com/watch?v=JuLPMCxvBf8

Timewatch, Hitler's Death: The Final Report, UK television broadcast (30/04/1995).

Websites

Bennet, Owen, 'Are These Classified FBI Files Proof Adolf Hitler Escaped by SUBMARINE to Argentina?', *Daily Express* (15/04/2014), http://www.express.co.uk/news/weird/470586/Are-these-classified-FBI-files-proof-ADOLF-HITLER-escaped-by-SUBMARINE-to-Argentina (accessed 24/01/2015).

Bojan, Anne-Marie, 'FBI Documents Claim Hitler Faked His Own Death and Fled to Argentina', UNILAD (12/01/2018), https://www.unilad.co.uk/tv/fbi-documents-claim-hitler-faked-his-own-death-and-fled-to-argentina/ (accessed 27/07/2018).

Dawson, James, 'Declassified Files Reveal CIA Investigated If Adolf Hitler Survived the War and Fled to Colombia', Lad Bible (31/10/2017), http://www.ladbible.com/news/weird-news-cia-investigated-if-adolf-hitler-survived-the-war-and-fled-to-colombia-20171031 (accessed 27/07/2018).

Dewsbury, Rick & Hall, Allan, 'Did Hitler and Eva Braun Flee Berlin and Die (Divorced) of Old Age in Argentina?' *Daily Mail* (18/10/2011), http://www.dailymail.co.uk/news/article-2050137/Did-Hitler-Eva-Braun-flee-Berlin-die-old-age-Argentina.html (accessed 02/04/2015).

Gadiano, Jerry, 'Submarine Found at Ocean Bottom Reveals 'Truth' About Hitler's South America Escape', UNILAD (18/04/2018), https://www.unilad.co.uk/news/submarine-found-at-ocean-bottom-reveals-truth-about-hitlers-south-america-escape/ (accessed 27/07/2018).

Hale, Beth, 'MI5 Obsession with Hitler's deputy Martin Bormann Led Britain on Nazi Goose Chase', *Daily Mail* (01/09/2009), http://www.dailymail.co.uk/news/article-1210412/British-obsession-Hitlers-deputy-Martin-Bormann-led-MI5-Nazi-goose-chase.html (accessed 24/11/2017).

Hayward, Ben, 'CIA Veteran Claims Hitler "Faked His Death, Moved to the Canary Islands"', UNILAD (08/01/2016), https://www.unilad.co.uk/news/cia-veteran-claims-hitler-faked-his-death-and-moved-to-the-canary-islands/ (accessed 27/07/2018).

Hitchens, Christopher, 'Mommie Dearest', *Slate* (2003), http://www.slate.com/articles/news_and_politics/fighting_words/2003/10/mommie_dearest.html (accessed 01/06/2018).

'Hitler No. 2 "to be found riding Nessie"', *Metro* (31/08/2009), http://metro.co.uk/2009/08/31/hitler-no-2-to-be-found-riding-nessie-369891/ (accessed 24/11/2017).

'How Hitler's deputy was Tipped to Ride on the Loch Ness Monster', *The Scotsman* (01/09/2009) http://www.scotsman.com/news/how-hitler-s-deputy-was-tipped-to-ride-on-the-loch-ness-monster-1-772342 (accessed 24/11/2017).

Lee, Adrian, 'Did Adolf Hitler Escape?' *Daily Express* (17/10/2011), http://www.express.co.uk/expressyourself/277962/Did-Adolf-Hitler-escape (accessed 02/04/2015).

Lusher, Adam, 'Adolf Hitler Really is Dead: Scientific Study Debunks Conspiracy Theories That He Escaped to South America', *Independent* (20/05/2018), https://www.independent.co.uk/news/world/europe/adolf-hitler-debunked-escaped-south-america-skull-fragment-woman-teeth-jawbone-scientific-study-a8360356.html (accessed 01/07/2018).

Osborn, Andrew, 'Adolf Hitler Suicide Story Questioned After Tests Reveal Skull is a Woman's', *Telegraph* (29/09/2009), http://www.telegraph.co.uk/history/world-war-two/6237028/Adolf-Hitler-suicide-story-questioned-after-tests-reveal-skull-is-a-womans.html (accessed 01/04/2015).

Percival, Tom, 'Shocking Revelation from US President's Diary Suggests Hitler Didn't Die', UNILAD (20/03/2017), https://www.unilad.co.uk/politics/shocking-revelation-from-us-presidents-diary-suggests-hitler-didnt-die/ (accessed 27/07/2018).

Reid, Claire, 'CIA Veteran Claims Hitler Faked His Suicide and Fled to Argentina', Lad Bible (16/01/2017), http://www.ladbible.com/now/weird-cia-veteran-claims-hitler-faked-his-suicide-and-fled-to-argentina-20170116 (accessed 27/07/2018).

Teal, Josh, 'CIA Documents Reveal Hitler "Still Alive" Following World War II', UNILAD (28/09/2017), https://www.unilad.co.uk/gossip/cia-documents-reveal-hitler-still-alive/ (accessed 27/07/2018).

UConn, 'The Hitler Project – Nick Bellantoni' (15/06/2011), YouTube, https://www.youtube.com/watch?v=ZqrrjzfnsVY.

Vandivert, Bill, Life War Correspondent to Churchill, Bill (03/07/1945), http://time.com/3524807/after-the-fall-photos-of-hitlers-bunker-and-the-ruins-of-berlin/ (accessed 05/04/2018).

NOTES

PREFACE

1 Simon Dunstan & Gerrard Williams, *Grey Wolf: The Escape of Adolf Hitler* (New York: Sterling, 2011).

2 Interrogations of Otto Günsche and Heinz Linge (1948–1949), in Henrik Eberle & Matthias Uhl (eds), *The Hitler Book: The Secret Report by His Two Closest Aides* (London: John Murray, 2005), p.238.

INTRODUCTION: IS HISTORY WRONG?

1 The National Archives (TNA), FO 1005/1700, Intelligence Bureau, Intelligence Review Number 3, 'The Hitlerian Myth' (09/01/1946).

2 Hitler's deteriorating emotional and physical condition is attested to by several eyewitnesses. See Hans Rattenhuber, Statement in Soviet Captivity (20/05/1945), Testimony of General Helmuth Weidling (04/01/1946) and Interrogation of Field-Marshal Ferdinand Schörner (10/05/1947) in V. K. Vinogradov, J. F. Pogonyi & N. V. Teptzov (eds), *Hitler's Death: Russia's Last Great Secret from the Files of the KGB* (London: Chaucer Press, 2005), pp. 185–186, 229, 242. See also Heinz Linge, *With Hitler to the End: The Memoir of Hitler's Valet* (Barnsley: Frontline Books, 2009), p.1; Interrogations of Otto Günsche and Heinz Linge (1948–1949), in Henrik Eberle and Matthias Uhl (eds), *The Hitler Book: The Secret Report by His Two Closest Aides* (London: John Murray, 2005), pp.205–206, 246; Antony Beevor, *Berlin: The Downfall 1945* (London: Penguin, 2003), p.350.

3 Testimony of General Helmuth Weidling (04/01/1946), in Vinogradov, Pogonyi & Teptzov, *Hitler's Death*, p.226; Interrogations of Otto Günsche and Heinz Linge (1948–1949) in Eberle & Uhl (eds), *Hitler Book*, p.255; Hugh Trevor-Roper, *The Last Days of Hitler* (London: Macmillan, 2002), p.143; Beevor, *Berlin*, p.268; James P. O'Donnell, *The Berlin Bunker* (London: J. M. Dent, 1979), p.91.

4 Hans Rattenhuber, Statement in Soviet Captivity (20/05/1945), in Vinogradov, Pogonyi & Teptzov, *Hitler's Death*, p.189. See also Interrogations of Otto Günsche and Heinz Linge (1948–1949), in Eberle & Uhl (eds), *Hitler Book*, p.219; Anton Joachimsthaler, *The Last Days of Hitler: Legend, Evidence and Truth* (London: Cassell, 2000), p.90.

5 Interrogations of Otto Günsche and Heinz Linge (1948–1949), in Eberle and Uhl (eds), *Hitler Book*, pp.206, 219. See also Trevor-Roper, *Last Days of Hitler*,

pp.87, 89; Beevor, *Berlin*, p.204; Cornelius Ryan, *The Last Battle* (London: NEL, 1980), p.227; Joachim Fest, *Inside Hitler's Bunker: The Last Days of the Third Reich* (London: Macmillan, 2005), p.14.

6   Testimony of General Helmuth Weidling (04/01/1946), in Vinogradov, Pogonyi & Teptzov, *Hitler's Death*, p.226; Beevor, *Berlin*, p.322; Fest, *Inside Hitler's Bunker*, pp.9, 152–153.

7   Hans Rattenhuber, Statement in Soviet Captivity (20/05/1945) and Interrogation of Field-Marshal Ferdinand Schörner (10/05/1947), in Vinogradov, Pogonyi & Teptzov, *Hitler's Death*, pp.187, 243. See also Interrogations of Otto Günsche and Heinz Linge (1948–1949), in Eberle & Uhl (eds), *Hitler Book*, pp.206–207, 227; Traudl Junge, *Until the Final Hour: Hitler's Last Secretary* (London: Orion, 2004), p.159; Joachimsthaler, *Last Days of Hitler*, p.103.

8   Fest, *Inside Hitler's Bunker*, p.47. See also Beevor, *Berlin*, p.275; Ian Kershaw, *Death in the Bunker* (London: Penguin, 2005), pp.4, 25; Joachimsthaler, *Last Days of Hitler*, p.103.

9   Trevor-Roper, *Last Days of Hitler*, pp.163–165. See also Linge, *With Hitler to the End*, pp.189–190; Fest, *Inside Hitler's Bunker*, p.47.

10   Trevor-Roper, *Last Days of Hitler*, p.98. See also Beevor, *Berlin*, p.251; Ryan, *Last Battle*, pp.291–292; Joachimsthaler, *Last Days of Hitler*, p.98; Fest, *Inside Hitler's Bunker*, p.48.

11   The National Archives and Records Administration (NARA II), RG 498, UD 993, Box 4629, 5917790, 'The Hairdresser and the Courtesan', HQ XX Corps G-2 Weekly Intelligence Summary No. 12 (14/08/1945). See also Linge, *With Hitler to the End*, pp.45–46.

12   NARA II, RG 498, UD 993, Box 4629, 5917790, 'The Hairdresser and the Courtesan', HQ XX Corps G-2 Weekly Intelligence Summary No. 12 (14/08/1945).

13   Ibid.

14   Oliver Hirschbiegel (dir.), *Downfall* (Constantin Film, released 16/09/2004).

15   Interrogations of Otto Günsche and Heinz Linge (1948–1949), in Eberle & Uhl (eds), *Hitler Book*, p.230. See also Trevor-Roper, *Last Days of Hitler*, p.105; Fest, *Inside Hitler's Bunker*, p.63.

16   Interrogations of Otto Günsche and Heinz Linge (1948–1949), in Eberle & Uhl (eds), *Hitler Book*, pp.248–249. See also Fest, *Inside Hitler's Bunker*, p.84; Ada Petrova & Peter Watson, *The Death of Hitler: The Final Words from Russia's Secret Archives* (London: Richard Cohen Books, 1995), pp.28–29.

17   Beevor, *Berlin*, p.288. See also Joachimsthaler, *Last Days of Hitler*, p.110; Petrova & Watson, *Death of Hitler*, p.27.

18   Joachimsthaler, *Last Days of Hitler*, pp.132, 134. See also Christa Schroeder, *He Was My Chief* (Barnsley: Frontline Books, 2012), pp.158–160; Ian Kershaw, *Hitler 1936–1945: Nemesis* (London: Penguin, 2000), p.198.

19   Kershaw, *Bunker*, pp.28–29. See also Joachimsthaler, *Last Days of Hitler*, p.116.

20   Beevor, *Berlin*, p.322. See also Joachimsthaler, *Last Days of Hitler*, pp.88, 116; Petrova & Watson, *Death of Hitler*, p.31.

21 Interrogations of Otto Günsche and Heinz Linge (1948–1949), in Eberle & Uhl (eds), *Hitler Book*, p.259. See also Joachimsthaler, *Last Days of Hitler*, p.126; Fest, *Inside Hitler's Bunker*, p.94; Petrova & Watson, *Death of Hitler*, p.33.

22 Fest, *Inside Hitler's Bunker*, pp.94–95.

23 Joachimsthaler, *Last Days of Hitler*, p.126. See also Fest, *Inside Hitler's Bunker*, pp.99–100; Petrova & Watson, *Death of Hitler*, p.34.

24 Joachimsthaler, *Last Days of Hitler*, p.126. See also Fest, *Inside Hitler's Bunker*, p.95; Petrova & Watson, *Death of Hitler*, p.34.

25 Beevor, *Berlin*, p.343.

26 Liddell Hart Centre for Military Archives (LHCMA), King's College London, Private Papers of Major-General John Sydney Lethbridge, 'end of the report to Robertson'. This undated report is a variation of Hugh Trevor-Roper's original intelligence report of November 1945, which it mostly copies verbatim throughout but expands slightly to include new evidence from Hitler's wills.

27 Junge, *Until the Final Hour*, p.183. See also Joachimsthaler, *Last Days of Hitler*, p.129.

28 Trevor-Roper, *Last Days of Hitler*, p.159.

29 Ibid., p.161.

30 Petrova & Watson, *Death of Hitler*, p.39. See also Trevor-Roper, *Last Days of Hitler*, p.178.

31 Petrova & Watson, *Death of Hitler*, p.39. See also Trevor-Roper, *Last Days of Hitler*, p.178.

32 Junge, *Until the Final Hour*, p.186. See also Petrova & Watson, *Death of Hitler*, p.38; Trevor-Roper, *Last Days of Hitler*, p.175.

33 Interrogations of Otto Günsche and Heinz Linge (1948–1949), in Eberle & Uhl (eds), *Hitler Book*, pp.268–269.

34 Linge, *With Hitler to the End*, p.199.

35 Erich Kempka, *I Was Hitler's Chauffeur* (Barnsley: Frontline Books, 2012), pp.89–90. See also Fest, *Inside Hitler's Bunker*, pp.114–115; O'Donnell, *Berlin Bunker*, p.179.

36 Kempka, *I Was Hitler's Chauffeur*, pp.89–90. See also Kershaw, *Hitler*, p.828.

37 Trevor-Roper, *Last Days of Hitler*, p.180. See also Petrova & Watson, *Death of Hitler*, p.40.

38 Trevor-Roper, *Last Days of Hitler*, p.180. See also Joachimsthaler, *Last Days of Hitler*, p.197; Petrova & Watson, *Death of Hitler*, p.40.

39 Kershaw, *Hitler*, p.830. See also Trevor-Roper, *Last Days of Hitler*, p.180; Joachimsthaler, *Last Days of Hitler*, p.198; Fest, *Inside Hitler's Bunker*, p.118; Petrova & Watson, *Death of Hitler*, p.40.

40 Fest, *Inside Hitler's Bunker*, pp.142–144.

41 Kershaw, *Hitler*, p.833.

42 O'Donnell, *Berlin Bunker*, p.217.

43 Kershaw, *Hitler*, p.833.

44 Ibid., p.831. See also Fest, *Inside Hitler's Bunker*, pp.136–137; Trevor-Roper, *Last Days of Hitler*, pp.186–187.

45 Charles Pigden, 'Conspiracy Theories and the Conventional Wisdom', *Episteme*, Vol. 4, No. 2 (2007), p.219.

46 Bob Baer, *Hunting Hitler*, History Channel, Season One, Episode One (10/11/2015).

CHAPTER 1: THE EVOLUTION OF FACTS AND CONSPIRACIES

1 The National Archives (TNA), CAB 146/438, Hugh Trevor-Roper, Oxford to Brian Melland, Cabinet Office, Historical Section (28/03/1966).
2 Hugh Trevor-Roper, *The Last Days of Hitler* (London: Macmillan, 2002), p.xx. See also Ada Petrova & Peter Watson, *The Death of Hitler: The Final Words from Russia's Secret Archives* (London: Richard Cohen Books, 1995), p.161.
3 Trevor-Roper, *Last Days of Hitler*, pp.x, xx, xxxix.
4 Ibid., pp.xx, xlv, xlvi. See also: Donald M. McKale, *Hitler: The Survival Myth* (New York: Stein and Day, 1983), pp.ix, 46–47, 50–51, 76; Anton Joachimsthaler, *The Last Days of Hitler: Legend, Evidence and Truth* (London: Cassell, 2000), pp.22–23, 59, 246–247; James P. O'Donnell, *The Berlin Bunker* (London: J. M. Dent, 1979), pp.301–302; Petrova & Watson, *Death of Hitler*, pp.14, 16, 44.
5 David R. Senn & Richard A. Veems (eds), *Manual of Forensic Odontology*, fifth edition (Boca Raton, FL: CRC Press, 2013), p.19.
6 Trevor-Roper, *Last Days of Hitler*, pp.178–183.
7 Ibid., p.xxi.
8 Ibid., pp.x, xxvii, xlvii.
9 Ibid., pp.x, xx, xxxvi.
10 W. Byford-Jones, *Berlin Twilight* (London: Hutchinson, 1947).
11 Ibid., pp.82–83.
12 Ibid., pp.118–119.
13 Herbert Moore & James W. Barret (eds), *Who Killed Hitler?* (New York: Booktab Press, 1947), pp.121–123.
14 Ibid., pp.114, 117.
15 McKale, *Hitler*, p.132. See also Moore & Barret, *Who Killed Hitler*, p.iii; Joachimsthaler, *Last Days of Hitler*, p.25.
16 NARA II, RG 319, ZZ6, Box 8, 6828925, 'Investigation of Hitler's Death' (28/11/1947).
17 Ibid.
18 Ibid.
19 NARA II, RG 319, ZZ6, Box 8, 6828925, HQ CIC EUCOM to Commanding Officer, CIC Region VIII (November 1947).
20 Peter Levenda, *Ratline: Soviet Spies, Nazi Priests, and the Disappearance of Adolf Hitler* (Lake Worth, FL: Ibis Press, 2012), pp.22, 25, 31, 34. See also Hugh Thomas, *Doppelgängers: The Truth about the Bodies in the Berlin Bunker* (London: Fourth Estate, 1995), pp.94, 96.
21 M. A. Musmanno, *Ten Days to Die* (New York: Doubleday, 1950).
22 Thomas White, 'A Pittsburgh Judge's Path to Nuremberg and Back', *Western Pennsylvania History*, Vol. 98, No. 1 (2015), p.99. See also Joachimsthaler, *Last Days of Hitler*, p.282.
23 According to Brian Melland, Musmanno made heavy use of 'purple prose' that put 'credibility to a severe test', resulting in a 'thoroughly sensational'

book. See TNA, CAB 146/438, Brian Melland, Cabinet Office Historical Section to Trevor-Roper, Oxford (23/03/1966) and Melland to Dr L. Kahn (15/03/1966).

24 TNA, CAB 146/438, Trevor-Roper to Melland, (28/03/1966).

25 TNA, CAB 146/438, 'Extracts from Ten Days To Die'.

26 White, 'Pittsburgh Judge's Path to Nuremberg', p.99.

27 McKale, *Hitler*, p.111. See also Joachimsthaler, *Last Days of Hitler*, p.24.

28 Roger Moorhouse, 'Introduction', in Heinz Linge, *With Hitler to the End: The Memoir of Hitler's Valet* (Barnsley: Frontline Books, 2009), p.xiii. See also Petrova & Watson, *Death of Hitler*, p.47.

29 Trevor-Roper, *Last Days of Hitler*, p.xxxvi.

30 Ibid., p.xxxvi.

31 Reuben Ainsztein, 'How Hitler Died: The Soviet Version', *International Affairs*, Vol. 43, No. 2 (1967), pp.307, 314, 318. See also Erich Kuby, *The Russians and Berlin: 1945* (New York: Ballantine Books, 1969), pp.174, 177.

32 Lev Bezymenski, *The Death of Adolf Hitler: Unknown Documents from Soviet Archives* (London: Michael Joseph, 1968), pp.44–51.

33 Ibid., p.49.

34 Reidar Sognnaes, 'Hitler and Bormann Identifications Compared by Postmortem Craniofacial and Dental Characteristics', *American Journal of Forensic Medicine & Pathology*, Vol. 1, No. 2 (1980), pp.109–111. See also Reidar Sognnaes, 'Dental Evidence in the Postmortem Identification of Adolf Hitler, Eva Braun and Martin Bormann', *Legal Medicine Annual* (1976), pp.197–200.

35 O'Donnell, *Berlin Bunker*, pp.182–184, 276, 299–301.

36 Joachimsthaler, *Last Days of Hitler*, pp.179–180.

37 Daniela Marchetti, Ilaria Boschi, Matteo Polacco & Julia Rainio, 'The Death of Adolf Hitler – Forensic Aspects', *Journal of Forensic Sciences*, Vol. 50, No. 5 (2005), pp.1148–1149. See also McKale, *Hitler*, p.188; Joachimsthaler, *Last Days of Hitler*, pp.227, 252–253; Henrik Eberle & Matthias Uhl (eds), *The Hitler Book: The Secret Report by His Two Closest Aides* (London: John Murray, 2005), p.283.

38 Joachimsthaler, *Last Days of Hitler*, pp.167, 174–175, 180–181, 222, 225, 227, 252–253. See also Joachim Fest, *Inside Hitler's Bunker: The Last Days of the Third Reich* (London: Macmillan, 2005), p.163; McKale, *Hitler*, p.188.

39 McKale, *Hitler*, p.197. See also Trevor-Roper, *Last Days of Hitler*, p.lvii; Ian Kershaw, *Death in the Bunker* (London: Penguin, 2005), p.26; Petrova & Watson, *Death of Hitler*, p.75.

40 McKale, *Hitler*, p.197.

41 Ibid.

42 Petrova & Watson, *Death of Hitler*, p.76.

43 Ibid., pp.76, 85, 90.

44 V. K. Vinogradov, J. F. Pogonyi & N. V. Teptzov (eds), *Hitler's Death: Russia's Last Great Secret from the Files of the KGB* (London: Chaucer Press, 2005), p.26. See also Petrova & Watson, *Death of Hitler*, pp.21, 126–127.

45 Vinogradov, Pogonyi & Teptzov, *Hitler's Death*, pp.18–20, 23–26.

46 Thomas, *Doppelgängers*, pp.185–189.

47 Petrova & Watson, *Death of Hitler*, p.100. Thomas is a conspiracy theorist par excellence who has found reason to write similar books about the deaths of Heinrich Himmler and Rudolf Hess; see Hugh Thomas, *SS-1: The Unlikely Death of Heinrich Himmler* (London: Fourth Estate, 2001) and Hugh Thomas, *The Murder of Rudolf Hess* (London: Hodder & Stoughton, 1979). See also Steve Clarke, 'Conspiracy Theories and Conspiracy Theorizing', *Philosophy of the Social Sciences*, Vol. 32, No. 2 (2002), p.131.

48 Thomas, *Doppelgängers*, p.91.

49 Traudl Junge, *Until the Final Hour: Hitler's Last Secretary* (London: Orion, 2004). See also Heinz Linge, *With Hitler to the End: The Memoir of Hitler's Valet* (Barnsley: Frontline Books, 2009); Erich Kempka, *I Was Hitler's Chauffeur* (Barnsley: Frontline Books, 2012); Christa Schroeder, *He Was My Chief* (Barnsley: Frontline Books, 2012); Bernd Freytag Von Loringhoven, *In the Bunker with Hitler* (London: Orion, 2006).

50 Joachimsthaler, *Last Days of Hitler*, pp.148, 150, 158–161. See also Moore & Barret, *Who Killed Hitler*, p.154; Fest, *Inside Hitler's Bunker*, pp.175–176; Levenda, *Ratline*, p.38; Thomas, *Doppelgängers*, pp.101–105; Bezymenski, *Death of Adolf Hitler*, p.71.

51 O'Donnell, *Berlin Bunker*, pp.180–182. See also Joachimsthaler, *Last Days of Hitler*, pp.148–149; Levenda, *Ratline*, p.36; Thomas, *Doppelgängers*, p.96; Ron T. Hansig, *Hitler's Escape* (Twickenham: Athena Press, 2005), p.52.

52 Fest, *Inside Hitler's Bunker*, pp.116, 175. See also Petrova & Watson, *Death of Hitler*, pp.110–115.

53 O'Donnell, *Berlin Bunker*, p.14.

54 Tudor Georgescu, 'Hitler's Downfall Revisited', *Totalitarian Movements and Political Religions*, Vol. 7, No. 3 (2006), pp.373, 375.

55 Ibid., p.376.

56 Luke Bennett, '*The Bunker*: Metaphor, Materiality and Management', *Culture and Organization*, Vol. 17, No. 2 (2011), pp.155, 160–162, 167.

57 David R. Beisel, 'The German Suicide, 1945', *Journal of Psychohistory*, Vol. 34, No. 4 (2007), pp.303–308. See also Christian Goeschel, 'Suicide at the End of the Third Reich', *Journal of Contemporary History*, Vol. 41, No. 1 (2006), pp.153, 155, 157–158.

58 Trevor-Roper, *Last Days of Hitler*, pp.4, 43, 64. See also Beisel, 'German Suicide', p.309; Goeschel, 'Suicide', p.155; Fest, *Inside Hitler's Bunker*, p.171.

59 Trevor-Roper, *Last Days of Hitler*, p.63. See also D. Doyle, 'Adolf Hitler's Medical Care', *Royal College of Physicians of Edinburgh* (2005), pp.75–80; McKale, *Hitler*, p.98.

60 Marchetti, Boschi, Polacco & Rainio, 'Death of Adolf Hitler', pp.1147, 1151–1152.

61 Joachimsthaler, *Last Days of Hitler*, pp.8, 40, 179.

62 Ibid., pp.8, 177.

63 Ibid., p.8.

64 McKale, *Hitler*, pp.6, 62, 131, 140–141.

65 Ibid., pp.59–61, 65. See also Petrova & Watson, *Death of Hitler*, p.15.

66 McKale, *Hitler*, pp.40–41. See also Roberts, in Vinogradov, Pogonyi & Teptzov, *Hitler's Death*, pp.10, 12.

67 McKale, *Hitler*, pp.106, 146.

68 Ibid., p.32.
69 David Coady, 'Are Conspiracy Theorists Irrational?', *Episteme*, Vol. 4, No. 2 (2007), p.202. See also Charles Pigden, 'Conspiracy Theories and the Conventional Wisdom', *Episteme*, Vol. 4, No. 2 (2007), pp.224, 230; David Aaronovitch, *Voodoo Histories: The Role of Conspiracy Theory in Shaping Modern History* (London: Jonathan Cape, 2009), p.5.
70 Coady, 'Are Conspiracy Theorists Irrational', p.202.
71 Ibid., pp.198–201. Gerrard Williams argues against 'the official history' on *Hunting Hitler*, History Channel, Season One, Episode One (10/11/2015).
72 Clarke, 'Conspiracy Theories', p.134.
73 Simon Dunstan & Gerrard Williams, *Grey Wolf: The Escape of Adolf Hitler* (New York: Sterling, 2011). See also Rick Dewsbury & Allan Hall, 'Did Hitler and Eva Braun Flee Berlin and Die (Divorced) of Old Age in Argentina?' *Daily Mail* (18/10/2011), http://www.dailymail.co.uk/news/article-2050137/Did-Hitler-Eva-Braun-flee-Berlin-die-old-age-Argentina.html (accessed 02/04/2015); Adrian Lee, 'Did Adolf Hitler Escape?' *Daily Express* (17/10/2011), http://www.express.co.uk/expressyourself/277962/Did-Adolf-Hitler-escape (accessed 02/04/2015); Sky News television interview with Gerrard Williams (16/10/2011), YouTube, https://www.youtube.com/watch?v=JuLPMCxvBf8; Sir David Frost interviews Gerrard Williams, YouTube, https://www.youtube.com/watch?v=o3aEr4SqVpM.
74 Dunstan & Williams, *Grey Wolf*, pp.xix, xxi, xxii. See also Harry Cooper, *Hitler in Argentina* (Hernando, FL: CreateSpace Independent Publishing Platform, 2014), pp.8, 16, 25–26, 129; Hansig, *Hitler's Escape*, pp.viii, 53–54; Levenda, *Ratline*, pp.18, 21–25, 27–28, 40, 43, 173, 229.
75 Dunstan & Williams, *Grey Wolf*, p.xix.
76 Ibid., pp.337–338.
77 *Hunting Hitler*, Seasons 1–3, History Channel (2015–2018).
78 Richard J. Evans, *Altered Pasts: Counterfactuals in History* (London: Little Brown, 2014), pp.84–86. To Evans' credit, he may have discussed these issues in more detail during a public talk (Professor Sir Richard Evans, 'Hitler Lives! "Alternative Facts" and Conspiracy Theories', at The National Archives [30/08/2017]), but he has yet to do so in print.
79 Pigden, 'Conspiracy Theories and the Conventional Wisdom', p.219.
80 J. Eric Oliver & Thomas J. Wood, 'Conspiracy Theories and the Paranoid Style(s) of Mass Opinion', *American Journal of Political Science*, Vol. 58, No. 4 (2014), p.953.
81 Pigden, 'Conspiracy Theories and the Conventional Wisdom', p.221.
82 Cooper, *Hitler in Argentina*, p.2.
83 Jerry Gadiano, 'Submarine Found at Ocean Bottom Reveals "Truth" About Hitler's South America Escape', UNILAD (18/04/2018), https://www.unilad.co.uk/news/submarine-found-at-ocean-bottom-reveals-truth-about-hitlers-south-america-escape/ (accessed 27/07/2018). See also Anne-Marie Bojan, 'FBI Documents Claim Hitler Faked His Own Death and Fled to Argentina', UNILAD (12/01/2018), https://www.unilad.co.uk/tv/fbi-documents-claim-hitler-faked-his-own-death-and-fled-to-argentina/ (accessed 27/07/2018); Josh Teal, 'CIA Documents Reveal Hitler "Still Alive"

Following World War II', UNILAD (28/09/2017), https://www.unilad. co.uk/gossip/cia-documents-reveal-hitler-still-alive/ (accessed 27/07/2018); Tom Percival, 'Shocking Revelation from US President's Diary Suggests Hitler Didn't Die', UNILAD (20/03/2017), https://www.unilad.co.uk/ politics/shocking-revelation-from-us-presidents-diary-suggests-hitler-didnt-die/ (accessed 27/07/2018); Ben Hayward, 'CIA Veteran Claims Hitler "Faked His Death, Moved to the Canary Islands"', UNILAD (08/01/2016), https://www.unilad.co.uk/news/cia-veteran-claims-hitler-faked-his-death-and-moved-to-the-canary-islands/ (accessed 27/07/2018); James Dawson, 'Declassified Files Reveal CIA Investigated If Adolf Hitler Survived the War and Fled to Colombia', Lad Bible (31/10/2017), http://www.ladbible.com/news/weird-news-cia-investigated-if-adolf-hitler-survived-the-war-and-fled-to-colombia-20171031 (accessed 27/07/2018) (this article was shared 12,000 times and was liked by 9,000 people on Facebook by 24/07/2018); Claire Reid, 'CIA Veteran Claims Hitler Faked His Suicide and Fled to Argentina', Lad Bible (16/01/2017), http://www.ladbible.com/now/weird-cia-veteran-claims-hitler-faked-his-suicide-and-fled-to-argentina-20170116 (accessed 27/07/2018) (this article was liked by more than 4,000 people on Facebook and shared by more than 6,000 by 24/07/2018). Social media will become an increasingly important source for historical analysis. The UNILAD Facebook page is followed by 39,115,009 people (figure correct on 24/07/2018), giving an indication of just how widespread stories of Hitler's escape have become.

84 Bojan, 'FBI Documents'.

85 Christopher J. Gilbert, 'Playing with Hitler: Downfall and its Ludic Uptake', *Critical Studies in Media Communication*, Vol. 30, No. 5 (2013), pp.419–420.

86 McKale, *Hitler*, pp.199–205. See also Dunstan & Williams, *Grey Wolf*, p.xxx

87 Major-General Sir Kenneth Strong, *Intelligence at The Top: The Recollections of an Intelligence Officer* (London: Cassell, 1969), pp.247–248.

88 John Bruce Lockhart, 'Intelligence: A British View', in K. G. Robertson (ed.), *British and American Approaches to Intelligence* (London: Macmillan, 1987), p.52. On MI6 in Bad Salzuflen, see Keith Jeffery, *MI6: The History of the Secret Intelligence Service 1909–1949* (London: Bloomsbury, 2011), pp.664, 668.

89 William D. Rubinstein, *Shadow Pasts: History's Mysteries* (Harlow: Pearson, Longman, 2008), p.2.

90 Ibid.

91 Ibid., p.4.

92 Petrova & Watson, *Death of Hitler*, p.75.

93 Caroline Sharples, 'The Death of Nazism? Investigating Hitler's Remains and Survival Rumours in Post-War Germany', in Shane McCorristine (ed), *Interdisciplinary Perspectives on Mortality and its Timings* (London: Palgrave Macmillan, 2017), p.88.

94 Ibid., pp.88–89.

95 Ibid., p.98.

96 Adam Lusher, 'Adolf Hitler Really is Dead: Scientific Study Debunks Conspiracy Theories That He Escaped to South America', *Independent* (20/05/2018),

https://www.independent.co.uk/news/world/europe/adolf-hitler-debunked-escaped-south-america-skull-fragment-woman-teeth-jawbone-scientific-study-a8360356.html (accessed 01/07/2018).

97 P. Charlier, R. Weil, P. Rainsard, J. Poupon & J. C. Brisard, 'The Remains of Adolf Hitler: A Biomedical Analysis and Definitive Identification', *European Journal of Internal Medicine* (2018), pp.1–3.

98 Ibid., p.2.

99 Jean-Christophe Brisard & Lana Parshina, *The Death of Hitler: The Final Word* (Boston: Da Capo Press, 2018).

100 Charlier *et al.*, 'Remains of Adolf Hitler', p.2.

101 Ibid.

102 Jonathan Evans, in Christopher Andrew, *The Defence of the Realm: The Authorized History of MI5* (London: Penguin, 2009), p.xv.

103 Stephen Twigge, Edward Hampshire & Graham Macklin, *British Intelligence: Secrets, Spies and Sources* (Kew: The National Archives, 2008), p.8. See also Stephen Dorril, *MI6: Fifty Years of Special Operations* (London: Fourth Estate Limited, 2000), p.xiii.

104 Dorril, *MI6*, p.xiii. See also Twigge, Hampshire and Macklin, *British Intelligence*, pp.7–8.

105 Richard J. Aldrich, *The Hidden Hand: Britain, America and Cold War Secret Intelligence* (London: John Murray, 2002), p.638. See also Dorril, *MI6*, p.xiv.

106 Aldrich, *Hidden Hand*, pp.5–7. See also Jeffery, *MI6*, p.xi.

107 Jeffery, *MI6*, p.xiv.

CHAPTER 2: BRITISH INTELLIGENCE AND RUMOURS OF SURVIVAL

1 Christopher Hitchens, 'Mommie Dearest', *Slate* (2003), http://www.slate.com/articles/news_and_politics/fighting_words/2003/10/mommie_dearest.html (accessed 01/06/2018).

2 Some of the documents analysed in this chapter are also analysed in Richard Overy, *Interrogations, Inside the Minds of the Nazi Elite* (London: Penguin, 2001), p.101. However, in that book this analysis is in the context of the Nuremberg trials and lacks detail. There is no book specifically about Hitler's death in which the documents are referenced.

3 The National Archives (TNA), FO 371/46748, Roberts (Moscow) to FO (02/05/1945) and WO, communication concerning 'Facts about Hitler's Death' (04/05/1945).

4 TNA, FO 371/46748, 'Draft Reply to Parliamentary Question No. 19' (15/05/1945).

5 TNA, FO 371/46749, *News Chronicle, Daily Telegraph* and *Daily Herald* (05/07/1945).

6 TNA, FO 371/46749, Roberts (Moscow) to FO (11/09/1945).

7 TNA, FO 371/46749, Roberts (Moscow) to FO (12/09/1945). See also Frank Roberts, *Dealing with Dictators* (London: George Weidenfeld & Nicolson, 1991), p.93.

8 TNA, FO 371/46749, FO Minutes (12/09/1945).

9 Ibid.

10   TNA, FO 371/46749, 'Hitler's Last Days', SHAEF Memorandum (30/07/1945).

11   TNA, FO 371/46749, *The Times* (13/10/1945) and Roberts (Moscow) to FO (09/10/1945). See also Hugh Trevor-Roper, *The Last Days of Hitler* (London: Macmillan, 2002), p.xlvii.

12   TNA, FO 371/46749, FO Minutes (09/10/1945).

13   TNA, FO 371/46749, Letter from the Dominions Office (29/09/1945). See also D.B. Sole, South Africa House to Miss B. Staple, Dominions Office (21/08/1945).

14   TNA, FO 371/46749, FO Minutes (29/09/1945).

15   TNA, FO 371/46749, Letter from British Legation Copenhagen (29/10/1945).

16   TNA, FO 371/46749, FO Minutes (29/10/1945).

17   Major-General Sir Kenneth Strong, *Intelligence at the Top: The Recollections of an Intelligence Officer* (London: Cassell, 1969), p.173.

18   TNA, FO 371/46749, FO Minutes (26/09/1945).

19   TNA, WO 208/4475, BBC monitoring service, 'Hadji Hitler' (25/10/1945) and 'Hitler in Ireland' (16/06/1945). See also Stephen Twigge, Edward Hampshire and Graham Macklin, *British Intelligence: Secrets, Spies and Sources* (Kew: The National Archives, 2008), p.97.

20   TNA, WO 208/3791, Capt N. Dewhurst, No. 1 Area Intelligence Office (AIO) to HQ ID, 'Operation Conan Doyle' (04/10/1946) and Signal Report, HQ ID to 1 AIO (October 1946) p.182 and C. E. R. Hirsch, WO to Major-General J. S. Lethbridge, ID HQ (28/09/1946).

21   TNA, WO 208/3791, Hirsch to Lethbridge (28/09/1946).

22   TNA, WO 208/3791, Lethbridge to Hirsch (09/10/1946).

23   TNA, WO 208/3791, Air Intelligence HQ to ID HQ (12/09/1947).

24   Ibid.

25   TNA, WO 208/3791, Memorandum (09/10/1947).

26   TNA, WO 208/3791, R. G. Hodges, HQ ID to Gordon Potter, British Liaison Officer (BLO), HQ EUCOM (10/12/1947) and TNA, WO 208/3787, 'Report on Possible Fate and Location of Hitler, Bormann and Fegelein' (27/10/1945).

27   TNA, WO 208/3791, Hodges to Potter (10/12/1947).

28   TNA, WO 208/3791, Deputy Director of Intelligence to BLO (11/03/1948).

29   TNA, WO 208/3791, Interrogation of Karl Gebhardt (24/02/1948).

30   TNA, WO 208/3791, Deputy Director of Intelligence to BLO (11/03/1948). The CIC summary of Skorzeny's interrogation along with the British ID request for information can also be found in the National Archives and Records Administration (NARA II), RG 319, ZZ6, Box 8, 6828925, 'Hitler's Last Days' (10/03/1948).

31   TNA, WO 208/3791, Hodges to Potter (10/12/1947).

32   TNA, WO 208/3791, *Hamburger Allgemeine* (07/10/1947), *Westdeutsche Rundschau* (04/12/1947), *The Times* (13/12/1947), *Lüneburger Landezeitung* (16/01/1948), *Express Wieczorny* (18/12/1947).

33   TNA, WO 208/3791, Hodges, Ops & Planning Branch, ID HQ Herford to 5 AIO, 'Rumours Concerning Whereabouts of Adolf Hitler' (02/03/1948).

34 TNA, WO 208/3791, *Lübecker Frei Presse* (31/12/1947) and Censorship Civil Communications (22/10/1947).

35 TNA, WO 208/3791, Hodges, 'Rumours Concerning Whereabouts of Adolf Hitler' (02/03/1948) and Hodges, 'Hitler Survival Rumours' (03/12/1947).

36 Harry Cooper, *Hitler in Argentina* (Hernando, FL: CreateSpace Independent Publishing Platform, 2014), p.26.

37 TNA, WO 208/3791, 'Rumours Concerning the Whereabouts of Adolf Hitler' (16/04/1948) and 'Hitler Survival Rumour' (16/01/1948) and 'Hitler Survival Rumour' (16/06/1948) and 'Baumgart is Telling Lies', p.25 and 'Hitler Survival Rumour (17/06/1948).

38 Simon Dunstan & Gerrard Williams, *Grey Wolf: The Escape of Adolf Hitler* (New York: Sterling, 2011), pp.163, 222, 225, 266–267, 282.

39 Cooper, *Hitler in Argentina*, pp.117–229.

40 Sky News interview with Gerrard Williams (16/10/2011).

41 Dunstan & Williams, *Grey Wolf*, pp.160–161.

42 Sky News interview with Gerrard Williams (16/10/2011).

43 Adam Sisman, *Hugh Trevor-Roper: The Biography* (London: Phoenix, 2011), pp.81, 88, 94, 117–118, 125.

44 Owen Bennet, 'Are These Classified FBI Files Proof Adolf Hitler Escaped by SUBMARINE to Argentina?', *Daily Express* (15/04/2014), http://www.express.co.uk/news/weird/470586/Are-these-classified-FBI-files-proof-ADOLF-HITLER-escaped-by-SUBMARINE-to-Argentina (accessed 24/01/2015).

45 Donald M. McKale, *Hitler: The Survival Myth* (New York: Stein and Day, 1983), pp.198–199.

46 Dunstan & Williams, *Grey Wolf*, pp.xx, 156–157. See also Cooper, *Hitler in Argentina*, p.62; Ron T. Hansig, *Hitler's Escape*, pp.25, 32, 38–39.

47 TNA, KV 4/354, Interrogation of Baroness von Varo (01/10/1945).

48 TNA, WO 208/3791, Memorandum, 'Release of Information re Hitler to the Press' (19/03/1948).

49 TNA, WO 208/3789, 'Record of Eye Examination made 2 Mar 44', p.163.

50 TNA, WO 208/3787, 'Hitler's Death' (07/11/1945) and Trevor-Roper to Ramsbotham, CIB Memorandum, p.55.

51 TNA, WO 208/3791, HQ ID Herford to Captain Frazier, USLO 'Adolf Hitler' (19/11/1947).

52 Helmuth Weidling made a similar point in Soviet captivity; see Testimony of General Helmuth Weidling (04/01/1946) in V. K. Vinogradov, J. F. Pogonyi & N. V. Teptzov (eds), *Hitler's Death: Russia's Last Great Secret from the Files of the KGB* (London: Chaucer Press, 2005), p.239. See also Ada Petrova & Peter Watson, *The Death of Hitler: The Final Words from Russia's Secret Archives* (London: Richard Cohen Books, 1995), pp.106–107.

CHAPTER 3: AMERICAN INTELLIGENCE AND RUMOURS OF SURVIVAL

1 The Vault, FBI Digital Archive, Adolf Hitler Volume 2, Los Angeles to Director FBI, 'Hitler Hideout' (14/08/1945).

2 The Vault, FBI Digital Archive, Adolf Hitler Volume 1, Office Memorandum, United States Government, James H. Merritt to D. M. Ladd, 'Adolf Hitler and Woman Aboard City of New Orleans' (28/02/1948).

3 FBI Hitler Volume 1, Office Memorandum, United States Government, D. M. Ladd to H. B. Fletcher, 'Adolf Hitler and Woman Aboard City of New Orleans' (03/03/1948).

4 FBI Hitler Volume 1, handwritten letter stamped October 1945.

5 FBI Hitler Volume 1, letter to Director FBI (25/07/1946).

6 FBI Hitler Volume 1, letter to Mr. Walter Winchell (03/10/1946).

7 FBI Hitler Volume 1, L. N. Conroy to H. B. Fletcher (10/10/1948).

8 FBI Hitler Volume 1, O. J. Auerswald to H. B. Fletcher (11/10/1948).

9 FBI Hitler Volume 1, L. N. Conroy to H. B. Fletcher (10/10/1948).

10 FBI Hitler Volume 1, SAC, St. Louis to Director, FBI (18/03/1949).

11 FBI Hitler Volume 2, Mr. Morrell to C. D. DeLoach (06/07/1960).

12 FBI Hitler Volume 2, Mr. Morrell to C. D. DeLoach (06/07/1960).

13 FBI Hitler Volume 2.

14 FBI Hitler Volume 2, *Washington Times-Herald* (09/06/1945).

15 FBI Hitler Volume 2, *Washington Times-Herald* (10/06/1945).

16 FBI Hitler Volume 2, *Washington Times-Herald* (05/07/1945).

17 FBI Hitler Volume 2, 'From Buenos Aires' (14/07/1945).

18 FBI Hitler Volume 2, 'From Buenos Aires' (14/07/1945).

19 FBI Hitler Volume 2, *Washington Star* clipping (21/07/1945).

20 FBI Hitler Volume 2, *Washington Star* clipping (21/07/1945).

21 FBI Hitler Volume 2, *Washington Star* clipping (21/07/1945).

22 FBI Vault Volume 2, C. H. Carson to D. M. Ladd, 'Reports that Adolf Hitler and Eva Braun are in Argentina' (31/07/1945).

23 Ibid.

24 FBI Vault Volume 2, 'Report that Adolf Hitler is in Argentina' (11/08/1945).

25 Ibid.

26 FBI Hitler Volume 2, SAC Los Angeles to Director, FBI, 'Report on Hitler Hideout' (14/08/1945).

27 FBI Vault Volume 2, FBI Radiogram from Buenos Aires (17/08/1945).

28 Ibid.

29 FBI Hitler Volume 3, Office Memorandum, Edw. A. Tamm to The Director (25/08/1945).

30 Ibid.

31 FBI Hitler Volume 2, John Edgar Hoover to Assistant Chief of Staff, G-2 (06/09/1945).

32 FBI Hitler Volume 1, American Embassy, Montevideo, Uruguay to Director, FBI (28/11/1945).

33 FBI Hitler Volume 1, Philadelphia to Director, FBI (31/07/1946).

34 Ibid.

35 FBI Hitler Volume 1, SAC, San Francisco to Director, FBI, 'Attempted Hoax' (23/09/1947).

36 Ibid.

37 Ibid.

38 FBI Hitler Volume 1, Investigation Department, Washington, DC, 'Translation from the Spanish' (30/05/1948).

39 Ibid.

40 The National Archives and Records Administration (NARA II), RG 263, UD 2, Box 3, Folder 1, 16966402, CIA to Chief WHD, 'Adolph Hitler' (03/10/1955).

41 NARA II, RG 263, UD 2, Box 3, Folder 1, 16966402, CIA to Chief WH, 'Adolf Hitler' (17/10/1955).

42 Harry Cooper, *Hitler in Argentina* (Hernando, FL: CreateSpace Independent Publishing Platform, 2014), pp.226–229.

43 James Dawson, 'Declassified Files Reveal CIA Investigated If Adolf Hitler Survived the War and Fled to Colombia', Lad Bible (31/10/2017), http://www.ladbible.com/news/weird-news-cia-investigated-if-adolf-hitler-survived-the-war-and-fled-to-colombia-20171031 (accessed 27/07/2018). See also Josh Teal, 'CIA Documents Reveal Hitler 'Still Alive' Following World War II', UNILAD (28/09/2017), https://www.unilad.co.uk/gossip/cia-documents-reveal-hitler-still-alive/ (accessed 27/07/2018).

44 NARA II, RG 263, UD 2, Box 3, Folder 1, 16966402, CIA to Chief WH, 'Adolf Hitler' (17/10/1955).

45 NARA II, RG 263, UD 2, Box 3, Folder 1, 16966402, CIA to Chief WHD, 'Adolph Hitler' (03/10/1955).

46 NARA II, RG 263, UD 2, Box 3, Folder 1, 16966402, Chief WHD to CIA 'Adolph Hitler' (04/11/1955).

47 Simon Dunstan & Gerrard Williams, *Grey Wolf: The Escape of Adolf Hitler* (New York: Sterling, 2011), p.281.

48 NARA II, RG 263, A1-27, Box 8, 7283100, 'Commentary'.

49 NARA II, RG 549, A1-52, Box 820, 563511, HQ EUCOM, Dep Dir Intell, 'Remarks', (15/10 – likely 1947).

50 NARA II, RG 549, A1-52, Box 820, 563511, *Stars and Stripes* (06/10/1947).

51 NARA II, RG 549, A1-52, Box 820, 563511, HQ ID Herford to USLO Captain Frazier (19/11/1947).

52 NARA II, RG 549, A1-52, Box 820, 563511, 'Is Hitler Dead?' (24/11/1947).

53 Ibid.

54 Ibid.

55 Ibid.

56 Ibid.

57 NARA II, RG 319, ZZ6, Box 8, 6828925, Ops Br to HQ 970th CIC Det (26/11/1947).

58 Ibid.

59 NARA II, RG 549, A1-52, Box 820, 563511, C.F. Fritzsche to Director of Intelligence OMGUS (21/01/1948).

60 NARA II, RG 549, A1-52, Box 820, 563511, C.R. Huebner to Lucius D. Clay (March 1948).

61 NARA II, RG 549, A1-52, Box 820, 563511, Heimlich Testimony (11/03/1948).

62 NARA II, RG 549, A1-52, Box 820, 563511, A.T. Netterblad, Jr. to Slayden, HQ EUCOM ID, 'Death of Hitler' (30/09/1948).

63 NARA II, RG 549, A1-52, Box 820, 563511, W. M. M. Slayden, R&A Branch, HQ EUCOM ID to Assistant Deputy Director ID, 'Hitler's Death' (27/08/1948). American intelligence came across this evidence only after several initially confusing interrogations. The fact that this information was derived from second- and third-hand sources added to the reluctance of American intelligence officials to publicise their findings, but their evidence was proved correct when the Soviets later published their own account of the incident. In the end, it was proved that Herr Fedor Bruck, who 'occupied the office formerly used by Prof. Dr. Blaschke, Hitler's Dentist', told CIC agent Mathews that Echtmann and Heusermann were taken by the Russians to identify Hitler and Eva's teeth. They revealed this to their families upon their release. Frau Heusermann's sister confirmed this story to Mathews. For the above, see NARA II, RG 549, A1 48, Box 734, 563465, R&A Br to Ops Br, 'Death of Hitler' (15/03/1948). The Soviet account of this event can be found in Bezymenski, *Death of Adolf Hitler*, pp.52–57. Heusermann and Echtmann were later imprisoned by the Soviets for many years; see Vinogradov, Pogonyi & Teptzov, *Hitler's Death*, pp.96, 102. Blaschke was captured by the CIC in May 1945; see Anton Joachimsthaler, *The Last Days of Hitler: Legend, Evidence and Truth* (London: Cassell, 2000), p.226.

64 NARA II, RG 549, A1-52, Box 820, 563511, W. M. M. Slayden, R&A Branch, HQ EUCOM ID to Assistant Deputy Director ID, 'Hitler's Death' (27/08/1948).

65 NARA II, RG 549, A1-52, Box 820, 563511, Ops Br to HQs 7970th CIC Gp, 'Hitler's Jawbone' (07/09/1948).

66 NARA II, RG 319, A1 134B, Box 101, 7356891, Herbert Bechtold, HQ 7970th CIC Group Region IV, Agent Report (14/09/1948).

67 NARA II, RG 319, A1 134B, Box 101, 7356891, Allen S. Stone, Agent Report (05/08/1948). Quotation from Herbert Bechtold, HQ 7970th CIC Group Region IV, Agent Report (14/09/1948).

68 NARA II, RG 319, A1 134B, Box 101, 7356891, Herbert Bechtold, HQ 7970th CIC Group Region IV, Agent Report (14/09/1948).

69 Max owned a bakery in Munich and the alleged Luftwaffe pilot who told this tale was an infrequent customer. It is likely that this pilot was simply repeating popular rumours, just as Max formed his opinions based on a mixture of such rumours. See NARA II, RG 319, A1 134B, Box 101, 7356891, Herbert Bechtold, HQ 7970th CIC Group Region IV, Agent Report (14/09/1948).

70 NARA II, RG 319, A1 134B, Box 101, 7356891, Ellington D. Golden, HQ CIC Region IV to Commanding Officer HQ 7970th CIC Group (14/09/1948).

71 NARA II, RG 549, A1 48, Box 748, 563465, 'Quarterly Historical Report: Operations Branch' (01/01/1949–31/03/1949).

72 Bob Baer, *Hunting Hitler*, History Channel, Season One, Episode One (10/11/2015).

73 Dave Hoffman (narrator), *Hunting Hitler*, History Channel, Season One, Episode One (10/11/2015).

74 Tim Weiner, *Legacy of Ashes: The History of the CIA* (London: Penguin, 2008), p.19.

75 Ibid., p.19. Weiner's works must, of course, be cited with caution after Nicholas Dujmovic convincingly argued that many of his statements were biased and unreliable. I have, as recommended by Dujmovic, also read Christopher Andrew's excellent *For the President's Eyes Only: Secret Intelligence and the American Presidency from Washington to Bush* (London: HarperCollins, 1995), but I believe that, in the context of Hitler survival rumours, Weiner's comments are appropriate (although overstated). To be fair to the CIA, they were also good at spotting such fraudulent intelligence and, like the FBI, discontinued investigations when sources were found to be unreliable. See Nicholas Dujmovic, 'Bonum Ex Malo: The Value of Legacy of Ashes in Teaching CIA History', in Christopher R. Moran and Christopher J. Murphy (eds), *Intelligence Studies in Britain and the US: Historiography since 1945* (Edinburgh: Edinburgh University Press, 2013), pp.90–111.

76 Cooper, *Hitler in Argentina*, p.26.

77 FBI, Hitler Volume 1, Hoover to Legal Attaché, Rio de Janeiro (09/07/1947). For a conspiratorial take on this rumour (including a typically selective use of documents), see Dunstan & Williams, *Grey Wolf*, pp.242–246.

78 Rhodri Jeffreys-Jones, *The FBI: A History* (Connecticut: Yale University Press: 2007), p.144.

79 FBI, Hitler Volume 1, Hoover to Censored (14/11/1945).

80 Jeffreys-Jones, *FBI*, pp.11, 138

81 Ibid., pp.11–12.

82 Ibid., pp.10, 12, 100, 116–118.

83 Ibid., pp.11, 143.

84 NARA II, RG 65, A1 136P, Box 38, 6133250, D. M. Ladd to The Director, 'Martin Bormann' (24/06/1948).

85 Christopher Hitchens, *Blood, Class and Empire: The Enduring Anglo-American Relationship* (London: Atlantic, 2006), p.322.

86 Jeffreys-Jones, *FBI*, pp.109, 152. See also Richard J. Aldrich & Rory Cormac, *The Black Door: Spies, Secret Intelligence and British Prime Ministers* (London: William Collins, 2016), p.110.

87 FBI, Hitler Volume 1, Letter to Hoover (03/11/1945).

88 Jeffreys-Jones, *FBI*, p.118.

89 NARA II, RG 549, A1-52, Box 820, 563511, Captain George T. Gabelia's testimony before Colonel Harold R. Booth (15/03/1948).

90 Peter Levenda, *Ratline: Soviet Spies, Nazi Priests, and the Disappearance of Adolf Hitler* (Lake Worth, FL: Ibis Press, 2012), pp.22, 25, 31, 34. See also Hugh Thomas, *Doppelgängers: The Truth about the Bodies in the Berlin Bunker* (London: Fourth Estate, 1995), pp.94–95.

CHAPTER 4: POLITICAL MOTIVATIONS? BRITISH, AMERICAN AND SOVIET CONDUCT

1 Peter Levenda, *Ratline: Soviet Spies, Nazi Priests, and the Disappearance of Adolf Hitler* (Lake Worth, FL: Ibis Press, 2012), p.22.

2 Ibid., pp.22, 25, 31, 34.

3 Simon Dunstan and Gerrard Williams, *Grey Wolf: The Escape of Adolf Hitler* (New York: Sterling, 2011), p.xxx.

4 James P. O'Donnell, *The Berlin Bunker* (London: J. M. Dent, 1979), p.14.
5 The Vault, FBI Digital Archive, Adolf Hitler Volume 2, 'Washington Times-Herald' (08/07/1945).
6 FBI, Hitler Volume 2, 'Evening News' (24/07/1945).
7 Adam Sisman, *Hugh Trevor-Roper: The Biography* (London: Phoenix, 2011), p.133. See also Hugh Trevor-Roper, *The Secret World: Behind the Curtain of British Intelligence in World War II and the Cold War* (London: I. B. Tauris, 2014), pp.29–30.
8 Sky News television interview with Gerrard Williams (16/10/2011), YouTube, https://www.youtube.com/watch?v=JuLPMCxvBf8.
9 P. R. J. Winter, 'A Higher Form of Intelligence: Hugh Trevor-Roper and Wartime British Secret Service', *Intelligence and National Security*, Vol. 22, No. 6 (2007), pp.848–849, 875.
10 Ibid, pp.849–850.
11 Edward Harrison (ed.), 'Introduction', in Trevor-Roper, *Secret World*, pp.2–3. See also Winter, 'Higher Form of Intelligence', pp.848, 873.
12 Sisman, *Hugh Trevor-Roper*, p.118.
13 Winter, 'Higher Form of Intelligence', pp.856, 873.
14 Trevor-Roper, *Secret World*, p.29.
15 The National Archives (TNA), WO 208/3787, White to Robertson (10/09/1945).
16 Sean Greenwood, *Britain and the Cold War* (London: Macmillan, 2000), p.6.
17 Hugh Trevor-Roper, *The Last Days of Hitler* (London: Macmillan, 2002), pp.lviii, 205.
18 TNA, FO 1050/583, 21 Army Group CI Sitrep No. 14 (02/08/1945).
19 Ibid.
20 TNA, FO 1050/583, 21 Army Group CI Sitrep No. 15 (11/08/1945).
21 Churchill Archives Centre, British Diplomatic Oral History Programme (BDOHP), Sir Peter Edward Ramsbotham Interviewed by Malcom McBain (09/01/2001).
22 TNA, FO 1005/1165, Joint Intelligence Committee CCG (BE) (18/09/1945).
23 The National Archives and Records Administration (NARA II), RG 498, UD964, Box 4563, 5891629, 'G-2 Weekly Intelligence Summary No. 7' (03/11/1945).
24 BDOHP, Ramsbotham Interviewed by McBain (09/01/2001).
25 NARA II, RG 319, NM382, Box 1847, 2155420, Intelligence Division Summary No. 15 (15/02/1947).
26 FBI, Hitler Volume 2, 'Hitler Lives!' clipping from *Washington Times-Herald* (20/02/1949).
27 Ibid.
28 Ibid.
29 Stephen Dorril, *MI6: Fifty Years of Special Operations* (London: Fourth Estate Limited, 2000), p.67.
30 TNA, KV 4/354, Minute from MI5 to JIC (03/06/1946).
31 TNA, KV 4/354, JIC Minutes (14/06/1946).
32 TNA, KV 4/354, JIC Minutes (24/06/1946) and Trevor-Roper to White (19/06/1946).

33 Ibid.

34 Liddell Hart Centre for Military Archives (LHCMA), King's College London, Private Papers of Major-General John Sydney Lethbridge, 'end of the report to Robertson'. This undated report is a variation of Trevor-Roper's original intelligence report of November 1945, which it mostly copies verbatim throughout but has expanded slightly to include new evidence from Hitler's wills.

35 Greenwood, *Britain*, pp.6, 8, 11.

36 Ibid., p.10.

37 Trevor-Roper, *Last Days of Hitler*, p.xxxi.

38 Ibid.

39 Ibid.

40 Ibid, pp.xxxi–xxxii.

41 Ibid, pp.xxxi–xxxii. See also Anton Joachimsthaler, *The Last Days of Hitler: Legend, Evidence and Truth* (London: Cassell, 2000), p.131.

42 Trevor-Roper, *Last Days of Hitler*, p.xxxii.

43 Ibid., p.xxx.

44 NARA II, RG 242, P 26, Box 1, 12008425, HQ Third United States Army, 303 CIC Det to AC of S G-2 (28/12/1945).

45 Trevor-Roper, *Last Days of Hitler*, p.xxxii.

46 NARA II, RG 242, P 26, Box 1, 12008425, HQ Third United States Army, 303 CIC Det to AC of S G-2 (28/12/1945).

47 Ibid.

48 Ibid.

49 Ibid.

50 Ibid.

51 Ibid.

52 Ibid.

53 Trevor-Roper, *Last Days of Hitler*, p.xxxiii.

54 Ibid., pp.xxxiii–xxxiv.

55 Ibid., p.xxxiv.

56 TNA, CAB 146/438, 'Hitler's Will: Points From Foreign Office Papers' (31/12/1945).

57 Ibid. See also Richard J. Aldrich, *The Hidden Hand: Britain, America and Cold War Secret Intelligence* (London: John Murray, 2002), p.181; Dorril, *MI6*, p.99.

58 Sisman, *Hugh Trevor-Roper*, pp.140–141.

59 TNA, CAB 146/438, FO to Washington (08/01/1946).

60 TNA, CAB 146/438, MI4, Top Secret Cipher Telegram (16/02/1946).

61 TNA, CAB 146/438, FO to Washington (08/01/1946).

62 NARA II, RG 242, P 26, Box 1, 12008425, British Embassy, Washington, DC, 'Aide Memoire' (09/01/1946).

63 Ibid.

64 TNA, WO 208/3788, Templer to Lethbridge (08/12/1945). For further information on Templer, see Dorril, *MI6*, p.98.

65 TNA, WO 208/3788, Lethbridge to Templer (04/12/1945).

66 TNA, WO 208/3789, Anonymous letter to Kopf (22/12/1945).

67 TNA, WO 208/3789, Trevor-Roper to Intelligence Bureau (IB) (23/01/1946).
68 TNA, WO 208/3789, Ramsbotham to Wethered (18/12/1945).
69 TNA, WO 208/3788, 'The Hitler Case' (02/12/1945) and TNA, WO 208/3789, 'Draft for Press Hand Out', p.123.
70 TNA, WO 208/3789, Secret Signal, Counter Intelligence Bureau (CIB) (08/01/1946).
71 TNA, WO 208/3789, MGI (CCG) to DMI WO (22/01/1946) and TNA, WO 208/3781, 'Hitler's Will', p.50.
72 TNA, CAB 146/438, *Daily Telegraph* (31/12/1945).
73 NARA II, RG 242, P 26, Box 1, 12008425, Edward M. Pickett, 'Circumstances of Discovery of Hitler's Wills' (11/01/1946).
74 NARA II, RG 242, P 26, Box 1, 12008425, Department of State, Washington, Secret Message (16/01/1946).
75 TNA, WO 208/3781, FO to Intelligence Group (IG), Adv HQ Berlin 'This Document Must Not Be Reproduced' (03/02/1946).
76 TNA, WO 208/3781, Lethbridge, IG HQ to Brigadier E. J. Foord, Deputy MGI, IG, Adv HQ, Berlin (22/01/1946).
77 TNA, WO 208/3788, Lethbridge, IG HQ to Head CIB (23/11/1945) and TNA, WO 208/3789, 'Hitler's Wills' (07/01/1946). Copies can also be found in the private papers of Major-General Templer and Major-General Lethbridge.
78 NARA II, RG 242, P 26, Box 1, 12008425, The President to Secretary of War (22/03/1946).
79 TNA, WO 208/3789, MGI (CCG) to DMI WO (22/01/1946).
80 TNA, CAB 146/438, 'Hitler's Will: Points From Foreign Office Papers', pp.3–4.
81 TNA, KV 4/354, JIC Minutes (14/06/1946) and JIC Minutes (24/06/1946).
82 TNA, WO 208/3789, USFET, 'Hitler As Seen By His Doctors' (29/11/1945) and TNA, WO 208/3790, USFET, 'Hitler's Teeth' and TNA, WO 208/3787, USFET, 'Hitler As Seen By His Doctors' (15/10/1945).
83 Thomas White, 'A Pittsburgh Judge's Path to Nuremberg and Back', *Western Pennsylvania History*, Vol. 98, No. 1 (2015), p.99. See also Joachimsthaler, *Last Days of Hitler*, p.282.
84 TNA, WO 208/3789, Haylor to Sands (08/01/1946).
85 TNA, WO 208/3787, 'Present position of enquiry and recommendations for further action in British and U.S. Zone', p.30 and 'Frau Christian', p.147.
86 Trevor-Roper, *Last Days of Hitler*, p.xx.
87 TNA, CAB 146/438, Trevor-Roper to Melland (28/03/1966).
88 Ibid.
89 Ian Sayer and Douglas Botting, *America's Secret Army: The Untold Story of the Counter Intelligence Corps* (London: Fontana, 1990), p.308.
90 Dorril, *MI6*, p.104.
91 TNA, CAB 146/438, Trevor-Roper to Melland (08/04/1966).
92 TNA, KV 4/354, Hodges to MI5 (04/11/1947). Also in TNA, WO 208/3791.
93 Dunstan & Williams, *Grey Wolf*, p.xxi.
94 TNA, FO 938/196, 299/MG/8482/PRISC (03/03/1948).

95 TNA, KV 4/354, Trevor-Roper's reply to Reitsch, published in *Die Welt* (14/10/1947).
96 TNA, KV 4/354, Trevor-Roper, Christ Church, Oxford (01/08/1946).
97 Sisman, *Hugh Trevor-Roper*, p.222.
98 TNA, CAB 146/438, Melland to Trevor-Roper (13/04/1966).
99 TNA, CAB 79/33, JIC Report (23/05/1945).
100 Aldrich, *Hidden Hand*, pp.21–22, 24, 37, 49, 69.
101 TNA, WO 208/4475, MI6 Political Report (07/06/1945).
102 TNA, WO 208/4475, MI14 (13/07/1945).
103 TNA, WO 208/4475, DDMI Minutes (14/07/1945).
104 TNA, FO 371/46749, Hodgson to Bevan. See also TNA, WO 208/3781 and TNA, WO 208/3787, pp.88–89.
105 TNA, FO 371/46748, *The Times* (07/06/1945), also in TNA, WO 208/4475. See also Donald M. McKale, *Hitler: The Survival Myth* (New York: Stein and Day, 1983), p.46.
106 McKale, *Hitler*, p.49.
107 Ada Petrova & Peter Watson, *The Death of Hitler: The Final Words from Russia's Secret Archives* (London: Richard Cohen Books, 1995), p.44.
108 Ibid.
109 TNA, FO 371/46748, *The Times* (09/07/1945).
110 TNA, WO 208/3790, Censorship Civil Communications (10/01/1946).
111 TNA, FO 371/46748, FO Minutes (16/05/1945).
112 TNA, FO 371/46749, 'Hitler's Last Days', SHAEF Memorandum (30/07/1945).
113 TNA, FO 371/46749, Draft Reply to Parliamentary Question (15/10/1945).
114 Sisman, *Hugh Trevor-Roper*, p.133.
115 TNA, WO 208/3787, White to Robertson (10/09/1945).
116 TNA, WO 208/3787, GSI HQ (24/10/1945).
117 TNA, WO 208/3787, 'Hitler's Death' (22/10/1945).
118 Sisman, *Hugh Trevor-Roper*, p.137.
119 TNA, WO 208/3788, Cameron to Ramsbotham (26/11/1945) and TNA, WO 208/3787, 'The Death of Hitler', p.35.
120 TNA, WO 208/3788, Searle to Trevor-Roper (30/11/1945).
121 TNA, WO 208/3789, Wethered to Ramsbotham (27/12/1945).
122 TNA, WO 208/3781, *Daily Telegraph* and *Der Kurier* (02/01/1946) and 'Alleged Discovery of Hitler's Body' (03/01/1946).
123 TNA, WO 208/3781, Memorandum (07/01/1946).
124 TNA, WO 208/3781, 'Alleged Discovery of Hitler's Body' (03/01/1946) and CIB, Berlin letter to Haylor, IB (07/01/1946).
125 TNA, WO 208/3789, QIC Minutes (10/01/1946).
126 Ibid.
127 TNA, WO 208/3781, Dubrovski to Jennings (12/06/1946).
128 TNA, WO 208/3781, 'Von Below' (14/06/1946) and 'Von Below' (03/06/1945). See also V. K. Vinogradov, J. F. Pogonyi & N. V. Teptzov (eds), *Hitler's Death: Russia's Last Great Secret from the Files of the KGB* (London: Chaucer Press, 2005), pp.22, 117–118.
129 Vinogradov, Pogonyi & Teptzov, *Hitler's Death*, p.26.

130 TNA, FO 371/46749, FO Minutes (09/10/1945) and (12/09/1945).
131 Herbert Moore & James W. Barret (eds), *Who Killed Hitler?* (New York: Booktab Press, 1947), pp.136, 138. See also McKale, *Hitler*, pp.40–41, 53–55, 63; Joachimsthaler, *Last Days of Hitler*, pp.248–250; O'Donnell, *Berlin Bunker*, p.302; Antony Beevor, *Berlin: The Downfall 1945* (London: Penguin, 2003), pp.425–426; Trevor-Roper, *Last Days of Hitler*, pp.l–li.
132 McKale, *Hitler*, p.73. See also Henrik Eberle & Matthias Uhl (eds), *The Hitler Book: The Secret Report by His Two Closest Aides* (London: John Murray, 2005), p.xxiv.
133 Professor Norman Stone, on *Timewatch, Hitler's Death: The Final Report*, UK television broadcast (30/04/1995). See also Petrova & Watson, *Death of Hitler*, pp.86–87.
134 Trevor-Roper, *Secret World*, p.viiii.

CHAPTER 5: HELPING HITLER ESCAPE? THE HUNT FOR HITLER'S HENCHMEN

1 The National Archives (TNA), KV 2/3033, R. J. T. Griffin, 'Interview with Karl Heinz Kaerner' (11/08/1949).
2 Simon Dunstan & Gerrard Williams, *Grey Wolf: The Escape of Adolf Hitler* (New York: Sterling, 2011), p.xix. See also Donald M. McKale, *Hitler: The Survival Myth* (New York: Stein and Day, 1983), pp.143–144.
3 The Vault, FBI Digital Archive, Adolf Hitler Volume 1, John F. Sembower, 'Hitler Mystery Deepens', Undated Newspaper Extract. This particular extract contains some hilarious images of Hitler in various disguises, one of which shows him wearing glasses and with an abundance of facial hair, whilst another has him with no hair at all!
4 The National Archives (TNA), WO 208/3789, Leo Barton Interrogation of Kempka (12/01/1946).
5 Kempka told Trevor-Roper in October 1945 that this was a 'Panzer IV', but Antony Beevor claims it was a Nordland Tiger Tank. See Antony Beevor, *Berlin: The Downfall 1945* (London: Penguin, 2003), p.382 and TNA, KV 4/354, Interrogation of Erich Kempka (07/10/1945). Also in the National Archives and Records Administration (NARA II), RG 242, P 26, Box 1, 12008425, Special Interrogation of Erich Kempka (07/10/1945). In the latter interrogation, Trevor-Roper included a doodle of the tank attack, though it is not nearly as detailed as the one included in Kempka's 1946 interrogation, reproduced as Figure 1 in this book. Quotations in main text are from TNA, WO 208/3789, Leo Barton Interrogation of Kempka (12/01/1946).
6 Apparently, the blast was the result of a 'Panzerfaust, thrown from a window'. See TNA, KV 4/354, Interrogation of Erich Kempka (07/10/1945). Also in NARA II, RG 242, P 26, Box 1, 12008425, Special Interrogation of Erich Kempka (07/10/1945). Quotations in main text are from TNA, WO 208/3789, Leo Barton Interrogation of Kempka (12/01/1946).
7 TNA, WO 208/3789, Leo Barton Interrogation of Axmann (14/01/1946).
8 Reidar Sognnaes, 'Dental Evidence in the Postmortem Identification of Adolf Hitler, Eva Braun and Martin Bormann', *Legal Medicine Annual* (1976), p.209.

9 Hugh Trevor-Roper, *The Last Days of Hitler* (London: Macmillan, 2002), pp.xxxvii–xxxviii.

10 NARA II, RG 263, ZZ 18, Box 15, Folder 6, 26186820, 'Martin Bormann' (06/12/1945).

11 NARA II, RG 263, ZZ 18, Box 15, Folder 6, 26186820, Memorandum for Mr. Jack D. Neal (23/01/1946).

12 NARA II, RG 263, ZZ 18, Box 15, Folder 6, 26186820, 'Intelligence Report, Madrid' (10/04/1946).

13 TNA, KV 2/3033, Minute Sheet, 'Mr. Curry' (29/10/1946).

14 Ibid.

15 TNA, KV 2/3033, Guy Liddell to Stewart Menzies (30/10/1946).

16 Ibid. See also Telegram from Liddell to Shoosmith (30/10/1946).

17 TNA, KV 2/3033, *Evening Standard*, 'Bormann "living in S. America"' (11 December, presumably 1946) and *Reynolds Newspaper*, 'Bormann is Alive, Says S.S. Officer' (November, likely 1946).

18 TNA, KV 2/3033, G. J. Jenkins, Defence Security Office, Egypt to Sir Percy Sillitoe, MI5 London (31/12/1946).

19 TNA, KV 2/3033, J. Chenhalls to H. A. R. Philby (14/01/1947).

20 TNA, KV 2/3033, J. Chenhalls to MI6 (25/02/1947). See also Special Branch, New Scotland Yard, London to MI5 (14/02/1947).

21 NARA II, RG 263, ZZ 18, Box 15, Folder 6, 26186820, Headquarters, Counter Intelligence Corps, 'Martin Bormann' (18/03/1947).

22 NARA II, RG 263, ZZ 18, Box 15, Folder 6, 26186820, Memorandum for Mr. Ross H. Ingersoll (27/03/1947).

23 TNA, KV 2/3033, Special Branch, Colombo, Ceylon to G. T. D. Patterson, MI5, London (19/05/1947).

24 Ibid.

25 TNA, KV 2/3033, Courtenay Young, Minute Sheet (28/05/1947).

26 TNA, KV 2/3033, Miss Gunn, Minute Sheet (04/06/1947).

27 TNA KV 2/3033, Sillitoe to Ceylon Police (11/06/1947).

28 'Hitler No. 2 "to be found riding Nessie"', *Metro* (31/08/2009), http://metro.co.uk/2009/08/31/hitler-no-2-to-be-found-riding-nessie-369891/ (accessed 24/11/2017). See also Beth Hale, 'MI5 obsession with Hitler's deputy Martin Bormann led Britain on Nazi goose chase', *Daily Mail* (01/09/2009), http://www.dailymail.co.uk/news/article-1210412/British-obsession-Hitlers-deputy-Martin-Bormann-led-MI5-Nazi-goose-chase.html (accessed 24/11/2017); 'How Hitler's deputy was tipped to ride on the Loch Ness Monster', *The Scotsman* (01/09/2009) http://www.scotsman.com/news/how-hitler-s-deputy-was-tipped-to-ride-on-the-loch-ness-monster-1-772342 (accessed 24/11/2017).

29 TNA, KV 2/3033, J. Chenhalls to SIS (11/06/1947).

30 TNA, KV 2/3033, G. Brammer, Area Intelligence Officer, 'International Nazi Organisation: Martin Bormann' (03/07/1947).

31 TNA, KV 2/3033, Hodges, HQ ID to MI5 (28/06/1947).

32 TNA, KV 2/3033, Minute Sheet, 'Mr Himsworth' (07/07/1947).

33 TNA, KV 2/3033, Censored to HQ ID (04/07/1947).

34 Trevor Roper, *Last Days of Hitler*, pp.xi–xii.

35 Ibid, p.xii.
36 TNA, KV 2/3033, Norman Himsworth, Minute Sheet (10/07/1947).
37 NARA II, RG 65, A1 136P, Box 38, 6133250, Edward J. Martin 'Martin Borman' (08/02/1946).
38 NARA II, RG 65, ZZ 20, Box 19, Folder 2, 26299481, CIC Milan to Washington (01/10/1947).
39 Ibid.
40 TNA, KV 2/3033, MI6 to Mrs. D. M. Quin, MI5 (11/08/1947).
41 NARA II, RG 263, ZZ 18, Box 15, Folder 6, 26186820, 'Repeated Rumours, Re. Presence Martin Bormann in Ecuador' (02/04/1948). See also Chief, Foreign Branch to Chief of Station, 'Whereabouts of Marin Bormann' (05/04/1948).
42 NARA II, RG 65, A1 136P, Box 38, 6133250, Ladd to Director FBI (06/05/1948).
43 NARA II, RG 65, A1 136P, Box 38, 6133250, Hoover, Memorandum to Tolson, Tamm and Ladd (06/05/1948).
44 Ibid.
45 NARA II, RG 65, A1 136P, Box 38, 6133250, Ladd to The Director (10/05/1948).
46 Ibid.
47 NARA II, RG 65, A1 136P, Box 38, 6133250, Ladd to The Director (19/05/1948).
48 NARA II, RG 65, A1 136P, Box 38, 6133250, Ladd, Top Secret Memorandum to The Director (15/05/1948).
49 Ibid.
50 TNA, KV 2/3033, J. Chenhalls, MI5 to J. A. Cimperman, American Embassy, London (10/06/1948).
51 Ibid.
52 NARA II, RG 65, A1 136P, Box 38, 6133250, American Embassy, London to Director FBI (15/06/1948).
53 NARA II, RG 65, A1 136P, Box 38, 6133250, Ladd to The Director, Top Secret Memorandum (01/06/1948).
54 Ibid. See also Dunstan & Williams, Grey Wolf, p.261.
55 NARA II, RG 65, A1 136P, Box 38, 6133250, Ladd to The Director, Top Secret Memorandum (01/06/1948).
56 NARA II, RG 65, A1 136P, Box 38, 6133250, Robert H. Jackson, Supreme Court to The President, The White House (16/06/1948).
57 Ibid.
58 NARA II, RG 65, A1 136P, Box 38, 6133250, Ladd to The Director, Memorandum (24/06/1948) and Ladd, Memorandum (08/09/1948).
59 NARA II, RG 65, A1 136P, Box 38, 6133250, Ladd to The Director, Memorandum (16/06/1948).
60 NARA II, RG 65, A1 136P, Box 38, 6133250, Ladd, Memorandum (08/09/1948).
61 Ibid.
62 Ibid.
63 Ibid.
64 Ibid.

65 NARA II, RG 65, A1 136P, Box 38, 6133250, Director, FBI to The Attorney General, 'Martin Bormann' (17/09/1948).

66 NARA II, RG 65, A1 136P, Box 38, 6133250, Ladd to The Director, Memorandum (28/09/1948).

67 NARA II, RG 65, A1 136P, Box 38, 6133250, V. P. Keay to Ladd, Memorandum (07/02/1949).

68 NARA II, RG 65, A1 136P, Box 38, 6133250, Hoover to Jack D. Neal, Department of State (09/02/1949). See also handwritten note on Keay to Ladd, Memorandum (07/02/1949).

69 NARA II, RG 65, A1 136P, Box 38, 6133250, Keay to Ladd, Memorandum (07/02/1949).

70 NARA II, RG 65, A1 136P, Box 38, 6133250, Ladd to The Director, Memorandum (06/05/1948).

71 NARA II, RG 65, A1 136P, Box 38, 6133250, Memorandum Re: Martin Bormann (14/05/1948).

72 Of course, some very nasty Nazis were hiding in Argentina, but, as the FBI acknowledged in 1946, '[t]he desire of the Argentine Resistance to embarrass the present Argentine government has led them to use any story which has come to hand without regard for its truthfulness'; see NARA II, RG 65, A1 136P, Box 38, 6133250, 'Military Attaché Report Argentina' (19/02/1946).

73 TNA, FO 1093/448, Warner to Aubrey (28/07/1948). On Aubrey Halford, see Keith Jeffery, *MI6: The History of the Secret Intelligence Service 1909-1949* (London: Bloomsbury, 2011), p.620.

74 TNA, FO 1093/448, Warner to Aubrey (28/07/1948).

75 Ibid. The facts about Eugen Dollmann's post-war career are shady to say the least. By virtue of his involvement in Operation Sunrise (the secret surrender of German forces in Italy during the Second World War), he was protected from prosecution after the war by some American intelligence officers. Nevertheless, his presence in American custody continued to be a source of friction between the Americans, the British and the Italians. At the time of his meeting with MI6 in 1948, his presence in Italy was against the advice of the CIA, although some evidence suggests he was still employed by the CIC. See NARA II, RG 263, ZZ 19, Box 29, 19049305, CIA History Staff, Kevin Conley Ruffner, 'Eagle and Swastika: Draft Working Paper' (2003).

76 TNA, FO 1093/448, Warner to Aubrey (28/07/1948).

77 Ibid.

78 Ibid.

79 Ibid.

80 Ibid.

81 TNA, FO 1093/448, J. E. D. Street to Halford (11/08/1948).

82 TNA, FO 1093/448, J. E. D. Street to Mr. Joy (14/09/1948).

83 Ibid.

84 Ibid.

85 TNA, FO 1093/448, J. E. D. Street to Mr. Joy (24/09/1948).

86 Ibid.

87 Ibid.

88 TNA, FO 1093/448, Handwritten Minutes (25/09/1948).

89 NARA II, RG 263, ZZ 18, Box 15, Folder 6, 26186820, Confidential Memorandum (21/07/1949).
90 Ibid.
91 Ibid.
92 Ibid.
93 Ibid.
94 NARA II, RG 263, ZZ 18, Box 15, Folder 6, 26186820, James E. Brown, Jr. to the Secretary of State, Washington (26/07/1949).
95 NARA II, RG 263, ZZ 18, Box 15, Folder 6, 26186820, Confidential Memorandum (21/07/1949).
96 NARA II, RG 263, ZZ 18, Box 15, Folder 6, 26186820, James E. Brown, Jr. to the Secretary of State, Washington (26/07/1949).
97 Ibid.
98 TNA, KV 2/3033, 'Hitler Lives, Say Nazis', *Evening Standard* (09/05/1950).
99 Ibid.
100 Ibid.
101 Ibid.
102 TNA, KV 2/3033, R. J. T. Griffin, 'Interview with Karl Heinz Kaerner' (11/08/1949).
103 Ibid.
104 TNA, KV 2/3033, Ashley Clarke to Pat (13/08/1949). On William Hayter's relations with MI6, see Jeffery, *MI6*, p.620.
105 TNA, KV 2/3033, J. E. D. Street, Foreign Office to B. G. Atkinson, MI5 (17/08/1949). See handwritten notes on this letter for MI5's opinion.
106 TNA, KV 2/3033, R. J. T. Griffin, 'Interview with Karl Heinz Kaerner' (11/08/1949).
107 NARA II, RG 263, ZZ 18, Box 15, Folder 6, 26186820, Robert A. Schow to Director, FBI (07/12/1949).
108 NARA II, RG 263, ZZ 18, Box 15, Folder 6, 26186820, Mr. Kurt Kirsch (15/08/1950).
109 Ibid.
110 TNA, KV 2/3033, 'From the Press Section' (22/09/1950); see also handwritten note (24/10/1950).
111 TNA, KV 2/3033, 'From the Press Section', handwritten note (24/10/1950).
112 TNA, KV 2/3033, Metropolitan Police, Special Branch, Special Report, 'Martin Borman' (25/08/1951).
113 Ibid.
114 Ibid.
115 Ibid.
116 Ibid.
117 Ibid.
118 TNA, KV 2/3033, Metropolitan Police, Special Branch, Special Report, '"Martin Borman" or "Henry Adcock"' (03/12/1951).
119 Ibid.
120 Ibid.
121 Ibid.
122 Ibid.

123 Ibid.
124 Ibid.
125 TNA, KV 2/3033, B. G. Atkinson, MI5 to HQ ID (15/01/1952).
126 NARA II, RG 263, ZZ 18, Box 15, Folder 6, 26186820, 'Operational, Franz Lange' (21/01/1952).
127 NARA II, RG 263, ZZ 18, Box 15, Folder 6, 26186820, Central Intelligence Agency, Security Information (08/02/1952).
128 NARA II, RG 263, ZZ 18, Box 15, Folder 6, 26186820, Hoover to Director CIA (03/08/1948).
129 Trevor-Roper, *Last Days of Hitler*, pp.xxxviii–xxxix.
130 TNA, KV 2/3033, L. Thompson, HQ ID to MI5 (14/03/1952).
131 Sognnaes, 'Dental Evidence', p.174.
132 Ibid, pp.209–222.
133 Charles Whiting, *The Search for 'Gestapo' Müller* (Barnsley: Leo Cooper, 2001), pp.135–136.
134 K. Anslinger, G. Weichhold, W. Keil, B. Bayer & W. Eisenmenger, 'Identification of the Skeletal Remains of Martin Bormann by mtDNA Analysis', *International Journal of Legal Medicine*, Vol. 114, No. 3 (2001), pp.194–196.
135 Ibid, p.194.
136 Ibid.
137 Ibid, pp.194–196.
138 Ibid.
139 Hugh Thomas spots 'forensic fraud' everywhere (see Hugh Thomas, *Doppelgängers: The Truth about the Bodies in the Berlin Bunker* [London: Fourth Estate, 1995], p.249), whereas the authors of *Grey Wolf* are apparently oblivious.
140 Timothy Naftali, Norman J. W. Goda, Richard Breitman & Robert Wolfe, 'The Mystery of Heinrich Müller: New Materials from the CIA', *Holocaust and Genocide Studies*, Vol. 15, No. 3 (2001), pp.454, 458.
141 NARA II, RG 263, UD 2, Box 4, Folder 2, 16967345, Central Intelligence Agency, Directorate of Plans, *Counterintelligence Brief: The Hunt For 'Gestapo Mueller'* (October 1971). See also Naftali *et al.*, 'Mystery of Heinrich Müller', p.458.
142 NARA II, RG 263, UD 2, Box 4, Folder 2, 16967345, Central Intelligence Agency, Directorate of Plans, *Counterintelligence Brief: The Hunt For 'Gestapo Mueller'* (October 1971).
143 Ibid.
144 Naftali *et al.*, 'Mystery of Heinrich Müller', p.458. See also NARA II, RG 263, UD 2, Box 4, Folder 2, 16967345, Central Intelligence Agency, Directorate of Plans, *Counterintelligence Brief: The Hunt For 'Gestapo Mueller'* (October 1971).
145 Naftali *et al.*, 'Mystery of Heinrich Müller', p.457.
146 NARA II, RG 263, UD 2, Box 4, Folder 2, 16967345, Central Intelligence Agency, Directorate of Plans, *Counterintelligence Brief: The Hunt For 'Gestapo Mueller'* (October 1971). See also NARA II, RG 263, UD 2, Box 4, Folder 3, 16967821, 'Fate of Gestapo Chief' (10/11/1970).
147 NARA II, RG 263, UD 2, Box 4, Folder 2, 16967345, Central Intelligence Agency, Directorate of Plans, *Counterintelligence Brief: The Hunt For 'Gestapo Mueller'* (October 1971).

148 Ibid.

149 NARA II, RG 263, UD 2, Box 4, Folder 3, 16967821, 'Fate of Gestapo Chief' (10/11/1970).

150 NARA II, RG 263, UD 2, Box 4, Folder 2, 16967345, 'Harz, Karl Rudolf' (18/02/1971).

151 Anton Joachimsthaler, *The Last Days of Hitler: Legend, Evidence and Truth* (London: Cassell, 2000), pp.32–34.

152 Ibid., p.34.

153 Ron T. Hansig, *Hitler's Escape* (Twickenham: Athena Press, 2005), p.32.

154 NARA II, RG 263, UD 2, Box 4, Folder 2, 16967345, Central Intelligence Agency, Directorate of Plans, *Counterintelligence Brief: The Hunt For 'Gestapo Mueller'* (October 1971).

155 Naftali *et al.*, 'Mystery of Heinrich Müller', p.453.

156 NARA II, RG 65, A1 1360, Box 6, 6136364, D. J. Brennan Jr. to W. C. Sullivan, 'Heinrich Mueller' (16/11/1967).

157 TNA, KV 2/2655, R. G. Hodges, ID HQ, Germany to MI5 London (17/08/1949).

158 The bombardment of the Reichschancellery garden by Russian guns explains the disappearance and almost unidentifiable state of many corpses, as will be seen in the final chapter in this book.

159 The Museum of Military Medicine (MMoM), Aldershot, RADC/CF/4/5/Himm, Second Army Defence Company, 'War Diary' (May 1945).

160 MMoM, RADC/CF/4/5/Himm, T. Selvester, 'Heinrich Himmler'.

161 TNA, WO 208/4431, Interrogation of Heinz Macher (10/11/1945). See also the latter's Preliminary Interrogation Report (24/05/1945); Preliminary Interrogation of Werner Grothmann (24/05/1945); C. A. Smith, Chief Interrogator, 031 Camp, 'Identification of Heinrich Himmler' (23/05/1945).

162 MMoM, RADC/CF/4/5/Himm, Second Army Defence Company, 'War Diary' (May 1945).

163 Christian Goeschel, 'Suicide at the End of the Third Reich', *Journal of Contemporary History*, Vol. 41, No. 1 (2006), p.158.

164 TNA, FO 1005/1700, Intelligence Division Review Number 14 (November 1946).

165 NARA II, RG 263, ZZ 18, Box 15, 26186820, Memorandum for Jack D. Neal (23/01/1946).

166 King's College Archive Centre, Cambridge University, The Private Papers of Noel Gilroy Annan, 'The Political Situation in the British Zone'. See also Wellington Long, *The New Nazis of Germany* (Philadelphia: Chilton, 1968), pp.20, 38.

167 TNA, FO 1005/1722, Rhineland-Westphalia Intelligence Staff, Political Summary No. 3 (15/11/1946).

168 Joachim Fest, *Inside Hitler's Bunker: The Last Days of the Third Reich* (London: Macmillan, 2005), p.90.

169 Ian Kershaw, *Death in the Bunker* (London: Penguin, 2005), pp.35, 54–55. See also Joachimsthaler, *Last Days of Hitler*, p.144.

170 Fest, *Inside Hitler's Bunker*, p.107. See also Ada Petrova & Peter Watson, *The Death of Hitler: The Final Words from Russia's Secret Archives* (London: Richard Cohen Books, 1995), p.25.

171 Beevor, *Berlin*, p.200.

172 Ibid.

173 Ibid.

174 Goeschel, 'Suicide', p.157.

175 Fest, *Inside Hitler's Bunker*, p.128.

176 David R. Beisel, 'The German Suicide, 1945', *Journal of Psychohistory*, Vol. 34, No. 4 (2007), p.303.

177 Ibid., p.304.

178 Goeschel, 'Suicide', p.160.

179 Ibid., pp.160, 172.

180 Ibid., pp.162, 167. See also Beisel, 'German Suicide', p.305.

181 Beisel, 'German Suicide', p.305.

182 Goeschel, 'Suicide', p.155.

183 Adolf Hitler, Gerhard L. Weinberg (ed.), Krista Smith (trans.), *Hitler's Second Book: The Unpublished Sequel to Mein Kampf* (New York: Enigma Books, 2003), pp.13–15.

184 Matthew Seligmann, John Davison & John McDonald, *In the Shadow of the Swastika: Life in Germany Under the Nazis 1933–1945* (Kent: Spellmount, 2003), p.25. See also Matthew Hughes & Chris Mann, *Inside Hitler's Germany* (London: Windmill Books, 2012), p.174.

185 Fest, *Inside Hitler's Bunker*, p.130.

186 Goeschel, 'Suicide', p.157.

187 Beisel, 'German Suicide', p.309.

188 *Los Angeles Times*, 'Hitler Fanatics Battle Allies' (31/03/1946), quoted in Scott Andrew Selby, *The Axmann Conspiracy: The Nazi Plan for a Fourth Reich and How the U.S. Army Defeated It* (New York: Berkley, 2012), p.225.

189 Norbert Frei, *Adenauer's Germany and the Nazi Past: The Politics of Amnesty and Integration* (Chichester: Columbia University Press, 2002), p.277.

190 Peter Levenda, *Ratline: Soviet Spies, Nazi Priests, and the Disappearance of Adolf Hitler* (Lake Worth, FL: Ibis Press, 2012), pp.20, 23, 31.

191 Selby, *Axmann Conspiracy*, pp.65, 79–80, 106, 118, 161. See also TNA, FO 1005/1700, ID, Intelligence Review Number 13, 'Nursery' (October 1946).

192 Long, *New Nazis*, p.45.

193 Hugh Thomas, *SS-1: The Unlikely Death of Heinrich Himmler* (London: Fourth Estate, 2001), pp.190–192.

194 Ibid., p.221.

195 NARA II, RG 319, NM3 82, Box 1846, 2155420, Intelligence Division, 'Intelligence Summary No. 21' (15/07/1947), p.3. See also NARA II, RG 319, NM3 82, Box 1847, 2155420, Intelligence Division Summary No. 15 (15/02/1947), 'Globetrotter'; NARA II, RG 498, UD 308, Box 1380, 5717055, 'Secret Report on Globetrotter' (10/04/1947).

196 TNA, FO 1005/1715, Hamburg Regional Intelligence Office (RIO), 'Monthly Security Intelligence Summary' (01/04/1947), 'Monthly Security Intelligence Summary' (30/04/1947), 'Monthly Security Intelligence Summary' (31/05/1947).

197 Much of this correspondence is preserved in TNA, WO 208/4431. For example, see Hodges, ID Herford to Potter, British Liaison Officer, HQ EUCOM, 'Himmler's Strong Boxes' (31/01/1948). See also British Liaison Officer, G-2 USFET to HQ ID (13/01/1947).

198 Ibid.

199 TNA, WO 208/4431, HQ BAOR to Intelligence Bureau (31/05/1946). This folder is useful for disproving other claims made by Hugh Thomas.

200 TNA, WO 208/4431, Photograph of Himmler.

201 TNA, FO 1005/1715, Hamburg RIO, 'Monthly Security Intelligence Summary' (01/04/1947), p.3.

202 TNA, WO 208/4431, CIC Region IV, Top Secret Memorandum 'Operation Globetrotter' (17/12/1946).

203 TNA, WO 208/3791, Hodges, 'Rumours concerning whereabouts of Adolf Hitler' (02/03/1948) and Hodges, 'Hitler Survival Rumours' (03/12/1947).

204 McKale, *Hitler*, pp.141, 143. See also Uki Goñi, *The Real Odessa: How Perón Brought the Nazi War Criminals to Argentina* (London: Granta, 2002), p.295.

205 McKale, *Hitler*, p.141.

206 See Goñi, *Odessa*, pp.xix–xx. See also Guy Walters, *Hunting Evil: How the Nazi War Criminals Escaped and the Hunt to Bring Them to Justice* (London: Bantam, 2009). Goñi's account does have some issues; see Ignacio Klich, 'Review of Uki Goñi, *The Real Odessa: How Perón Brought the Nazi War Criminals to Argentina* (London: Granta, 2002)', *Journal of Latin American Studies*, Vol. 37, No. 2 (2005), pp.400–402. There is still much research to be done on this topic.

207 Walters, *Hunting Evil*, p.3.

208 Perry Biddiscombe, 'Operation Selection Board: The Growth and Suppression of the Neo Nazi "Deutsche Revolution" 1945–47', *Intelligence and National Security*, Vol. 11, No. 1 (1996), pp.59–77. See also TNA, CAB 191/1, HQ ID, '"Deutsche Revolution" Appreciation of Investigations into German Subversive Movements culminating in Operation Selection Board' (03/04/1947) Report submitted to the JIC.

209 David Aaronovitch, *Voodoo Histories: The Role of Conspiracy Theory in Shaping Modern History* (London: Jonathan Cape, 2009), p.10.

210 Ernst Haiger, 'Fiction, Facts, and Forgeries: The "Revelations" of Peter and Martin Allen about the History of the Second World War', *Journal of Intelligence History*, Vol. 6, No. 1 (2006), pp.105–106.

211 Ibid., p.106.

212 Ibid., pp.108, 110–111, 115.

213 Aaronovitch, *Voodoo Histories*, p.12.

214 Frei, *Adenauer's Germany*, p.277. See also Walters, *Hunting Evil*, p.150; TNA, FO 371/103904, Major-General J. M. Kirkman, Commander, British Intelligence Organisation (Germany), 'Operation "Terminus" 14/15 January 1953' (05/02/1953).

215 Joachimsthaler, *Last Days of Hitler*, pp.165, 195.

216 TNA, FO 371/103896, Sir I. Kirkpatrick, Wahnerheide to Foreign Office (12/01/1952). Although they claimed that they could 'manage the interrogation with … [their] own resources', further help from Nazi experts was requested.

217 The British High Commissioner believed that Trevor-Roper would be 'ideal'; see TNA, FO 371/103896, Sir I. Kirkpatrick, Wahnerheide to Foreign Office (12/01/1952). Minutes in this folder show that Foreign Office officials did in fact try to contact Trevor-Roper to see if he was available for these interrogations, but due to their 'work at Oxford', Frank Roberts confirmed that both Trevor-Roper and Alan Bullock would 'not be available'. History was thus denied another excellent Trevor-Roper intelligence investigation. See Frank Roberts to Sir W. Strang (13/01/1953).

CHAPTER 6: THE EVIDENCE STILL STANDS

1 The National Archives (TNA), FO 1005/1700, Adolf Hitler speaking at a conference on 01/02/1943 quoted in Intelligence Division, 'Intelligence Review No. 16' (January 1947).
2 Herbert Moore & James W. Barret (eds), *Who Killed Hitler?* (New York: Booktab Press, 1947), p.114. See also Peter Levenda, *Ratline: Soviet Spies, Nazi Priests, and the Disappearance of Adolf Hitler* (Lake Worth, FL: Ibis Press, 2012), pp.21–22.
3 The National Archives (TNA), HW 1/3760, Japanese Ambassador to Tokyo (30/04/1945) and TNA, HW 5/767, CX/MSS/SC.2. See also Richard J. Aldrich, *The Hidden Hand: Britain, America and Cold War Secret Intelligence* (London: John Murray, 2002), p.27 for further information on Signals Intelligence (SIGINT) from the Japanese Ambassador.
4 TNA, FO 371/4764, *The Times* (02/05/1945).
5 TNA, FO 371/46748, Sir Orme Sargent Minute to Prime Minister (02/05/1945).
6 TNA, FO 371/46748, Prime Minister to Sir Orme Sargent (03/05/1945).
7 TNA, WO 208/4475, Interrogation of Johanna Wolf (31/05/1945).
8 TNA, KV 4/354, Report on Interrogation of Hermann Karnau (19/06/1945).
9 TNA, KV 4/354, Interrogation of Hermann Karnau (28/05/1945), Report on Interrogation of Hermann Karnau (19/06/1945).
10 V. K. Vinogradov, J. F. Pogonyi & N. V. Teptzov (eds), *Hitler's Death: Russia's Last Great Secret from the Files of the KGB* (London: Chaucer Press, 2005), pp.67, 80.
11 The National Archives and Records Administration (NARA II), RG 549, A1-52, Box 820, 563511, Captain George T. Gabelia's testimony before Colonel Harold R. Booth (15/03/1948).
12 TNA, KV 4/354, 'Verbal statement' by 'Kurt Samuel' (20/07/1945).
13 TNA, FO 371/46749, 'Hitler's Last Days', SHAEF Memorandum (30/07/1945).
14 Ibid.
15 TNA, WO 208/3787, CX CF/IV/73 (July 1945).
16 TNA, KV 4/354, Interrogation of Karnau (26/09/2945).
17 TNA, WO 208/3787, Interrogation Report of Hilco Poppen (30/09/1945).
18 TNA, WO 208/3787, Interrogation Report of Hilco Poppen (06/10/1945).
19 TNA, KV 4/354, Interrogation of Erich Kempka (07/10/1945). Also in NARA II, RG 242, P 26, Box 1, 12008425, Special Interrogation of Erich Kempka (07/10/1945).

20 NARA II, RG 263, UD 2, Box 4, Folder 2, 16967345, Erich Mansfeld, Interrogation Report, Bremen Interrogation Centre (30/07/1945). Mansfeld was arrested and interrogated on British orders by a CIC agent named J. Finer; see Arrest Report in this file dated (14/07/1945) and details of the British instructions in 'Memorandum to the Officer in Charge' (26/07/1945). See also NARA II, RG 242, P 26, Box 1, 12008425, Special Interrogation of Erich Kempka (07/10/1945).

21 NARA II, RG 263, UD 2, Box 4, Folder 2, 16967345, Erich Mansfeld, Interrogation Report, Bremen Interrogation Centre (30/07/1945).

22 Ibid.

23 Ibid.

24 Ibid.

25 Ibid.

26 Ibid.

27 Ibid.

28 TNA, WO 208/3787, USFET, Interrogation of Hanna Reitsch (08/10/1945).

29 Ibid., and TNA, KV 4/354, Interrogation of Albert Speer (11/09/1945) and TNA, WO 208/3791, USFET, Interrogation of Gerda Christian (25/04/1946).

30 TNA, WO 208/3781, 'The Death of Hitler', also in TNA, WO 208/3787.

31 TNA, FO 371/46748, The Times (09/07/1945).

32 TNA, WO 208/3791, Kurt Hewe, 'My Service in the Shelter of the Reich Chancellery' (18/12/1946).

33 TNA, KV 4/354, Interrogation of Baroness von Varo (01/10/1945) and 'Points Emerging from special interrogation of Else Krueger' (29/09/1945) and USFET, 'Interrogation of Junge, Gertrud' (30/12/1946) and TNA, WO 208/3791, USFET, Interrogation of Gerda Christian (25/04/1946).

34 NARA II, RG 242, P 26, Box 1, 12008425, Robert P. Patterson, Secretary of State for War to The President (19/03/1946). A less clear copy of this letter can be read in FBI, Hitler Volume 2.

35 TNA, WO 208/3788, Statement by William James Skardon (01/12/1945) and TNA, WO 208/3781, undated, 'Second Interrogation of Von Below'.

36 NARA II, RG 242, P 26, Box 1, 12008425, Hoover to Assistant Chief of Staff, G-2, Washington, DC, 'Report of the FBI Laboratory' (13/03/1946).

37 NARA II, RG 242, P 26, Box 1, 12008425, Robert P. Patterson, Secretary of State for War to The President (19/03/1946). A less clear copy of this letter can be read in FBI, Hitler Volume 2.

38 TNA, CAB 146/438, Forensic Science Laboratory Report by Ronald M. Mitchell (16/06/1966).

39 TNA, CAB 146/438, 'Note on Hitler's 1945 Wills' (1971).

40 TNA, CAB 146/438, Melland to Trevor-Roper (23/03/1966) and Melland to Dr. L. Kahn (09/12/1966).

41 TNA, CAB 146/438, 'Note on Hitler's 1945 Wills' (1971).

42 TNA, CAB 146/438, Translation of Marshal Chuikov's memoirs (1964) and John Erickson to Melland (28/09/1965).

43 TNA, CAB 146/438, 'Note on Hitler's 1945 Wills' (1971) and Erickson to Melland (31/03/1965).

44 TNA, CAB 146/438, 'Note on Hitler's 1945 Wills' (1971).

45 TNA, FO 938/196, 'Report on "The Last Days of Hitler" By Trevor-Roper For North Rhine Westphalia' (1948).

46 TNA, KV 4/354, JIC 'Bibliographical Note' (03/06/1946).

47 TNA, WO 208/3790, Trevor-Roper to Searle (07/03/1946) and 'Time Table of Events in Hitler's Bunker'.

48 For example, see questions for Gerda Christian from Trevor-Roper in TNA, WO 208/3790, and resulting USFET interrogation in TNA, WO 208/3791.

49 TNA, WO 208/3789, USFET, Interrogation of Axmann (14/01/1946).

50 TNA, WO 208/3790, USFET, 'Supplement to interrogation of Kempka etc.' (25/01/1946).

51 Hugh Trevor-Roper, *The Last Days of Hitler* (London: Macmillan, 2002), p.178. See also TNA, KV 4/354, 'Points Emerging from special interrogation of Else Krueger' (29/09/1945) and USFET, 'Interrogation of Junge, Gertrud' (30/12/1946) and TNA, WO 208/3791, USFET, Interrogation of Gerda Christian (25/04/1946) and TNA, WO 208/3790, 'Time Table of Events in Hitler's Bunker'.

52 Simon Dunstan & Gerrard Williams, *Grey Wolf: The Escape of Adolf Hitler* (New York: Sterling, 2011), p.xxi.

53 Harry Cooper, *Hitler in Argentina* (Hernando, FL: CreateSpace Independent Publishing Platform, 2014), pp.8–16.

54 TNA, WO 208/3788, USFET, Interrogation of Kempka (12/01/1946).

55 TNA, WO 208/3789, Searle, IB to USFET (26/01/1946) and TNA, WO 208/3790, Trevor-Roper to Garvey (CIC), USFET (11/02/1946).

56 Anton Joachimsthaler, *The Last Days of Hitler: Legend, Evidence and Truth* (London: Cassell, 2000), p.159.

57 Ada Petrova & Peter Watson, *The Death of Hitler: The Final Words from Russia's Secret Archives* (London: Richard Cohen Books, 1995), pp.114–115.

58 Charles Pigden, 'Conspiracy Theories and the Conventional Wisdom', *Episteme*, Vol. 4, No. 2 (2007), p.224. Although this argument is challenged in Pigden's article, in the context of Hitler conspiracies, Coady still has a point.

59 Joachimsthaler, *Last Days of Hitler*, pp.155–156, 161, 163–164, 166, 173, 176–177, 182.

60 TNA, FO 371/46748, 'Some thoughts on Hitler's death' (02/05/1945).

61 TNA, FO 371/46748, 'Top Secret Cypher Telegram' (02/05/1945).

62 TNA, FO 371/46748, 'Some thoughts on Hitler's death' (02/05/1945) and 'Top Secret Cypher Telegram' (02/05/1945).

63 TNA, FO 371/46748, 'Top Secret Cypher Telegram' (02/05/1945) and C1958/31/18 (04/05/1945).

64 Moore & Barret, *Who Killed Hitler*, pp.121–123.

65 TNA, HW1/3760, 'Brazilian Ambassador, London, Reports on Death of Hitler' (03/05/1945).

66 TNA, FO 371/46748, *The Times* (24/05/1945).

67 TNA, WO 204/2349 (entire folder) and TNA, FO 371/46748, FO Minutes (07/06/1945) and TNA, WO 208/3787, 'Nazi Underground Installation' (21/09/1945).

68 TNA, WO 208/4475, BBC Monitoring (17/10/1945).

69 Moore & Barret, *Who Killed Hitler*, pp.117, 123.

70 TNA, KV 4/354, Interrogation of Hermann Karnau (28/05/1945).

71 TNA, WO 208/3790, Memorandum on 'Mueller, Willi Otto' (04/02/1946).

72 NARA II, RG 263, UD 2, Box 4, Folder 2, 16967345, Erich Mansfeld, Interrogation Report, Bremen Interrogation Centre (30/07/1945).

73 TNA, KV 4/354, Interrogation of Werner Grothmann (26/09/1945).

74 Trevor-Roper, *Last Days of Hitler*, p.xxiii.

75 TNA, KV 4/354, Report on Interrogation of Hermann Karnau (19/06/1945).

76 TNA, KV 4/354, 'Top Secret: Ref:- Hermann Karnau' (21/06/1945) and TNA, WO 208/3790, Memorandum on 'Mueller, Willi Otto' (04/02/1946).

77 Ian Kershaw, *Hitler 1936–1945: Nemesis* (London: Penguin, 2000), p.1038.

78 TNA, CAB 79/33, JIC SHAEF 'Political Intelligence Report' (14/05/1945).

79 Dunstan and Williams, *Grey Wolf*, p.xix. See also Levenda, *Ratline*, p.18.

80 Petrova & Watson, *Death of Hitler*, p.90. See also Joachimsthaler, *Last Days of Hitler*, pp.21,180; Vinogradov, Pogonyi & Teptzov, *Hitler's Death*, p.24.

81 Petrova & Watson, *Death of Hitler*, p.53. See also Lev Bezymenski, *The Death of Adolf Hitler: Unknown Documents from Soviet Archives* (London: Michael Joseph, 1968), p.33.

82 Joachim Fest, *Inside Hitler's Bunker: The Last Days of the Third Reich* (London: Macmillan, 2005), p.158.

83 NARA II, RG 263, UD 2, Box 4, Folder 2, 16967345, Central Intelligence Agency, Directorate of Plans, *Counterintelligence Brief: The Hunt For 'Gestapo Mueller'* (October 1971).

84 Winston S. Churchill, *The Second World War, Volume VI: Triumph and Tragedy* (Boston: Houghton Mifflin, 1985), pp.545–546. See also Lord Moran, *Winston Churchill: The Struggle for Survival, 1940–1965* (London: Constable, 1966), p.270.

85 Imperial War Museums (IWM), Private Papers of J. E. Rhys, 'Memoirs of a Soldier', p.56.

86 W. Byford-Jones, *Berlin Twilight* (London: Hutchinson, 1947), p.122.

87 IWM, Private Papers of J. E. Rhys, 'Memoirs of a Soldier', pp.54–55.

88 Liddell Hart Centre for Military Archives (LHCMA), King's College London, Lethbridge Private Papers, 'greeting card taken from Adolf Hitler's marble topped desk (now in pieces) by Maj. General Lethbridge'.

89 IWM, Private Papers of J. E. Rhys, 'Memoirs of a Soldier', p.55.

90 TNA, KV 4/354, statement of John L. McCowen (30/05/1947) and Trevor-Roper to White (20/06/1947).

91 NARA II, RG 549, A1-52, Box 820, 563511, Heimlich Testimony (11/03/1948).

92 Petrova & Watson, *Death of Hitler*, pp.53–56.

93 Ibid., p.81.

94 Ibid.

95 'Post-Mortem of the Corpse of the German Shepherd Dog' (22/05/1945), in Vinogradov, Pogonyi & Teptzov, *Hitler's Death*, pp.92–94.

96 NARA II, RG 549, A1-52, Box 820, 563511, Heimlich Testimony (11/03/1948).

97 Petrova & Watson, *Death of Hitler*, p.82.

98 Ibid.

99 TNA, CAB 79/33, JIC Report (29/04/1945).
100 Petrova & Watson, *Death of Hitler*, pp.85, 87. See also Vinogradov, Pogonyi & Teptzov, *Hitler's Death*, p.24.
101 Petrova & Watson, *Death of Hitler*, p.86.
102 Ibid.
103 Ibid., p.87. See also Professor Norman Stone, on *Timewatch, Hitler's Death: The Final Report*, UK television broadcast (30/04/1995).
104 Petrova & Watson, *Death of Hitler*, pp.2, 3, 76.
105 TNA, WO 208/4475, Interrogation of Axmann (16/10/1947). See also Joachimsthaler, *Last Days of Hitler*, pp.217, 252.
106 Trevor-Roper, *Last Days of Hitler*, pp.182–183. See also TNA, KV 4/354, White to Shoosmith (04/10/1946).
107 Joachimsthaler, *Last Days of Hitler*, pp.225, 231, 236, 253. See also Vinogradov, Pogonyi & Teptzov, *Hitler's Death*, pp.95–107; P. Charlier, R. Weil, P. Rainsard, J. Poupon & J. C. Brisard, 'The Remains of Adolf Hitler: A Biomedical Analysis and Definitive Identification', *European Journal of Internal Medicine* (2018), pp.1–3.
108 Fest, *Inside Hitler's Bunker*, p.164.
109 Joachimsthaler, *Last Days of Hitler*, pp.214, 218, 221, 252.
110 Bill Vandivert, Life War Correspondent to Bill Churchill (03/07/1945), http://time.com/3524807/after-the-fall-photos-of-hitlers-bunker-and-the-ruins-of-berlin/ (accessed 05/04/2018).
111 Petrova & Watson, *Death of Hitler*, pp.118, 161.
112 On Hitler's alleged monorchism, see Petrova & Watson, *Death of Hitler*, pp.56–57, 122.
113 Out of fear, the Soviets had altered other evidence concerning Hitler in an effort to please Stalin; see Henrik Eberle & Matthias Uhl (eds), *The Hitler Book: The Secret Report by His Two Closest Aides* (London: John Murray, 2005), pp.xxviii–xxix.
114 Adam Lusher, 'Adolf Hitler Really is Dead: Scientific Study Debunks Conspiracy Theories That He Escaped to South America', *Independent* (20/05/2018), https://www.independent.co.uk/news/world/europe/adolf-hitler-debunked-escaped-south-america-skull-fragment-woman-teeth-jawbone-scientific-study-a8360356.html (accessed 01/07/2018). See also Charlier *et al.*, 'Remains of Adolf Hitler', p.2.
115 The University of Connecticut posted a useful video featuring the scientists involved in the 2009 DNA analysis; see UConn, 'The Hitler Project – Nick Bellantoni' (15/06/2011), YouTube, https://www.youtube.com/watch?v=ZqrrjzfnsVY.
116 My suspicion is based on evidence. According to Dr Nicholas F. Bellantoni, '...it was the DNA that made it conclusive and the conclusion was that this is a woman, not a male. So it's a female. So it can't possibly be Adolf Hitler.' See UConn, 'The Hitler Project – Nick Bellantoni' (15/06/2011), YouTube, https://www.youtube.com/watch?v=ZqrrjzfnsVY.
117 Joachimsthaler, *Last Days of Hitler*, pp.180–181, 252–253. See also Fest, *Inside Hitler's Bunker*, p.163; Kershaw, *Hitler*, p.1039.

CONCLUSION: 'THE ONUS IS ON HITLER'

1   Alan Bullock, quoted in the National Archives and Records Administration (NARA II), RG 263, ZZ 20, Box 20, 26300439, Morris Leikind, 'Studies in Pathography: Adolph Hitler'.

2   If my words here seem a little strong, one should consider them a paraphrasing of Alan Bullock's analysis of earlier conspiracy theorists quoted at the start of this chapter.

3   Charles Pigden, 'Conspiracy Theories and the Conventional Wisdom', *Episteme*, Vol. 4, No. 2 (2007), p.219.

4   Ernst Haiger, 'Fiction, Facts, and Forgeries: The "Revelations" of Peter and Martin Allen about the History of the Second World War', *Journal of Intelligence History*, Vol. 6, No. 1 (2006), p.118.

5   Keith Jeffery, *MI6: The History of the Secret Intelligence Service 1909-1949* (London: Bloomsbury, 2011), p.xv.

6   Richard J. Aldrich, *The Hidden Hand: Britain, America and Cold War Secret Intelligence* (London: John Murray, 2002), p.182.

7   Jonathan Evans, in Christopher Andrew, *The Defence of the Realm: The Authorized History of MI5* (London: Penguin, 2009), p.xvii.

8   Simon Dunstan & Gerrard Williams, *Grey Wolf: The Escape of Adolf Hitler* (New York: Sterling, 2011), p.xxi. See also Adam Sisman, *Hugh Trevor-Roper: The Biography* (London: Phoenix, 2011), p.504.

9   I was unsuccessful in my attempt to gain access to FO 1093/276 under the Freedom of Information Act.

10 The National Archives (TNA), FO 371/46749, C7164 (15/10/1945).

INDEX